Yoni Bashan is a two-time award-winn  who has worked at News Corporatic 2008. His work has been published in *the Daily Telegraph* and the *Sunday Telegraph* newspapers, as well as overseas mastheads including the *Wall Street Journal*. In 2012 he was named Most Outstanding Crime Reporter at the Kennedy Award Foundation's inaugural ceremony.

THE SQUAD

YONI BASHAN

HarperCollins*Publishers*

HarperCollins*Publishers*

First published in Australia in 2016
by HarperCollins*Publishers* Australia Pty Limited
ABN 36 009 913 517
harpercollins.com.au

Copyright © Yoni Bashan 2016

HarperCollins*Publishers*
Level 13, 201 Elizabeth Street, Sydney NSW 2000, Australia
Unit D1, 63 Apollo Drive, Rosedale, Auckland 0632, New Zealand
A 53, Sector 57, Noida, UP, India
1 London Bridge Street, London, SE1 9GF, United Kingdom
2 Bloor Street East, 20th floor, Toronto, Ontario M4W 1A8, Canada
195 Broadway, New York NY 10007, USA

National Library of Australia Cataloguing-in-Publication entry:

Bashan, Yoni, author.
The squad / Yoni Bashan.
ISBN: 978 1 4607 5181 7 (paperback)
ISBN: 978 1 4607 0670 1 (ebook)
Organised crime – Australia.
Islamophobia – Australia.
Social conflict – New South Wales.
Islamophobia – New South Wales.
Drug traffic – Australia.
Muslims – Australia.
Islam – Australia.
Australia – Race relations.
364.1060994

Cover design by Hazel Lam, HarperCollins Design Studio
Cover image by Yolande De Kort / Trevillion Images; background textures
by shutterstock.com
Typeset in Adobe Garamond Pro by Kirby Jones
Printed and bound in Australia by Griffin Press
The papers used by HarperCollins in the manufacture of this book are natural, recyclable
products made from wood grown in sustainable plantation forests. The fibre source and
manufacturing processes meet recognised international environmental standards, and carry
certification.

To the owners of the original Double D record store.
This one's for you.

Contents

Preface

The story of the Middle Eastern Organised Crime Squad (MEOCS) canvassed in this book spans the years from 2006 to 2011, an era immortalised as a 'golden age' by many of its staff, and a time when big personalities were in charge. In some ways criminals had the upper hand in the lead-up to this period, and in parts of southwestern Sydney they intimidated officers, running amok on the streets of certain neighbourhoods. MEOCS was established as an ironhanded response. Its officers were a brotherhood, something tribal, almost an outlaw gang in themselves. They didn't break the rules, but they wrangled with them at times. The Squad's official charter spoke of crime reduction but, unofficially, there was a deeper imperative to take back the streets.

This era produced a plethora of strike force investigations, hundreds of them, too many to unpack in one book. Telling the story right meant I had to choose the Squad's most defining cases. Within these pages are the ones I felt best captured their work – tales of daring undercover missions, informants making deals, spectacular detective work and, as with any great story, painful losses.

The point of it all was to give people a view of the landscape of organised crime within Sydney's Middle Eastern community. I wanted to shed some light on the elusive crime barons, many of whom are still around today, and try to give some insight into their evolving tradecraft. But, really, this is a story about the officers who were shadowing them. Their work was at risk of being forgotten. Hopefully this book goes a little way towards acknowledging their slice of history.

Yoni Bashan

THE SQUAD

Prologue

Adnan Darwiche sat cross-legged on the kitchen floor of his safe house and picked up a bullet from the pile in front of him; Winchester brand, 9 millimetre. He sprayed it with gun oil and then wiped it carefully with gloved hands to remove any fingerprints and DNA. He didn't want either to be left behind at the scene.

'Make sure you wipe them properly,' he said to the three men sitting with him. Dozens more bullets were laid out in front of them and each one had to be polished. They had to be clean.

Darwiche's safe house was a ground-floor unit in the suburb of Punchbowl, an enclave of southwestern Sydney brimming with gang activity. Safe houses were everywhere, each one a place where street deals of drugs could be weighed and then sold, or weapons stored for attack. Darwiche's unit was empty of furniture but he used it to store an arsenal. In the kitchen cupboards, he'd been storing military-grade SKS assault rifles, modified handguns that could empty a magazine in less than two seconds, and a MAC-10 sub-machine gun so powerful it could cut a person into two pieces. In a black garbage bag under the kitchen sink he'd hidden his latest acquisition: a live, loaded and fully operational rocket launcher stolen from the army.

Sitting on the kitchen floor with Darwiche were three of his trusted lieutenants. Each one helped him with the bullets, picking them up between thumb and forefinger to wipe them clean according to their boss's instructions. They worked in silence but occasionally Darwiche spoke, giving directions. 'Make sure you don't get any hairs on them,' he said, according to one of the men sitting there, his closest friend, who would later turn Crown witness.

These men were mere hours away from one of the most violent nights in Sydney's history, prepping for an act of carnage that would redefine the city's struggle with Middle Eastern organised crime.

The concept of MEOC, as it would become known, had been germinating across the suburbs of southwestern Sydney for years, eventually manifesting in a tentative criminal strata, a world of dog-eat-dog where drug dealing and car rebirthing had become their own industries, and were treated like trade skills that could be handed down within families – father to son, brother to brother, cousin to cousin. You could start your career at the bottom and work your way up.

In this world, violence was a by-product of a broken alliance, a wounded ego or a deal that had fallen through. Even this had been organised to an accepted scale: bashings were doled out to send a message; kneecappings were a punishment; and if your house got shot up that was often a final warning. Any of these were enough to start a war between crime families or the many street crews sharing borders in a suburb. If someone got whacked it meant the battle lines had been drawn.

Amid this jail-yard environment, certain characters became like prospectors, looking ahead to identify lucrative markets and new ways of making money. They moved in early to the nightclubs of the inner city, the beach suburbs of the south, the hip bars and property markets of the east, and the taverns in the northwest.

Among them was Adnan Darwiche, known to both his enemies and crew as 'Eddie': a drug dealer who had battled his way to dominance. This high-functioning crim, who could spot a surveillance detail a mile away and was surrounded by a community of good people too frightened to speak up for fear of retribution, epitomised the struggle to rein in the burgeoning organised crime problem in Sydney. When Darwiche first started dealing pot circa 1996 it was to a few friends around Bankstown. He was sixteen back then and his business was too small to pose a threat. Later, he went on to do muscle work for Danny Karam, a MEOC pioneer and gang leader who overplayed his hand for control of Kings Cross and died young in a hail of bullets. By twenty-five Darwiche had been charged over a slew of executions and blood-soaked crime scenes, having built himself a drug empire that stretched from Bankstown to Hurstville. He had stamped out rivals, wrested control of their turf, and was turning over dazzling profits each week. He'd cemented himself as one of the most notorious criminal identities in Australia's gangland folklore.

And in October 2003, the only thing Darwiche was thinking about was war with the Razzak clan.

The Razzaks were a large extended family. Some members were heavily in the drug trade and controlled the runs around Hurstville, a lucrative patch, a staging point and corridor to customers west and south of Darwiche's turf.

The acrimony between Darwiche and the Razzaks was both complex and personal. Family honour and pride was at stake; their feuding had amped up over time from bashings to home invasions to kneecappings to drive-by shootings. People on both sides were marked for death. The tipping point had come in mid 2003 when the Razzaks had tried to kill Darwiche's close friend Khaled 'Crazy' Taleb, a high-school dropout who carried a gun so often and so freely that he started wearing a holster. Taleb had been shot five times during the Razzak ambush, the holster ironically preventing him from pulling out his own gun and firing back. From then on Darwiche had banned anyone in his crew from wearing holsters – and he planned to carry out an almighty blitzkrieg of thunderous retribution. Darwiche wanted something memorable and permanent. If he failed he faced a lifetime in prison, or death. But if he succeeded it would restore a pride that had slipped.

After cleaning the bullets, Darwiche and his crew left the Punchbowl unit and relocated to David Street, Greenacre, to another safe house where Darwiche's weapons had been moved ahead of the shooting. It was a few minutes past midnight. He took a seat at the kitchen table, grabbed a paper and pen, and began mapping out the logistics of the upcoming attack. He plotted the route he and his men would take to the Razzak safe house and marked out where everyone would stand during the attack. Then he planned their getaway route.

Just after 3am they rolled out in a stolen car and pulled up minutes later outside a fibro house at the bottom of Lawford Street, a cul-de-sac in the same suburb. It was a brittle-looking home, the kind that might sway if you pushed it hard enough. They didn't know exactly who would be inside, but they knew at least some Razzaks would be there. It didn't matter which ones.

Masked in balaclavas, they lined themselves up on the road in their pre-marked positions to avoid hitting each other in friendly fire.

On Darwiche's signal they started blasting the house, moving their guns in an 'S' shape for maximum damage, so if anyone inside the house tried to dive for cover a bullet would still catch them. They shelled the house with bullets until all they could hear were the dull metallic clicks of cartridge casings hitting the tarmac. It was over in seconds. Out of ammunition, they drove off, dumping the car on a nearby street and setting it alight, incinerating any evidence they might have left behind. Another vehicle, left there in advance, was waiting for them. They hurried to yet another safe house, where they changed clothes and then sat in front of the TV, waiting for the morning news to reveal the body count.

Crime scene officers got to Lawford Street within minutes of the shooting and began counting the cartridge shells strewn all over the road. There were ninety-nine in total. The recoil from the guns had sent many bullets wide of their mark; rounds were found in the trees and soil outside the property. They had shot clean through the chimney and side gate, into roof tiles that had exploded into shrapnel, and into the blue-and-white awnings that were hanging above the home's shattered windows.

The bullets that made it into the house had cut a chaotic path through kitchen cupboards and couches in the living room, perforating anything in their path and boring their way upwards into the bodies of two people who had been trying to sleep at the time.

In the bedroom was Mervat 'Melissa' Nemra, twenty-two, a mother of two small children. She was a bystander, an unintended casualty. Her husband, Ali, had opened their home to members of the Razzak family, granting them safe haven while their war with Adnan Darwiche continued to rage. For weeks she and the kids had avoided the house, coming back only to clean up and do the laundry. But that night she'd decided to stay over, leaving the kids with her mother. The bullet that had passed through her neck was medium-to-large calibre, the kind made to pierce an armour-plated vehicle. She had died within minutes.

Death had not come as quickly for Ziad 'Ziggy' Razzak, one of Darwiche's arch-rivals. The paramedics found him slumped on a sofa in the lounge room, barely breathing but somehow still alive. His legs had been shot out and there was an exit wound in his forehead. For seven hours he fought to stay alive on the operating table at St George Hospital, succumbing to his injuries at 10:05am.

The only survivor of the shooting was Melissa's husband, Ali Hamka. He'd been sitting in a chair next to Ziggy when the shooting began. His recollection of the incident, given to police later, was a vivid re-enactment that seemed to play out in his retelling in slow motion, like a scene from a movie with the sound cut for dramatic effect. Bullets travel faster than the speed of sound, which might explain why Hamka hadn't heard the gunfire at first; instead he'd seen an orange glow atop of his television set getting brighter and brighter. Half-asleep, he'd looked at Ziggy as the windows started popping, the blinds swaying as though pushed by a gentle breeze and not by the whir of bullets slamming into the house. Small black holes appeared in random locations along the walls. He told police he'd dived to the ground and kept his head covered as glass from the windows pulsed through the air. When the shooting was over he had crawled to the bedroom and found his wife's body. He held her hand and dialled Triple 0, the operator instructing him to press a towel into her neck.

The events of that night, later known as the 'Lawford Street shooting', galvanised the NSW Police Force and the state government into action. The ferocity of the attack, the players involved, the access to military-grade weaponry and the threat to community safety were emblematic of a much greater problem that had been festering without an adequate response. Many people have an opinion on why the police weren't containing the MEOC situation, but the majority view is that everything traced back to the shakeup of police tactics after the Wood Royal Commission of the mid 1990s.

Led by Justice James Wood, the Royal Commission into the then NSW Police Service exposed a toxic culture of graft and corruption. Bent cops were named and shamed in sensational hearings. Some quit the force; others committed suicide. The commission took a blowtorch to the organisation, applying heat to everyone. Clean officers, the good guys, were ordered to give evidence against their colleagues and grilled over basic law enforcement tradecraft, long-standing tactics that had been abused by bad eggs and were now considered suspicious. Search warrants were seen as a corruption risk because of the easy access to cash and jewellery. Recruiting informants was suddenly a bad thing, encouraging collusion with the enemy. Paranoia reigned. What followed was a drop-off in sources, which had always been the lifeblood of intelligence gathering.

At the time, Middle Eastern organised crime was still a fledgling industry, but in this demoralised law enforcement environment, gangs and crime began to thrive in vulnerable areas where police were MIA. Areas like Telopea Street, Punchbowl, became a drive-through drug market – outside one house you could buy cocaine; at another you could buy cannabis. In Kings Cross, rival gangs went to war over the nightclub scene, the most notorious of them led by Danny Karam. His crew, known as DK's Boys, battled over drug turf and then came after the police, taking violence to the next level. On 1 November 1998, they shot sixteen bullets into Lakemba Police Station, narrowly missing officers standing at the counter inside. Ten days later, thirteen shotgun rounds were fired into eleven houses on Eveleigh Street, Redfern, the heartland of Sydney's Indigenous community. This was in response to a fight between Aboriginal and Lebanese inmates at Lithgow Correctional Centre. As the gunmen sped away in their car, they chucked an Aboriginal flag out the window, scrawled with a message that said: 'Fuck with our brothers inside. We fuck with all your families outside. Blood for blood. P.S. LITHGOW GAOL ... 2 DIE 4?'

With these shootings at Lakemba and Redfern, the public got their first taste of MEOC – a new wave of criminal, more aggressive and daring. Politicians felt the blowback, coming under fire for a lack of action. The response from police in some southwestern Sydney commands was to conduct sweeping targeting of Middle Eastern men; a zero tolerance approach that created hostility and broke whatever fragile trust was still left after the Royal Commission. Victims of crime, family men, potential witnesses – all of whom wanted to achieve the same objective as the police: safer streets – felt bitter about getting jacked up on the streets, frisked and forced to answer questions. This was not the way to win hearts and minds. Those who did the right thing and tried reporting crimes got only a sporadic response from officers. Crimes weren't getting solved, and as a law enforcement agency, the police had become impotent.

In the days after the Lawford Street shooting, newspaper headlines depicted southwestern Sydney as a rogue territory controlled by armed gangs and drug dealers. The city's biggest tabloid newspaper, the *Daily Telegraph*, ran a prominent editorial demanding action. 'All of us must demand an end to the violence, a return to civility, a return to the Sydney we all know is the best city on earth,' the editorial read.

Even Police Commissioner Ken Moroney branded the violence 'urban terrorism'. His response was to set up Task Force Gain, a contingent of 160 police officers whose job would be to dedicate themselves to the problem of Middle Eastern organised crime.

In the past there had been similar efforts but these were piecemeal in the scheme of things, Band-Aid solutions. There had never been a dedicated, overarching law enforcement response to what were viewed as isolated incidents, like a gunshot victim staggering into a hospital, or a half-naked body found floating in a creek. The reality was these incidents and others like them were all symptomatic of a much deeper and clandestine industry of organised crime. They pointed to family structures, business relationships, tentative alliances, and cunning methodologies.

To preserve the fragile relationship police had with the Middle Eastern community, there was no public mention of the fact that Task Force Gain was specifically geared towards the issue of Middle Eastern organised crime. When it was launched on 22 October 2003, its officers immediately took control of ten active murders and nine separate strike forces. They were divided up into teams of criminal investigators, uniformed police, highway patrol officers, and a unit known as the Target Action Group (TAG), whose role would become something of a new concept in policing methodology.

One thing that quickly became apparent was that every crime scene had its roots in drugs and drug territory. Every shooting, every murder, every conflict was somehow planted in a conflict about drugs: a disagreement over money, an import that went awry or a runner who had ventured into rival turf. 'All roads lead back to drugs,' became one police chief's memorable refrain.

Within a year, coming off a relatively cold start with few informants or inroads, Task Force Gain had proven its worth. It made 1069 arrests, seized twenty-three handguns and recovered around $3.5 million worth of drugs.

The only problem was the price tag attached: Task Force Gain was a bloated, expensive initiative. It took up too much manpower and couldn't keep going forever.

For years prior, some senior officers had been making quiet submissions to police brass for a permanent Middle Eastern Organised Crime Squad, but they had been met with resistance from state politicians and representatives of the Middle Eastern community, some of whom saw the notion as racist and unfair, a form of ethnic profiling. The work of Task Force Gain seemed to soften their stance, but by the end of 2005 there was still no firm commitment to create a permanent task force, and warnings were being sounded about the ramifications of doing nothing: crime would creep back up, new players would emerge, intelligence would become outdated. This type of crime wasn't going away, and the most dire predictions forecast that another expensive Task Force Gain–style initiative would be necessary within a few years. If, however, the state acted to establish a scaled-down replacement, as one briefing paper suggested, the problem could be managed and it would ultimately save the state money.

A turning point in the argument came on a warm December afternoon in 2005 when a short fight erupted between three lifeguards and a group of Middle Eastern beachgoers on the sand at Cronulla Beach. Construed as an assault on Australian values, what followed were three days of ugly, roiling scenes of public bashings and anti-Muslim sentiment that would become known as the 'Cronulla Riots'. In retaliation, convoys of Middle Eastern men wreaked havoc across the beach suburbs, trashing cars and local businesses, catching police off guard and testing the law enforcement response to sudden and fluid eruptions of violence.

The job of investigating the Cronulla Riots and reporting back on the police response fell to Detective Chief Superintendent Ken McKay, a fixer of sorts and a maverick operator. McKay was regarded as a cool head by Police Commissioner Ken Moroney, someone who could parachute into a tricky situation, handle the television cameras, and bat away questions from journalists.

Under great pressure to respond to the riots, the NSW government made a sudden announcement in January 2006: a permanent Middle Eastern Organised Crime Squad would be set up within months. It was an ironic twist considering the Middle Eastern men arrested during McKay's investigation of the riots were not even remotely involved in organised crime; most were ordinary guys with wives and day jobs, who had been whipped up in the week's hysteria. After seven years of gangland violence and multiple reports urging a permanent solution to the MEOC problem, it was a punch thrown on a beach that made all the difference.

Moroney asked McKay to be the commander of this new Squad and gave him 108 officers: forty-seven criminal investigators, twenty-two Target Action Group detectives, sixteen uniformed police on general duties, twelve highway patrol officers, eight intelligence analysts, two Arabic interpreters and one executive assistant.

On Monday, 1 May 2006, these officers and their support staff formed up for duty.

CHAPTER ONE

NO PAIN, NO GAIN

INDUCTION DAY, MEOCS HEADQUARTERS
MONDAY, 1 MAY 2006

A corpse flashed up on a projector screen in front of a darkened lecture hall full of police officers. The dark brown eyes were fixed in a stare as the body cooled on a concrete floor of a western Sydney car yard. The arms were slung out to the side like they were strung up to a crucifix and the blood had stopped pooling just past the elbow, oozing in a puddle that started from beneath the torso. If you looked hard enough the puddle almost passed for an angel's wing. The cause of death: a volley of gunshots, five at close range. He hadn't even seen it coming – four in the back, one in the head. A classic gangland hit, said Detective Inspector Mick Ryan, curating the slideshow at the front of the room. He clicked a button to load up the next image. It was another death scene, this time a bedroom – a man lying face-down on a mattress, the sheets soaked wet with blood and the body turning purple; a drug runner, Ryan said. The next slide was a two-storey mini-mansion, renovated with a driveway and Christmas lights dangling from a balcony – a picture of good living. The only thing out of place was the bonnet of a police car jutting out from the corner of the frame, its presence explained in the next slide, a wide shot of the front door with another body on the ground, a well-dressed man who'd gone outside for a cigarette. A trickle of blood had been caught mid-rush as it coursed down the tiled walkway past an exhibit marker at his feet – the victim of a drive-by shooting, Ryan told the officers, all there on day one of their new assignment.

Mick Ryan's induction speech at MEOCS HQ was a welcome of sorts, a macabre presentation with a bit of everything: ugly mugshots, grisly death scenes, videos of drug dealing, crime theory 101. Sitting there taking it all in were 100-odd police representing a cross-section of careers and disciplines: detectives in black suits and cargo shorts, beat cops in soft vests, wide-eyed rookies, veterans who had seen it all, and a smattering of dead weight shanghaied from police commands across the city, there to make up the numbers in those early days.

Their office was inside a sad-looking mid-rise, constructed with too much red brick and too little character – like a dreary science block from a suburban high school. This was probably intentional. It was supposed to be a covert building, its exact address kept a secret as a security measure. Criminals were never brought back there, and if charges were laid they were done at an actual police station.

MEOCS had been given two levels of office space in the building, a place that in its heyday had been a prestigious NSW Police Region Command, a nerve centre where top brass gathered and big decisions were made. Since then it had been allowed to dilapidate. The Region office moved out and a rolling cavalcade of strike forces, task forces and incident responses moved in. By the time it was gifted to MEOCS, its rooms had been abandoned for years. Relics from these bygone eras were still there when Ken McKay, the Squad's newly appointed commander, first arrived for an inspection in April 2006. In one corner was a rickety metal cupboard sealed with crime scene tape. Kitschy Christmas decorations pointed the way to Santa's village. A map of southwestern Sydney the size of a small suburb was still hanging on a wall from previous strike force operations; largely ornamental, its utility for planning search warrants had been made redundant by GPS technology. As McKay surveyed the room he could detect a faint stench of mildew. Pigeons were flying in and out through open windows.

He had the two floors industrially cleaned and set up a bullpen of desks on both levels. Level Three would be assigned to his Criminal Investigation (CI) teams while the rest of the Squad – the Uniform branch, Highway Patrol, Target Action Group, Intelligence division, Telephone Intercept translators – were told to share the space on Level Two.

Few detectives under McKay had more experience policing Middle Eastern organised crime than Mick Ryan, which was why he was up there on Day One with his slideshow, giving the rest of the Squad a three-hour primer on the lessons he had learned from Task Force Gain.

Ryan was a very fit 46-year-old, a triathlete in his spare time. He was gruff, like Clint Eastwood, with a slight squint in one eye – hence his nickname 'Dirty Harry'. Years of working in organised crime had given him an intense manner. Before Task Force Gain he'd worked at the Gangs Squad. Before that it was the Drug and Organised Crime Strike Force Program (East Coast), another forerunner to MEOCS. It was a unit of pioneers who had made their careers during the late 1990s, a time when Middle Eastern organised crime was still a nascent industry and the police force was rudderless after the Royal Commission. Informants had dropped off and crime figures had risen, but even in this climate several cops had thrown it all to the wind and gone out on their own. Celebrated cases like Strike Force Mask, Strike Force Lancer and Strike Force

Ranger routed out the drug dealers of Telopea Street and ended the shooting rampages of DK's Boys. These were investigations that had won awards and gone on CVs, creating a distinguished alumni out of the detectives who were part of them; it was like being at the Sydney 2000 Olympics, or Woodstock. Being on just one of these cases was enough to cement a cop's credentials. Ryan, a veteran, had worked on all three.

He rarely smiled while he was on the job, but his humour was wicked and biting. After an argument about overtime pay with a disgruntled detective, he dumped a box full of babies' dummies on the guy's desk, $50 worth, laughing as he walked away. But he was also fiercely protective of his staff. Prior to his job at the Squad, he had once heard a rumour about an underworld figure making plans to assassinate one of his detectives; Ryan had gone out of his way to track the criminal down, hauling him into a police station and locking the door behind him in an interview room.

'I'm the one telling him to go after you,' Ryan had told the criminal, getting in close to the guy's face and thumping a finger into his chest. 'It's me you've got to be worried about. Threaten me,' he'd said, the words coming out as an invitation. The rumours ceased after that.

Even as he gave his induction speech and clicked through his slideshow, Ryan's demeanour made colleagues wary, signalling he was not to be trifled with. When a reasonably senior highway patrol officer yawned at the halfway point, Ryan stopped everything and pointed at the officer.

'Am I fucking boring you?' he asked, stunning the room, before moving on.

Ryan likened organised crime to a sickness; the violence and crime scenes weren't the causes, but the symptoms, emblematic of something bigger. Every street dealer, every gangland execution, every drive-by shooting or half-baked extortion was a shift in a broader narrative: a patch of drug turf under threat; a broken alliance; a powerplay beneath the surface. The key players were revealed to the room as super-savvy villains who changed their phone numbers twice a month and used high-frequency scanners to look for bugs planted in their homes. One guy even drove the length of his street every night with a torch to check parked cars for surveillance operatives.

Historically, Ryan told the Squad, the Vietnamese had their heroin imports and the Italians had their 'grass castles'. Those were their niches and they stuck with them; violence was a last resort. Middle Eastern organised crime was a new beast in this arena. Whatever had come previously was no match. One of Ryan's slides had the word 'MEOC' written in the middle of it and a series of straight lines sticking out, each one joining with a sub-heading – rape, serious assault, murder, arson, explosives, extortion, prostitution, money laundering, immigration offences, insurance fraud, identity fraud, terrorism, car rebirthing, weapons offences.

Task Force Gain had revealed this concept in practical terms. There were guys involved in arms trafficking who were wanted by the Arson Squad. A suspect in a homicide was running a home-loan scam. A standover man was rumoured to be holding C4 explosives. A family in Punchbowl was sending pot to South Australia and buying handguns with silencers from Melbourne. Every case was like a fractal pattern moving out in all directions, each job leading to three more.

The arrival of Task Force Gain had come as a shock to these crims. Working like a ground radar, it mapped out two distinct layers of underworld character. Beneath the topsoil were the sloppy criminals, many of whom were rounded up through routine work like pat-downs, search warrants and vehicle stops. These low-hanging fruit were quickly flipped into 'street assets' and given benefits if they worked as informants – small cash payments, a reduction on their sentence. The intelligence they fed back to detectives was harvested to track the second type of targets, those at the bedrock, the drug bosses who stayed ahead of the law by hiding their stash in telephone pits, or who used encrypted walkie-talkies to prevent their conversations being intercepted. These were the people who carried modified handguns with thirty-bullet magazines and imported new weapons via the Melbourne ports. Having never been fired, the guns had no scent for the sniffer dogs to pick up.

These people had been Ryan's world.

But even though Task Force Gain had locked up many of these targets, its work had unearthed a legion of others. It had swept through the MEOC community and identified the breadth of the problem, but arrived late to the game. By the time MEOCS was formed, the criminals who had been arrested by Task Force Gain were, in many cases, either out of prison or due for parole. For the fledgling Squad, this meant figuring out the lay of the land all over again, the who's who in the zoo. The work of Task Force Gain, Ryan told the men and women before him, had only scratched the surface. Now it was up to them.

CHAPTER TWO

THE LAY OF THE LAND

By mid 2006, at the time the Squad was formed, the world of Middle Eastern organised crime – a world of drug empires, notorious families, hired guns, street dealers, run managers, big-noters, grifters and bullshit artists – had settled into a hierarchy of status. Picture it in your mind like a triangle partitioned into several tiers, kind of like the food pyramid.

At the very top were senior members of powerful families with surnames like Ahmad, Ibrahim, Kalache and Darwiche, each with their own pseudo-governance over a patch of Sydney. They controlled turf and wielded power, mediated disputes and maintained order. The Ahmads had Punchbowl. The Ibrahims had Kings Cross. Successive police investigations had failed against them. In some areas it wasn't a family but a street gang. In Fairfield it was DLASTHR, an Assyrian crime group, its members Christian and mostly Northern Iraqi in heritage. In Villawood, the suburb next door, it was the Bronx Boys, now a footnote in history after their leader was murdered.

In the same league as these families and street crews were outlaw motorcycle gangs – Hells Angels, Nomads, Bandidos, Comancheros and Rebels. They provided muscle, manufactured drugs, did the importations, or helped with distribution; they were omniscient actors who sat outside the MEOC triangle but established partnerships with its top tier players. Some of these arrangements were closer than others. When Hassan 'Sam' Ibrahim, the eldest brother of the Ibrahim clan, joined the Nomads in the 1990s his membership immediately gave him an army and, in exchange, created an opening for the gang in Kings Cross, where Sam and his siblings had cemented themselves in the nightclub scene.

Beneath this upper echelon was a middle tier of movers who paid protection money to operate within patches of turf. These people were known as the upline suppliers; they were the backbone of the drug industry, the wholesalers who distributed big bags of ecstasy and cocaine to syndicates feeding the end users. In routine swindles common to the trade, they artificially inflated the volume by adding lignocaine, the dental anaesthetic, or Glucodin, the energy powder.

Under them were the syndicate bosses, the retail side of the industry, the franchisees who dealt direct with the customers. Their ventures were run like small businesses, each one requiring a run manager to handle operations and street dealers to do the dealing. They worked in shifts. Each day the run manager would get up early, bag the drugs at the safe house, count the cash, plan the roster, dole out the drug phones, make sure the delivery cars were fuelled up, and work any security.

Then came the triggermen and toughs who settled scores and collected debts. They were freelancers who worked for anybody, getting paid to do dirty work ranging from a bashing to a murder. There were tales of runners getting severely beaten just for crossing the street and dealing in the wrong territory, incidents that almost always led to war.

Finally, at the very bottom, were the dealers and delivery drivers, the cockatoos and gofers. These aspiring gangsters were often teenagers, or junkies who got paid in their drug of choice or worked to pay off a debt. They were the easiest targets for MEOCS, the low-hanging fruit who could easily be snatched off the street and shaken down for intelligence – the address of a safe house, the run cars doing the deliveries, the name and phone number of their bosses.

Ken McKay, the commander of MEOCS, was a man whose philosophies were captured in football metaphors and a handful of phrases – 'You can do 100 things right,' he'd say, often, 'but fuck one goat and you'll forever be known as a goatfucker.' He wanted this hierarchy organised into a priority list of the top 100 MEOC identities and crime families across Sydney. He gave this task to Mick Ryan, one of the most experienced detectives in the Squad. Ryan came up with a list of forty-two. These were the captains of industry, a grab bag of Teflon-coated figures: godfather types who never got their hands dirty, drug importers with low profiles, street bosses juggling five or six runs at a time, and tattooed musclemen just out on parole. The official name of this document was the MEOC Risk Assessment Register, but within the Squad it was simply called the Most Wanted List.

Making the cut was a carefully managed process. A big name wasn't enough; you had to be a risk to the community as well. Prospective names were run through an intelligence matrix and assigned a risk rating – medium, high or critical – and then given a corresponding number to quantify their risk. Anything above 190 was deemed critical. High risk started at 150 and medium at 125.

The twelve names on McKay's original 'critical list' were heavy with authority. They were survivors who are still around today, characters like Sam Ibrahim, Mahmoud 'Brownie' Ahmad, and Nasser Kalache who was a tow truck operator and, at one time, the owner of a pizza shop.

In the 'high-risk' category were people like Shadi Derbas, a Telopea Street original; Abdul Darwiche, another authority figure in the Darwiche family; Moustapha 'Wak' Assoum, a professional boxer and gun-for-hire; and Tony Haddad, a gifted conman with an unflappable poker-face. Known for his grifting, Haddad had once shown up to a drug deal with an empty suitcase, handing it over in exchange for $300,000. There were twenty-one others in this category.

As the commander, McKay had several options to deal with the players on his Most Wanted List. The 'critical' targets were mostly assigned to his criminal investigators: MEOCS CI. They were teams of detectives who were prepared to take on months of telephone eavesdropping and risky undercover operations. Microphones were snuck into houses and tracking devices planted on cars. This all made for slow-burning investigations, but the outcome was almost always a straitjacket of charges, the kind that left no wriggle room when the case ended up at court, resulting in lengthy prison terms.

The less-sophisticated targets, the drug-addled who rampaged through the suburbs and needed to be caught because of the risk they posed to the community, were assigned to the Uniform branch, a company split into Highway Patrol and General Duties officers. They were the public face of MEOCS, the only staff who deliberately looked like police. Cruising hot-spot neighbourhoods like Punchbowl, Bankstown, Auburn and Granville each day, their cars were instantly recognisable by the green and yellow paint, or the word MEOCS emblazoned on the bonnet.

For those cops working General Duties, each shift started with a printout of names and addresses: criminals on bail, parolees with curfews, repeat offenders and fugitives wanted for anything from car theft to assault. The idea was to find as many of them as possible and disrupt their routine. Catch them buying milk, or driving to their girlfriend's house. If they weren't wanted for arrest, the objective was to search them for weapons, ask questions, make them feel paranoid about being watched. In this way the MEOCS brand itself became a powerful tool, a passive crime deterrent, creating the impression of an all-seeing, all-knowing Squad with endless resources for close surveillance. That, of course, wasn't the case – but if a crim thought twice about leaving the house with a gun, well, that was half the job done. Informants were soon reporting back to their handlers about the psychological effect these constant interactions were having, telling MEOCS officers that carrying anything was no longer tenable when their Squad cars were live in their area.

It was the same routine for the Highway Patrol – constant interaction. McKay didn't want them running breath tests and speed traps. Let the local cops do that, he said. The job of the MEOCS Highway Patrol, in his mind, was to focus solely on top gang members and their associates, the troublemakers doing burnouts and running red lights. Sure, these were relatively minor infractions, but they presented all kinds of opportunities.

Most of the MEOCS Highway Patrol officers had spent their careers on the road; they were family men, avuncular and paunchy, sages of the front line who were known for their quick talk. They gathered intel under the guise of general banter. Each question, friendly and casual, was loaded with an angle: *Where are you headed? Who's that sitting next to you? Are you still living round here?* As a support unit, they were an in-house luxury at MEOCS that no other crime squad had at its disposal. If a listening device was being installed in a house and the target was spotted coming home earlier than expected, the Highway Patrol could discreetly stop the car and buy the operatives a few extra minutes. It was the same with the General Duties cops: if a target was having their phone tapped but wasn't making enough calls, a uniformed officer could knock on their door, ask them a few questions, and rattle the cage to stimulate some nervous dialling to associates.

These were just the small bonuses to having these units available. But being the public face of MEOCS put them in a prime position to win back the community's trust, to build up the kind of alliances and back channel sources of information that were needed to stop crime in the neighbourhood. The community was filled with good people, families and business owners all fed up with the drive-by shootings and gangster mentality. It was their shops being stood over, their children being lured into street life, their houses broadcast on the nightly news when shots were fired.

One practical measure McKay implemented to keep the community onside was to use discretion on the roads. One morning while flicking through the overnight Traffic Infringement Notices, McKay realised that way too many 'mum and dad' members of the community were being hit with petty traffic fines. Stinging these people did nothing for the MEOCS cause. McKay gave his officers an edict that from then on any motorist caught doing a low-level offence could be let off at the officer's discretion. McKay wanted to show the community – his potential eyes and ears on the ground – that not all cops were bad. 'Win hearts,' he said.

At a corporate level, McKay was working the same concept, organising training days for his staff with community representatives and getting himself spots on local Arabic radio stations. At every turn, he encouraged the community to align itself with the police. Help us help you, that was the message. Talk to us. Tell us where to look. Tell us where the crime is happening. Fridge magnets were handed out with the MEOCS logo on one side and the phone number of an anonymous crime tip-off line on the other. When the magnets became too expensive, the letterbox dropping started, a job delegated to the uniform staff.

Of course, there were missteps along this route of goodwill too, but these were corrected fast. The MEOCS emblem itself became a source of unexpected controversy. A complaint was lodged about its central design feature, a wood wasp, the natural enemy of the cedar tree. Given the cedar tree's iconic and central role in the design of the Lebanese flag, the emblem underwent a hasty redesign. It was the kind of faux pas that could derail all the effort going into strengthening community relations. Ties belonging to some Squad members had to be replaced – the wood wasp featured on them as well. An email went around inviting officers and staff to contribute to the redesign process. Some took it more seriously than others. One suggestion, which someone actually drew up, was a mullet being trimmed off with a pair of scissors – the mullet was a popular hairstyle among some Squad targets. 'Cutting out crime,' was the suggested tagline.

Eventually, a more neutral design with a sword, feathered wings, and a Latin motto was agreed upon. The motto – Auspicium Melioris Aevi – meant 'Omen of a Better Age', but it didn't quite catch on with staff.

An unofficial motto – 'but fuck one goat' – got repeated more often.

CHAPTER THREE

MEOCS TAG: THE EARLY YEARS

REVESBY, WEDNESDAY, 24 MAY 2006

He was lanky and jittery, with messed-up hair and an unusual bulge protruding from the front of his jacket. A junkie. Detectives Dave Roberts and Andrew Mitchell had spotted him from their car. Years of street policing had taught them to spot the odd and unusual in a neighbourhood. And sure, there was nothing illegal about a man walking through a park after dark; but to them something felt unsavoury about him.

'What's in the front of your jacket?' Roberts asked him, more curious than suspicious. A big man with a deep voice, Roberts looked more like a debt collector than a cop. He was dressed in faded blue jeans and a t-shirt – the standard dress of a MEOCS TAG detective. In a bumbag around his waist was capsicum spray and spare ammunition. Handcuffs and a Glock pistol were just visible at his hip.

The junkie reached into the pockets of his jacket and produced a collection of sexual lubricants clenched in each fist – squishy KY Jelly sachets, the kind that look like McDonald's ketchup packets. There were seven in total, all stolen, he admitted. The plan was to sell each one for a dollar.

Roberts had been expecting cannabis, maybe cocaine; you could never tell with junkies. Whenever he thought he'd seen it all, the street would show him something new. He turned to Mitchell. On the surface this looked like a waste of everyone's time, but, technically, the KY Jelly was stolen property. It was also leverage.

A brief check over the police radio revealed the guy had form as a skilled thief. He had a lengthy rap sheet and was fresh out on parole. Roberts played the bad cop, telling the thief his situation was more serious than it looked. His parole could be revoked. Mitchell stepped in with the lifeline. 'Is there anything you want to tell us?' he asked, signalling the start of that subtle interplay between cop and criminal, the invitation to barter in exchange for assistance. The man understood the implication immediately, happy to turn informant for the night.

He told them about a heroin dealer in Riverwood, a guy selling directly from his apartment. It wasn't much, barely a lead, but enough to get started. 'I don't know his name,' the junkie told the detectives, 'but he drives a red BMW.' If he was lying they'd come back and find him, Roberts said.

The next morning, as always, McKay flipped through the overnight paperwork from each team inspecting each arrest, a type of quality control as he saw it. He stopped at the Revesby incident and scanned through the notes about seized KY Jelly packets. The finer details about the drug dealer in Riverwood with the red BMW had been left out. That kind of follow-up intelligence wasn't normally included on standard paperwork.

'Is this what MEOCS has come to?' McKay asked, bemused but laughing. He had taken the printout and walked into the bullpen, pulling up a swivel chair next to Roberts and Mitchell at their desks in the Target Action Group (TAG) section of the room. He held the report up in the air and squinted at it, like it might be exposed as a fake in better light. With each read-through McKay found something else to laugh about, a new detail he'd missed. 'He's not even Middle Eastern!' he ribbed, which was true; the man Mitchell and Roberts had stopped did not fall within the Squad's usual charter – he was more Mediterranean than Middle Eastern – and didn't come close to being an organised crime figure. Roberts assured McKay there was more to the story, a heroin seizure potentially.

Had it been any other detectives with the same explanation, McKay might have stayed dubious. But Roberts and Mitchell had reputations behind them. They had started at the TAG office like everyone else only a couple of weeks earlier, but had already proven themselves to be heavy lifters.

They first met at Burwood back in 2003 where Roberts had been part of a proactive crime unit, a scaled-down version of what was to come at MEOCS. Burwood was an incubator, a testing ground where tactics could be trialled and tweaked. They were a team of four who practised surveillance and broke up gangs: Islanders, Asians and Middle Eastern crews who loitered on the steps of the Uniting Church and walked in packs through the street malls.

As a team they cruised the suburb in a 4WD with their windows down and their forearms planted on the door frames, their eyes scanning for faces, their ears listening to the streets. There was a hint of the Riot Squad about the Burwood Proactive Team, particularly Roberts and Mitchell – both men were six-foot something, hair carved to the scalp, their bodyweights never below 110 kilograms. Roberts had been a bouncer in a previous life. Mitchell had played rugby in England.

The Target Action Group's first arrest had been theirs, a coke dealer stopped in Punchbowl with a gram tucked into his underwear.

Four days later they hit a small milestone: the TAG's first raid: a home in Roselands, a villa among the modest brick houses and churches of suburbia that concealed boxes filled with the remains of a drug lab – dismantled glassware, chemistry equipment, beakers, funnels and baking trays. In the freezer were two bags of freshly made crystal methamphetamine worth about $25,000. In the living room was a phone book peppered with bullet holes. The phone book led the detectives to their second milestone: the unit's first gun seizure, a sawn-off rifle found leaning against a wall. The owner of the house, newly married and looking for a deal, told Roberts he would plead guilty to everything if he spared his wife who, on account of living in the house, was charged with the same offences.

Given this track record, McKay didn't doubt his detectives were onto a good thing with their lead about the Riverwood dealer and his red BMW. Both officers showed up to work the next morning, grabbed a set of car keys and drove laps through the suburb looking for the car. The streets were like a snapshot out of the 1950s, all triple-front housing and local bakeries. An old service station looked like it might have once had a mechanic on duty. After three hours, they spotted the car turning right onto Belmore Road and pulled it over, quizzing the driver, Anwar Elabbas. He had cash in his pocket – about $1600 – but no drugs. His passenger had a small rock of heroin in his underpants. The two detectives were familiar enough with crims by then to know what these guys must have been thinking: cops won't search underpants. Some cops were too squeamish for it, but any suspected dealer unlucky enough to cross Roberts and Mitchell got a gloved hand, a torch and a series of orders: squat down, cough three times, lift that up, move that to the side, cough again. No gloves? No problem. Mitchell went in anyway, probing deep.

Elabbas's apartment was in a complex of low-rise buildings on Roosevelt Avenue, a public housing estate across the road from a childcare centre. As the TAG officers stood guard at the entrance, waiting for someone back at the office to type up a search warrant, customers turned up and made lame excuses for why they were there. 'He wanted me to come and fix his air-conditioning,' one buyer told them.

Four hours later, the search warrant approved, Roberts and Mitchell burst inside the apartment with a team behind them. They were looking for heroin but stumbled instead on a .22-calibre revolver loaded with five bullets. They discovered it in a bedroom wardrobe; it was a prized find, their second weapons seizure in a fortnight. At MEOCS, finding a gun was a coup, worth more than a bag full of drugs – firearms arguably posed a more immediate threat to the community.

But gun charges were difficult to prosecute in court and filled with gaps for defendants to argue their innocence. Elabbas's lawyers argued that he'd never seen the gun before, and used the lack of DNA or fingerprints on the weapon to advance their point. Unable to prove Elabbas had ever touched the gun, even though it was found in his bedroom, the charge was withdrawn. However he was charged and convicted over the cash offence.

This brand of fast-moving arrest became a specialty of the TAG office, creating a surge in firearm and drug seizures. Within months, search warrant statistics were off the chart: eleven raids in June, seven in July, four in August, then back to eight in September. Rival commands couldn't come close to those numbers; they averaged one, maybe two in a month. A handful of officers thrived in this environment, spurring each other on, creating a kind of revved-up rivalry. But few were more talked about, by police and the criminals themselves, than Roberts and Mitchell. McKay called them 'the Breaker Brothers'. They were huge characters with a style of their own, magnets for trouble.

On slow afternoons they rode out to Telopea Street, Punchbowl, or Pine Road, Auburn, both difficult neighbourhoods considered too unsafe to go without backup. There they would park outside the most notorious family's house and eat lunch on the bonnet of their MEOCS car, turning up the radio to attract attention, sitting back and waiting for a dirty look, an insult, any kind of interaction. That was their MO: work the streets, start a dialogue, recruit informants, get the tip-offs.

Within a few months criminals were asking about them, dropping their names on intercepted calls, warning friends to look out for them. They were respected, feared and hated. They were exactly what McKay had wanted in his Target Action Group.

MEOCS TAG would over time become its own community within the Squad's general apparatus, walled-off and rife with its own code and jargon. It was a mix of personality types and male dominated: alphas and easy-going beta types, rookies with big egos, quiet achievers, loud achievers and mild-mannered detectives with families, mortgages and golf on Sunday.

As a unit they comprised roughly twenty-two officers, plain-clothed and spread across two teams. A team was eight detectives plus two team leaders ranked detective sergeant. They answered to the TAG's commander, Detective Inspector David Adney, who in turn reported to Ken McKay, the Squad's commander.

Adney was old school in attitude, but new school in strategy. He was a scrupulous details man, a man who believed in spreadsheets. He meticulously recorded every arrest, every gun, every drug seizure, and typed them up alongside street names, suburbs, logos and colours – green Mitsubishi ecstasy pills in Roselands; purple dolphins in Campbelltown. He worked the stats to find the trends, trace the drug runs, scan for hotspots.

Adney called this proactive policing, the art of self-generating, *finding* crimes and then solving them. It could be street dealing in a nightclub or a drug run taking over a suburb; the point was to work informants, figure out the problem, and then attack it with solutions: drugs dogs, undercover officers, uniform police, more visibility. This was Adney's niche, something that wasn't pushed at the academy, and something he developed as the TAG commander during Task Force Gain. As a mainstream tactic, it was under-utilised. Of course Adney, with a background in special tactics, was anything but mainstream.

As a police officer, Adney straddled the worlds of commando and cop, a by-product of his early career in the Tactical Response Group and Tactical Operations Unit. They were the big guns, the men of last resort, the guys who arrived not by car, but by armoured vehicle and helicopter. Their world was counter-terrorism and high-risk resolution, days filled with fast roping, stress shoots, kill houses. If you were in that group it meant you were comfortable with the sound of gunfire. If you excelled it meant being handpicked to train with the nation's elite, the SAS commandos in Perth. Adney was one of them, thrown into night manoeuvres and embassy assault missions. It was there he got the nickname 'the Frag'. Most cops say it's a nod to his fighting style, explosive and uncontrollable like a fragmentation grenade. Adney tells people, wryly, that it's because he's 'fragile'.

Six years as a tactical operative gave him a militaristic edge to his bearing. He brought this mindset to MEOCS. He was methodical, a goal-setter. He wanted at least two guns off the streets each month.

At least one search warrant a week. If presented with an elevator or a set of stairs, Adney always took the stairs. 'Incidental exercise' he called it. That's what cops working for him remembered.

When he first arrived, the TAG office was a motley bunch of officers, each one with varying skills and capabilities. Some had never breached a door. Others couldn't use a surveillance camera. Most had never heard gunfire.

There wasn't much support from the police hierarchy to upskill these detectives with tactical training. Their work fell into a grey zone: on the one hand, it was accepted that they would routinely deal with high-risk targets. On the other hand, as detectives, they hadn't been trained to deal with the basic risks. No one had shown them what to do in a gunfight or how to properly clear a house. From the police hierarchy's perspective, there were tactical police who were better suited to those challenges but, in reality, those teams were a finite commodity, not always available when called, and not always willing to take a job if it didn't meet certain risk thresholds.

With no formal support, Adney came up with his own ad hoc training package. He put it together in his spare time. With money donated from the NSW Crime Commission – $10,000 seized from a criminal – he bought a second-hand van, decking it out with tinted windows, sound equipment and gadgetry. The TAG detectives used it for practice; if the Highway Patrol was conducting routine vehicle stops, they piggybacked, following them in the van to hone their surveillance technique, perfecting the art of the clear, crisp shot.

Adney took his team to the trenches at the Anzac Rifle Range in Malabar so a range of guns could be fired over their heads. He wanted them to hear the difference between the various bullet calibres. The idea was to train them to recognise the guns they might come up against in a shoot-out. He strapped a bulletproof vest to a garbage bin and had it shot up to show them the limitations of standard police armour. The vests, as was revealed, were not indestructible.

There were also other insights that day. House doors that had been left out on the side of the road on council clean-up days were collected and set up for breaking practice. Adney showed them where the stress points were located and the proper way to use a Halligan bar, the pronged metal tool that firemen often carry.

The Target Action Group's brief was low- to mid-level drug investigations, a broad ambit that covered the legion of street dealers, run bosses and upline suppliers working patches of southwestern Sydney. Attacking this problem could be done quick and fast, one person at a time – Roberts and Mitchell–style – or it could be done slowly, over weeks and months, rolling from one target to the next until a net was ready to close around an entire supply chain. In a best-case scenario this ended with a cast of characters under arrest – the dealer, the driver, the run manager and the drug boss. One of the first TAG cases to tread this path was Strike Force Crotty.

Though there were many investigations like it, Strike Force Crotty symbolised many of the TAG's early forays into mid-level drug work, a time when detectives were still finding their feet at the Squad. Crotty was assigned to Ben Gray, a likeable young detective still in his twenties, barely three years out of the academy. Before MEOCS he'd been at Macquarie Fields working general duties, point duty and menial tasks; his last shift there was spent checking tickets at Minto railway station.

Gray's arrival at the TAG office was like a revelation, something wondrous. At MEOCS he got a kaleidoscopic view of policing: tapped phone lines, listening devices, body wires, undercover operations. Adney wasted no time dispatching Gray to Bankstown for his first assignment: a small pot run with a crew of street dealers. Their leader was Hassan Bazzi, twenty-two years old, a budding entrepreneur trying to run a clean, simple drug business. Gray was given Bazzi's phone number and told to infiltrate the syndicate using an undercover operative – or UC as they're known by the cops. He'd never done that before, but Adney didn't mind – he was there at the helm, shadowing Gray and showing him the ropes, guiding his new recruit through each step.

Bazzi knocked back the UC's call, telling him to deal with one of his runners, a sneaky little man who liked to rip off his customers, as Gray would soon learn.

The goal was to buy slowly and work towards big amounts. This took patience; rush in too soon and walls would go up, phone numbers would change. The sting would look obvious.

Gray's first deal with the runner was for a 'fifty' of cannabis, organised via text message, which equated to about three grams and cost $50. The pick-up location was an apartment block in Bankstown, a huge building that took up the entire corner of Stanley and Cross streets. The UC was back within an hour with a resealable bag of green buds. The buy went off without a hitch.

Two days later, Gray sent the UC back to the apartment block for another buy, the same amount, a fifty of cannabis. The runner slapped a bag into the officer's hand. It was hard and filled with pellets. Somehow, wires had been crossed – the runner had just handed over fifty ecstasy tablets instead of a fifty of cannabis, a terrible mistake on his part and an incredible coup for Gray's investigation.

It was a stroke of dumb luck that provided a huge leap in the case. Gray didn't know Bazzi was supplying ecstasy – no one did. Besides, the law couldn't care less about cannabis. As a threat to the community it ranked somewhere around Xanax tablets. But ecstasy? That was a different story, a harder drug that attracted serious prison time.

Through the body wire worn by the undercover officer Gray could hear the conversation on the ground.

'I meant a fifty like last time,' the undercover officer said, pretending to be annoyed. Gray called Adney to tell him the good news, but also to raise a slight hitch: the UC was only carrying $50 in buy-money. The fifty pills were priced at $2000, Gray said. What should they do? he asked.

Adney rushed out of the office and found an ATM. It was late and the banks were closed, so he pulled out $2000 from his personal savings account, marked down the serial numbers, and then drove into Bankstown to personally deliver the cash. Gray took the money when he arrived.

Later that night, back at the office, the pills were emptied onto a table, spread out, and counted one by one. It was a superb result. In a single buy the case had gone from a low-level pot run to a mid-level syndicate moving good amounts of ecstasy. From here, the awkward positioning for bigger deals was over.

Ten days later Gray made his next move, sending the UC back to the same corner, this time with $4000 in a wad of bills, enough to buy 100 MDMA tablets. The runner was waiting outside when the officer arrived. He took the money and said he'd be right back with the pills, disappearing into the apartment block and taking the elevator upstairs.

Ten minutes passed, then twenty minutes. Calls went unanswered. Messages were left. Gray started getting nervous. After a while it became obvious the runner wasn't coming back. He had taken them in a classic drug rip.

Gray was beside himself, convinced his career was finished. His first run at a big investigation had just ended with $4000 lost in a drug rip. There was no coming back from that, he thought. He called Adney to break the news, preparing himself for the worst.

As they spoke the undercover officer stayed outside the apartment block furiously dialling numbers in his phone. He refused to stand down. It wasn't the money, it was the principle – there was an indignity about being robbed. When he finally reached Bazzi he started shouting into the phone, putting in an Oscar-worthy performance. 'That little fucker took my money! He fucking ripped me off!' He said he wasn't leaving until he'd gotten his money back.

Bazzi might have been a drug boss, but he was also a businessman. He didn't like what he was hearing. Ripping off customers was a fast way of making enemies, the kind who leave anonymous tip-offs on police hotlines.

A car arrived a few minutes later, pulling up outside the apartment block. Bazzi stepped out and walked over to the UC, shaking his hand and apologising. This shouldn't have happened, he said. Then he disappeared into the building. Gray, watching from an unmarked car, felt his mood lifting. A surveillance team took photographs as Bazzi emerged holding a bag with 100 pills. He apologised a second time and told the UC to deal with him directly from then on. The UC's performance on the phone, it seemed, had cemented his credibility.

The next time they met, ten days later, Bazzi handed over 1000 tablets embossed with the Chanel logo. Another 500 pills followed, pink ones, then another 1000 tablets in a deal a few days later. Within three weeks more than $120,000 had been spent buying back drugs off Bazzi, deals that were almost inconceivable considering how they had come about. It was a crisis converted into a jackpot and it had taken a drug rip to make it possible – if it had happened in a movie people would have shouted at the screen and thrown popcorn, convinced the script wasn't believable.

These were extraordinary deals that put the Drug Squad to shame. Their cases would need to run for months to replicate this kind of work – large commercial quantity charges – and yet here was Ben Gray, a rookie, knocking it out of the park in less than a month.

On 23 September, barely eight weeks after that first cannabis deal, TAG detectives arrested Bazzi and the rest of his syndicate in a swoop on a handful of Bankstown addresses. He was ordered to serve a minimum of five and a half years in prison.

These short-term but high-yield investigations set apart the MEOCS Target Action Group from their colleagues working upstairs on Level 3 in the Criminal Investigation branch, known as MEOCS CI. The CI branch was split into three teams, each one led by a detective inspector with twelve officers reporting up to them. As Strike Force Crotty moved into its arrest phase, one of these teams, after weeks of negotiation, was preparing to pull off one of the Squad's most stunning coups of all.

CHAPTER FOUR

ROCKET MAN

BANKSTOWN, SATURDAY, 30 SEPTEMBER 2006

Ken 'Slasher' McKay, Commander of MEOCS, stepped out of his car onto Stacey Street and walked towards the two shady-looking men standing in a driveway across the road.

If McKay was nervous, he didn't show it. There was a loaded gun down the back of his footy shorts. In his shirt pocket was a mobile phone, its line open for detectives nearby, ready to broadcast any signs of distress. It wasn't the world's most sophisticated body wire, McKay thought, but it would have to do. Flanking him as he crossed the street was Mark Wakeham, a gifted 20-something-year-old detective and the architect of this gathering. Wakeham was very familiar with the men they were meeting. He'd studied them, knew the dangers; there was no way he was letting McKay meet them on his own.

They were leaning against a car and popped the boot as McKay and Wakeham got closer. Inside was a torn-up garbage bag with an olive-coloured tube sitting on top of it. The tube was about one metre long with capped covers on both ends and had a shoulder strap that hung loose. On the side were helpful, illustrated, step-by-step instructions: pull pin, remove rear cover, extend, release safety, aim and fire.

McKay looked at the tube then back at the men.

'Is that it?' he asked.

They said nothing, just nodded.

It was a rocket launcher, one of an untold number that had been stolen from the army and, as the lore suggested, sold into the underworld. It was a one-shot device, light enough to hold up with one hand and capable of causing heavy casualties in a civilian setting. In policing terms, this was the Holy Grail, El Dorado and the lost city of Atlantis rolled into one: after years of conjecture and fruitless searching, McKay was finally looking at something the Australian Defence Force (ADF) insisted had never gone missing from its stockpiles, and from what he knew there were others still out there. Military brass had been adamant that all their rocket launchers were accounted for – either secured in their armouries or destroyed via decommissioning. The notion that even one device, let alone several, had made it into the hands of a criminal was scandalous.

McKay probably should have called the Bomb Squad on the way out to Stacey Street, but he didn't. Too much fuss, he thought. Protocol would have called for the street to be shut down and homes to be evacuated, but McKay, an old-school type, couldn't be bothered. He didn't have time to organise all those 'bells and whistles', as he called them, and it wasn't his style anyway. He was a larrikin, a swashbuckler, a throwback to a time when the rules were bent just enough to get the job done, a larger-than-life character who could have stepped right off the script of a 1970s cop show, the ones that open with a montage.

Detectives still trade Ken McKay stories, passing them around like football cards, each time embellishing them just a little more in his favour. In this one he's chucking a live rocket launcher into the boot of his car, ignoring every workplace safety protocol imaginable; in another one he's being demoted to the Property Crime Squad as punishment for telling his boss – who had pulled the plug on one of his more ambitious investigations – that he was the 'best fucking friend organised crime ever had'; and in yet another one he's being presented with a bottle of Chivas Regal by Phillip Bradley, head of the NSW Crime Commission, who had lost a bet that McKay couldn't lock up Tony Vincent, an untouchable Sydney crime figure of his day.

Friends called him 'Slasher', a nod to the 1950s and 1960s Australian cricketer with the same name and, aptly, a wink to his management style – he was a chainsawer of red tape, a commander with a never-ending budget allocation. One time a federal police counterpart confided in McKay that he didn't have the money to keep an investigation going. McKay just laughed and said: 'It's the government, mate, it's never gunna run out of money.'

His journey to Stacey Street that afternoon had started an hour earlier at the Cronulla Hotel, a pub about forty minutes' drive from Bankstown. The sky was overcast and strong offshore winds had killed off his plans to go sailing, a favourite off-duty pastime. He pulled up a bar stool and resigned himself to an afternoon of drinking with a few buddies. He was either on his first beer or fourth, depending on who's telling the story, but just after midday his phone started vibrating. Private number.

'I've got that thing,' the voice said. It was male and vaguely familiar, a call McKay had been told was coming, part of a secret deal that his detectives had hashed out with Adnan 'Eddie' Darwiche. Housed behind the five-metre walls and concertina wire of Lithgow Correctional Centre, Darwiche had first revealed in a series of clandestine meetings with detectives Mark Wakeham and Jenny Nagle that he was prepared to hand back several rocket launchers in his possession if he could get a reduction on his murder sentences. They hadn't been handed down yet, but he was facing life for the 2003 Lawford Street shootings that killed Mervat 'Melissa' Nemra and drug boss Ziad 'Ziggy' Razzak. Nearly three years to the day after the incident, Darwiche had been convicted of the shooting by a jury. Aware that he may never see daylight outside of a prison, Darwiche was weighing his options. In that sense, the rocket launchers weren't just a bargaining chip, but also a ransom demand, a pressure point not just for the police but also the national security services. Darwiche knew damn well they wanted those weapons back. If nothing else, he had everyone listening.

Wakeham and Nagle's work had drawn out his first and only admission that he was currently storing, somewhere in Sydney, a number of rocket launchers that had been taken from the army. Previously, this hadn't been clear. The army denied that any were missing. McKay had joined the dialogue with Darwiche a bit later as these negotiations escalated. He had the rank and pull of a superintendent, and could make these sort of deals possible; but he wouldn't be held hostage by big talk. He had laid things out plainly for Darwiche, telling him his admissions meant nothing without some kind of proof. If he wanted to talk deals, he'd have to hand back one of the launchers to get the ball rolling. As a goodwill gesture, Darwiche said he would deliver one rocket launcher through an intermediary, who would call in good time. Deal, McKay said, and he would find a way to return the favour in kind.

And so it went: that afternoon at the Cronulla Hotel, the call came through. McKay hung up the phone, set his beer aside and started dialling numbers, putting together a team to head out to Bankstown to meet his mystery caller. First he called Detective Sergeant Belinda Dyson, a trusted colleague. Dyson was home, off duty, doing the washing.

'What are you doing?' McKay asked.

'Nothing. Why?'

He asked if she had a gun.

'Yeah, it's in the safe,' she said.

'I'll pick you up in ten minutes,' McKay said. 'Bring your shooter and your bullets.'

They took the M5 out to Bankstown, calling Mark Wakeham and Mick Adams along the way and arranging to meet them at Punchbowl Park. Adams, Wakeham's team leader at MEOCS, had been pivotal to the Darwiche negotiations; a lateral thinker and a problem solver, it was his idea to get McKay to use his mobile phone as a makeshift listening device. He'd even had a warrant typed up at the office before arriving at Punchbowl so any admissions recorded over the line could, potentially, be used in a courtroom.

At Punchbowl Park they formulated a plan. Dyson would drive with Adams and provide security from a distance. Wakeham would stay with McKay and shadow him at the meeting. Their biggest concern was an ambush. To let an unguarded commander walk into the heartland of Middle Eastern gang activity and pick up a rocket launcher linked to Adnan Darwiche seemed like an unwise move, especially without appropriate security precautions, of which they had none.

It was a five-minute drive from Punchbowl to the townhouse on Stacey Street where the two men were waiting. McKay picked up the launcher with a towel to avoid transferring any fingerprints onto it, then he walked back to his car and carefully rolled it into the boot.

'That wasn't too hard,' he said, getting into the passenger seat. They drove slowly back to the MEOCS HQ, careful not to let the device roll around too much in the back. No one knew the capability of the thing – would it go off if another car bumped into them? Could it be activated just from rolling around? McKay knew the weapon had a safety catch, but he was damned if he knew where it was. He'd never seen a rocket launcher before. No one had. Tailing them close behind was Dyson and Adams who provided a buffer from other cars.

Back at the office they all posed for photographs with the launcher, hamming it up for the camera, gathering around it like a trophy. Naysayers had said this day would never come. Bets had even been taken around the office on how quickly this mission would fail. One guy had said he would run naked down George Street if they recovered it successfully.

Dyson called the Bomb Squad and explained the situation to an on-call supervisor: they'd just picked up a rocket launcher from a community source and needed an expert to come out and pick it up. The supervisor laughed. It was an obvious joke.

'You're geeing me up, aren't you?'

'No,' Dyson said, deadpan. 'It's sitting here in the middle of the office.'

The supervisor's tone darkened. He ordered her to evacuate the building as a matter of urgency and set up a clearance zone. Dyson said that wasn't possible; the building shared its real estate with a police station that couldn't just be cleared out. 'There are guys in the cells downstairs,' she said.

Another, unforeseen logistical problem soon emerged. In something of an ironic twist, the Bomb Squad was not equipped to store a live rocket launcher at its depot in Zetland. The same problem arose at every police station across the city as Dyson tried to find a suitable gun safe. No one, it seemed, had the capacity or willingness to babysit the rocket launcher they'd just recovered. Normally, she would have just called the army, but that wasn't possible either; giving back the weapon could tip off the person who had stolen it, and therefore jeopardise enquiries into how it went missing. As a last resort Dyson called the Forensic Services Division. But they also refused to take the device for safety reasons. As the minutes ticked by, McKay began running out of patience. Sure, there were safety issues, but the meddling bureaucracy of it all gave him the shits. His team had just brought home the most sought-after weapon in the country and suddenly no one wanted to go near it.

'Well, where the fuck are we going to put it?' he asked, loudly. 'We can't just leave it in our office.'

He called back the Bomb Squad and pulled rank with the supervisor, coming up with a deal to reach a compromise – if their people could just pick up the launcher and store it for the rest of the weekend, then the Australian Federal Police would take it into their charge on Monday. Fine, said the supervisor. A forensics officer tried to examine the device when it arrived at the Bomb Squad's depot but was so nervous about touching it that only a few surfaces were given a dusting.

That Monday morning it was taken from the Zetland depot to the AFP's headquarters in Sydney's CBD. Forensic technicians went to work on the device. They pulled it apart until it was in pieces on the floor, removing its wings and examining its panels for any serial numbers. Each component was run through an X-ray machine to find any details that might have been scratched off. Envious types in the MEOCS office joked that the weapon was probably a dummy, nothing more than a tin tube handed over by a scheming criminal wanting a discounted prison sentence.

When the AFP was done with its examination they sent a 24-page report back to Detective Sergeant Mick Adams with their findings, concluding, in no uncertain terms, that the launcher was not a fake. A full profile of the weapon followed. The device was an M72 Light Anti-Tank Weapon, model number L1A2-F1, assembled using imported parts (the 'M' in M72 denoting manufacture in the United States) at an ammunition-filling factory in St Marys, a suburb of western Sydney. The launcher had been fitted with a high-explosive, Norwegian-made A3 warhead that had detonated on impact during live test firing in Adelaide. These tests showed the missile had been capable of penetrating twenty-eight centimetres of steel plate, seventy-five centimetres of reinforced concrete or 180 centimetres of soil.

Records suggested the weapon had been brought to Sydney around 1990 or 1991 for assembly, had a lifespan of about a decade, and was one of several devices scheduled to be destroyed on 8 June 2001 at the Myambat Ammunition Store near Muswellbrook, an army outpost several hours north of Sydney. Somehow this had never happened. Whoever stole it seemed to have a thorough working knowledge of where the important serial numbers were located, because they were all scratched off. But they were sloppy with the warhead itself. Its unique identifier, RAN90, was still intact on the side of the rocket fuse, allowing a trace to begin.

As McKay noted in a memorandum to superiors much later, the recovery represented a reality check for law enforcement, proof of the raw power at the fingertips of some MEOC identities. It was also a massive coup for the fledgling Squad; barely five months after its formation its detectives had not only recovered a weapon of enormous significance, but they had also confirmed that a much larger stockpile was still in the community, somewhere. Most concerning of all was the people with access to the devices, jihadists looking to cause heavy casualties in a civilian setting.

'For a number of years there had been talk within the criminal community of the existence of rocket launchers,' McKay wrote in his memorandum, a circular that went high up the chain of command. 'The validity of the information was difficult to judge. As a result of this investigation we now know for a fact that this weaponry exists and is [in] the possession of criminals/terrorists.'

Two months prior, when the launchers had still been a rumour, Mark Wakeham and Jenny Nagle got together one night to try to figure out whether the weapons really existed. This was done at a dive bar, somewhere. The actual place has long since been forgotten, but you can imagine something low-lit with neon, Dwight Yoakam playing in the background. It was over drinks when one of them came up with a novel suggestion: asking. This might have seemed like an obvious strategy, but the man they wanted to ask – Adnan Darwiche – had been sitting in a jail cell for almost two years and not once had anyone even tried to talk to him about the rocket launchers. It was during his murder trial for the 2003 shootings on Lawford Street that Khaled 'Crazy' Taleb, the star witness and main informant, had given up the first reliable intelligence about Darwiche's arsenal of rocket launchers. Taleb's statement ran to eighty-odd pages and provided the court with the inside scoop on life in Darwiche's crew. At the time of the Lawford Street shootings, Darwiche had allegedly brought the rocket launchers to a safe house at Greenacre but had decided against using them in the attack on the Razzaks. Concerns were raised that the warheads would pass right through the fibro home and hit an unintended target.

The prevailing view at MEOCS was that Darwiche had nothing to gain by making any admissions about the rocket launchers. If the ADF's assertions were true – that there were no launchers missing from their stockpiles – then, technically, there was also nothing to ask about.

The other reason why approaching Darwiche may not have been tried during this time was because he loathed police, few more so than Wakeham and Nagle. They were the plucky young detectives who had put him in prison for the Lawford Street shootings in the first place. They were the heartbeat of Strike Force Grapple, one of the state's largest investigations in recent years.

They were a partnership, a duo – young and feisty with a rare energy for the job. They were adventurous but practical, sticklers for detail who believed in letting ideas flow and trying new things. Crusty old bosses, with their textbooks and formulas, didn't know what to do with them.

For three years, their world had been Adnan 'Eddie' Darwiche and his war with the Razzak family. During Strike Force Grapple, on any given night, you could walk into the office and still find them at their desks, re-reading statements and poring over timelines, making sure their evidence married up. Some nights were spent guarding cheap motel rooms, sometimes in other parts of the country, where witnesses had been holed up for their safety. Some were illiterate; others were simple. Each had their own quirks. Khaled 'Crazy' Taleb wouldn't speak without first receiving a family pack meal from Red Rooster. And he always got it.

Throughout the nine-month trial for the Lawford Street shootings, Wakeham and Nagle had sat in court each day and watched Darwiche protest his innocence; he was convinced that Wakeham and Nagle had skewed evidence against him as part of a corrupt police conspiracy.

Naturally their relationship with him had become frosty. Threats had been made to both detectives. Teams of security staff had to be organised each day at the courthouse to manage the risks, not just to Wakeham and Nagle but also their witnesses, some of whom were top gang lieutenants giving evidence in exchange for immunity. Having worked so hard to put him in prison, the idea that he would now talk to these two detectives candidly, let alone admit he had a cache of stolen rocket launchers, which could add extra years to his sentence, was ludicrous.

To everyone, that is, except Wakeham and Nagle.

Before Taleb's admission, the rocket launchers had only existed in the spook stories and gossip of big-noting criminals, always talked about but never actually seen. Dozens of intelligence reports were collected but enquiries were put to bed when the ADF laughed off the suggestions. After that, any mention of rocket launchers was almost mischief-making. People got tired of hearing about them. Even in law enforcement circles it became unfashionable to bring them up for investigation. Trying to find them was akin to a wacky crusade, a mark of naïve ambition.

Wakeham and Nagle didn't care. Strike Force Grapple was over, Darwiche had been found guilty of two murders, and both detectives wanted a new challenge, their zest for the job starting to wane. Like many transplants from Task Force Gain, they arrived at MEOCS with reputations trailing them. McKay had heard the stories. Insubordination, freewheeling – whatever, McKay thought. He assigned them to Mick Adams, a team leader at MEOCS CI, a big man with a big heart who everyone knew as 'Grizzly'. In Adams, McKay knew he had someone to keep the two detectives in check.

Adams had come up as a beat policeman in Pyrmont during the early 1990s. It's different there now to what it was back then. He walked the beat alone, the streets filled with wharfies and tuna fishermen, loaders and unloaders, rowdy old salts who could walk into a bar with a roll of coin and drink for two days straight. For fun, they beat the crap out of each other. It was Adams's job to make sure innocent bystanders didn't get hurt – he'd step in when things got out of hand. Brawlers would turn on him, two men at a time, his backup a good fifteen minutes away. After a while they learned to leave him alone; he never went down.

His next move was to Kings Cross, back when it was still a seedy red-light district. It had all the familiar types: the spruiker, the pimp, the whore, the addict. Everyone knew Adams, trusted him. These were the Royal Commission days when cops in Kings Cross were viewed as especially corrupt. And that might have been the case, but everyone knew Adams, trusted him. He emerged as an emissary, a cop who was clean but shook hands with everyone and wasn't judgemental. If you needed help, advice, someone to talk to off record, you went to see Adams.

But he was also an ideas man and a thinker, a former undercover detective who never got tired of working up cover stories and angles. In Wakeham and Nagle, he saw a younger version of himself and gave them a loose rein.

Their first trip to visit Adnan Darwiche at Lithgow Correctional Centre was on 30 August 2006, a Wednesday morning. They drove out alone, telling no one where they were going. Despite Adams's trust in them, they knew that asking his permission would have meant weeks waiting for legal advice and a half-dozen committee meetings to get a decision, which would have invariably been 'no'.

So they just went, figuring out their strategy as towns drifted by along the Great Western Highway. Experience told them both to make no promises, but that was if Darwiche spoke at all. What if he went berserk? What if he attacked them? Backed into a corner and facing a double life sentence, Wakeham thought an assault charge would have meant nothing to him.

The interview room was cramped, a table and few chairs taking up most of the space. A guard brought Darwiche in and removed his handcuffs. He pulled out a chair, sat down and said nothing.

Nearly three years in prison had made him only slightly leaner than before his arrest. He still looked vaguely threatening, thick-necked and solid even in a loose orange jumpsuit. His beard was long again, grown out as a show of piety. And there was a brooding, caged-bear quality to him.

There had already been one police investigation into Adnan Darwiche during his time in custody. A few months after his arrest in August 2004, Taskforce Gain detectives had learned he was trying to corrupt a prison guard to help him escape from prison, asking questions of the officer about how a breakout might be possible. The officer showed a tentative interest in helping and agreed to come up with some examples: passageways and blind spots. Really, the officer was taking notes the whole time and passing them back to detectives. They monitored the situation under Strike Force Mansell and wired up the prison guard to get Darwiche recorded on tape. Somehow Darwiche got spooked at the last minute, and mysteriously told the officer he was no longer interested in escaping.

'I'll take my chances at court,' he said. By the time Wakeham and Nagle arrived to meet him his plan had fallen through – the jury had found him guilty of two murders, an attempted murder, and a violent home invasion dating back to 2001 that had left a member of the Razzak family partially paralysed. He was weeks away from being sentenced, so in Wakeham's and Nagle's minds the timing was right for a deal.

'Adnan, I believe you know who we are,' Wakeham said.

And then it came, several tantalising, candid and off-record admissions. Yes, he had rocket launchers. Sure, they were hidden somewhere. True, they had come from a 'government agency' and, sure, he could hand them back to authorities, along with any other weapons at his fingertips: hand grenades, plastic explosives, detonators.

'I'll give you so much information you'll be the next police commissioner,' he said.

Wakeham and Nagle were stunned, nodding along like this was all no big deal, but punching the air inside, hands slightly shaking under the table.

Of course, this was all just a teaser. Darwiche had a lot more information to give them, but there'd be conditions attached, he said. He wanted to be moved out of isolation in Lithgow's maximum-security wing and back into the general population where he could have privileges restored. He also had a personal request: in the event that his mother passed away, he wanted to attend the funeral, or at least say goodbye to her body at the morgue.

As he had decided with Nagle in the car, Wakeham made no promises. Those were the kinds of requests that would have to be approved by the chain of command, he said.

Back at the MEOCS office later that day, he typed furiously, the keyboard whirring at his desk as he prepared the paperwork to start a formal investigation into Darwiche's claims. Even though the information from the meeting was vague – Darwiche had been careful not to specify where the launchers were hidden or how many he was holding – there was a palpable excitement about what they'd been told.

Ultimately it was McKay's decision whether or not to push ahead and cut a deal. Anyone could sit in a room and make those kinds of promises. At best, Darwiche was telling the truth and willing to give back what he had in his possession. But it could also be a pack of lies, a play to sell police a dud in exchange for prison privileges, or, at worst, a setup to lure them into a remote location for an ambush. McKay said he wanted proof.

He joined Wakeham and Nagle for their next meeting with Darwiche a week later, commandeering the negotiations and putting his influence on the table. He had a direct line to well-placed individuals in the NSW government, most notably the police minister, Carl Scully. Middle Eastern organised crime was the hot-button topic of the moment and Scully regularly bypassed the commissioner to speak directly with McKay over the phone.

The atmosphere changed with McKay in the room. With the Squad's commander involved, it would have become obvious to Darwiche how seriously the police were taking the matter. Darwiche played this to his advantage, billing himself as a keeper of secrets and making cryptic suggestions about what he could do for authorities.

'You wouldn't have any idea what really goes on out there,' he said to McKay, who'd seen this sort of front before and was already bored with the mindgames. He pulled out a sheet of paper from his pocket and laid it out flat on the table in front of Darwiche. On the paper were pictures of various rocket launchers. Darwiche examined the photos and then stopped at the M72, pointing at it. 'That one,' he said.

McKay's offer was simple: since Darwiche's arrest, the NSW Crime Commission had been hounding him over a proceeds of crime forfeiture worth $50,000, a payment the commission considered that he owed to the state of NSW from his time as a drug dealer. McKay said in exchange for a rocket launcher, he would have the debt wiped.

Darwiche was intrigued, but said he wanted a guarantee of immunity; no secret charges coming to bite either him or his younger brother Mohamed, who he would get to help him, once they had met their end of the bargain.

McKay agreed to this arrangement, formalising this promise on 15 September under Controlled Operation 06/365, a document broad enough and vague enough to allow both Darwiche and his younger brother to purchase and possess virtually any conceivable weapon that could be fired or detonated 'from persons whose identity is yet to be established'.

Two weeks later, it was Mohamed Darwiche who rang McKay while he was enjoying an afternoon beer at the Cronulla Hotel. Even with ongoing scrutiny of Darwiche and his family – eavesdropping on his prison phone calls, placing listening devices in the jail's visiting areas, surveillance on his brother – Mohamed and another man were still able to deliver the rocket launcher to McKay at the townhouse on Stacey Street without revealing where the rest were hidden – or who was handling them.

The only person missing that day as the first rocket launcher was recovered was Jenny Nagle. She had already stepped on an overseas flight booked months in advance, a reward for seeing through the Lawford Street shootings to their bitter finality. The nine-month murder trial had been its own kind of prison for Nagle, a physically exhausting routine that left her burned out and, at one stage, needing a short stay in hospital. Her bosses in management had let her down, leaving her dispirited about the work, which she loved. As the plane took off she sank into her seat and looked out the window, watching as Sydney was gently cast off beneath her, deciding there and then to quit the NSW Police Force entirely.

*

The recovery of the M72 launcher sent police and national security agencies scrambling for answers. High-level briefings were sought. Questions were fired off in all directions, but the two at the forefront of everyone's mind were: how had the launchers gone missing, and who had supplied them to Darwiche. A task force comprising Australian Federal Police, the NSW Crime Commission and detectives attached to the NSW Terrorism Investigations Squad set out to address these pressing unknowns. It was given the code name Strike Force Ridgecrop. Suddenly, finding rocket launchers was back in fashion again, and everyone wanted a piece of the glory.

Meanwhile Strike Force Torpy, Wakeham and Adams's investigation, continued with negotiations at Lithgow Correctional Centre. While the Ridgecrop detectives were figuring out how the launchers went missing, the Torpy case worked on getting more weapons back.

By now Darwiche had engaged the services of John Doris, the same shrewd barrister who had dissected the police case at his trial over the Lawford Street murders. With Doris's entry into the discussions, Darwiche's original manifesto got a slight tweaking. Realising the potential value of what he was hiding, Darwiche's reasonable and realistic conditions, which he had first given to Wakeham and Nagle, had now been usurped by a series of unrealistic and non-negotiable ultimatums. At the very top of this list was a request for a royal pardon to be considered, one that would commute his sentence and give him an eventual release. Darwiche knew that quashing the sentence entirely was never going to happen. But commuting his sentence was achievable, he thought; he could do twenty-five years and then leave the country for good, he said. He even vowed to tear up his passport as a guarantee he would never come back.

McKay, still leading the negotiations, thought the idea was insane. A royal pardon was never going to happen. Darwiche wasn't some political prisoner jailed for his subversive views. He was a twice-convicted murderer, someone who, in the eyes of the law, was still a very serious threat to the community.

McKay told him that everything was on the table, but if he wanted a royal pardon then he would have to hand back more weapons. It was the only way to win favour with the NSW attorney-general, the person who could lobby the governor-general to sign a Royal Prerogative of Mercy.

At this, Darwiche agreed to make another handover, offering McKay twenty kilograms of Powergel explosives if he wanted it. These were commercial-grade 'busters', pudgy salami sticks that could blast holes in quarries and mines. Used correctly they could probably flatten half a city block. Darwiche said he had fourteen of them ready to go and could get another 400 kilograms by Christmas. They weren't rocket launchers, but McKay still jumped at the offer. It was also a tidy opportunity for the joint investigation team to try to track the hiding place of these explosives. Chances were they were hidden with the rest of his arsenal. But, already, this had proven to be surprisingly difficult.

All of Darwiche's contact with the outside world was closely monitored in prison. The exception to this were his face-to-face meetings with his brother Mohamed in the prison visiting area. These conversations were recorded through a listening device, but were almost always drowned out by the ambient noise of banging on the table and crying children. Mohamed was excellent at outsmarting law enforcement efforts to track him. During one meeting with McKay he slid a piece of paper across the table with four licence plate numbers written down, each one belonging to a different AFP surveillance car that had been following him that day.

The Powergel explosives were handed back to police on 17 October 2006. McKay did the pickup, arriving at a predetermined rendezvous point where fourteen 'busters' were handed over with a reel of bright red detonator cord. It was another low-key affair, one with barely any security and no Bomb Squad in tow, though McKay had called them for advice on the way out. In a brief chat to the on-call supervisor, he explained what was going on and asked for any advice on handling the explosive sticks. The supervisor kicked up a fuss, urging him to abort, insisting it was too dangerous.

McKay laughed. 'I'll ring you back when I've got it,' he said. Then he hung up and kept driving.

The next day, Darwiche was escorted from Lithgow Correctional Centre to a police station a short drive away. His barrister, John Doris, was waiting for him along with Wakeham and Adams. They had come to take a statement from Darwiche, capitalising on his hope of having a royal pardon considered. The other reason for the meeting was to mentally prepare Darwiche for his upcoming sentence. Wakeham didn't want these negotiations destroyed by what was coming. He anticipated the judge was likely going to hand down life sentences for the Lawford Street murders. Darwiche said he'd accept the sentences, so long as his lawyers could at least meet with the attorney-general and make his case for a royal pardon.

In the spirit of co-operation and still acting in good faith, Darwiche spoke even more openly and candidly during this meeting, revealing key details for the first time about how many rocket launchers he'd bought, what he had done with them, and how he'd gone about getting them in the first place. These were important admissions. He told the detectives he'd bought six rocket launchers towards the end of 2003 at the height of his war with the Razzak family. He refused to name his contact, but said they were people with links to the army. As for the launchers themselves, he said he'd sold most of them to a person by the name of Mohamed Ali Elomar, a man well known to authorities as the leader of a Sydney-based terrorist cell. It was Elomar who had been charged in 2005, one year earlier, after being overheard on a phone call throwing out ideas to blow up Sydney's Lucas Heights nuclear reactor and possibly the NSW Parliament building on Macquarie Street. In one call Elomar was overheard by the cops listening in as he talked about a worldwide war against Muslims, saying that 'we should do something about it over here'.

A letter from John Doris arrived on Ken McKay's desk one week later and was forwarded up through the NSW Police Force's chain of command, not stopping until it had reached the commissioner's office. The document was a contract of sorts, a formal agreement that summarised the promises made between Darwiche and the detectives over their recent meetings. Among them was a pledge from Darwiche that he would accept the life sentences to be handed down against him; that he would continue to collaborate with police to deliver more weapons; and that he would give evidence in future court proceedings against the people involved with the rocket launchers, if required.

In return, the police were asked to agree to seven undertakings, among them being that they would write to the attorney-general in support of a submission to commute Darwiche's sentence, and that they would move Darwiche to the main prison at Lithgow Correctional Centre once his assistance had been provided.

The document was hand-delivered to the police minister's office a few days later and then forwarded to the attorney-general, Bob Debus. His reply, emailed to John Doris on 7 November, seemed to offer nothing concrete and only stalled Darwiche for an answer. If anything it hinted strongly that more weapons would have to be returned for any kind of undertaking to be signed off. Debus wrote:

> It would be appropriate for me to consider as part of the application for the Royal Prerogative of Mercy, not only the extent of the applicant's co-operation, but also the quality and timeliness of that co-operation. It is important that I point out that I expect your client will not withhold information which might put the public safety at risk. Indeed, it is in your client's interests to maintain his co-operation because, as I have stated, its quality and timeliness are relevant to my decision.

When Darwiche read the letter he was sure he was being screwed. In his mind, all of his good-faith gestures had been for nothing. He'd given police a rocket launcher and fourteen sticks of Powergel and what did they want? More. What had he been given? Zilch. It was to be the beginning of the end of his co-operation. Two months had passed since the negotiations with police had started. At this point, his two life sentences had been sealed in court. And as a final insult, he'd been moved from Lithgow Correctional Centre to Goulburn's Supermax prison, the famous jail-within-a-jail, the most secure facility in the southern hemisphere.

At his last meeting with Adams and Wakeham, he made it clear that he wouldn't be tempted by any more deals. Their notes from the day tell the story:

Adnan Darwiche stated if police could not provide him with some form of guarantee that his sentence would be reduced to somewhere in the vicinity of twenty years then he was not prepared to assist any further. Police advised him that what he wanted was simply not possible and that the current arrangements with the attorney-general was the best that he could expect. Adnan Darwiche then told police that he could not assist anyway. He stated that he had made the relevant enquiries with his supplier of the rocket launchers and was unable to obtain them.

It was a disappointing end to a stellar few months. With Darwiche bowing out of the negotiations, Wakeham and Adams turned back to the few leads they still had in the hope of recovering the rocket launchers without him. This was no time to be giving up, they thought. There were still mounds of intelligence files and intercepted phone calls to transcribe and pick apart.

Around this time it had also become apparent that the joint investigation, Strike Force Ridgecrop, had amassed a few of its own promising leads. Efforts to trace back the rocket warhead's serial number were continuing. Paperwork was being pulled. Another angle the joint investigation had been working on was the identity of a mysterious person known as 'Taha', whose name had come up on an intercepted phone call. It could have been a first name, a last name, or even a nickname. It could have been a dead end; no one knew. But finding 'Taha' was pivotal – the Ridgecrop detectives believed he was somehow linked to the rocket launchers.

His name had been mentioned in a call about a month earlier, around the time John Doris's letter had arrived on Ken McKay's desk. The AFP had given up following Mohamed Darwiche in their cars but they were still tapping his mobile phone, listening to the calls between him and his older brother, Abdul, a tow truck driver with a tough reputation in the Middle Eastern community. Neither of them were under investigation for any crimes but they were considered by police to be the gateway to the launchers. During one of their calls, detectives overheard them planning to meet 'Taha' who, just by the way they spoke about him, sounded like he might be important. Efforts were made to follow Mohamed to the meeting and monitor his movements using a police helicopter, but heavy rain grounded both the aircraft and, coincidentally, one of Abdul's tow trucks as well, which forced both men to cancel the meeting. Plans to reschedule it never eventuated and the lead got away from police – the name 'Taha', however, stuck with them.

One person who knew more about Taha was Khaled 'Crazy' Taleb, the star witness in Darwiche's trial and former right-hand man. He had already been working with the NSW Crime Commission for several months, feeding them information about Darwiche and others in the underworld in exchange for his indemnity, one of the most generous pacts with a criminal ever signed off by the NSW government. Hundreds of thousands of dollars were spent on Taleb – relocation, allowances, rental payments, flights for his family from Lebanon to Australia, as well as visas so they could stay in the country. He was to be paid a weekly stipend of $721 for four years. The commission even bought him a boat so he could go fishing, but only on the condition that he pay for the fuel.

Among the many details he had already told the NSW Crime Commission about Darwiche – from their discussions about Islam to how they melted down handguns used to shoot people – emerged a story about an arms dealer who shopped guns around in the boot of his car. Taleb used to buy off him regularly. He was twenty-seven, married with a kid, and living in the southwestern suburb of Leumeah. His full name was Taha Abdul-Rahman.

Taleb told the commission that sometime in October 2003 he got a phone call from Taha Abdul-Rahman asking if he and Darwiche wanted a weapon of a different kind, something heavier and fit for a real battle. Within a couple of days, after a few short meetings, they cut their first deal for a rocket launcher: Darwiche paid $15,000 for it. A few weeks later they met again at a townhouse in Eagle Vale, where six more launchers were packed in two black garbage bags, a deal worth $55,000.

Wakeham and Adams took this information and ran with it, trawling through Darwiche's old intelligence archives and telephone intercept transcripts to find links between him and the arms dealer known as Taha Abdul-Rahman. These transcripts had been gathered years earlier, around the time of the Lawford Street murders. Anyone listening back then would have struggled to pick up on the true nature of the discussions; most were in code, droning on endlessly about car parts, tyres and tubing. But now, with the code broken, these exchanges conveyed a whole new meaning. In one call Darwiche asked for an 'instruction manual'. In another, the words 'fifty-five thousand dollar discount' were used. At the time, this meant nothing – instruction manual? Discount?

'It's one hundred per cent,' Darwiche had said on the intercepted phone call.

'I'll get everything ready,' Abdul-Rahman had replied.

Wakeham and Adams studied these conversations and saw the makings of a case against Abdul-Rahman staring back at them. A statement from Taleb plus the coded conversations would be enough evidence to satisfy a magistrate to approve a search warrant on Abdul-Rahman's house in Leumeah. With any luck, a rocket launcher would be sitting inside. McKay lit up with excitement when Adams briefed him on the plan. They were back in the game.

The only catch was Taleb, who wanted more money in exchange for his evidence about the rocket launchers. By now he'd learned to work the system and had realised his value to police. It's not known how much he was eventually offered, or whether he was paid, but such was the willingness to keep him satisfied that both the NSW Crime Commission and the AFP agreed to stump up the money together.

On 15 December, a team of officers surrounded Taha Abdul-Rahman's property and knocked on the front door. He was given two pieces of paper: a search warrant in one hand and a summons to appear before the NSW Crime Commission in the other. Rather than arresting him, the investigators were compelling him to appear before one of the commission's secret hearings, a star chamber inquisition where refusing to answer questions, or lying, can land a person in prison for two years. As he was escorted to the CBD for the hearing, members of the joint investigation team went room by room, rifling through desks, scrutinising documents and examining his garage. They seized his computer hard drive and downloaded the lot to be analysed in the search for any evidence that linked him to the rocket launchers. It had been more than three years since Abdul-Rahman had allegedly sold the weapons to Darwiche, so any hope of finding evidence in his house was something of a long shot.

In the end they found nothing tying him back to the launchers, but they did walk away with thirty rounds of ammunition, $7000 cash, numerous mobile phones, some banking records, and pictures of mutilated soldiers downloaded off the internet. In policing terms, that wasn't particularly fruitful, but the raid itself and the experience at the NSW Crime Commission had done wonders for the investigation. This was Adams's hope from the beginning. If the warrant didn't yield any evidence then at least it could act as a smokescreen, a cage rattler that might scare Abdul-Rahman into talking about the weapons.

In a phone call the next day, recorded by police, detectives got the incriminating, corroborating evidence they were looking for: 'They fucked me, bro ... about those things that fly ... that dick [Khaled Taleb] has spoken, man.'

Charges followed within weeks. At first Abdul-Rahman said nothing, but not long after he agreed to make full admissions to the Ridgecrop team, telling them everything – from how much he had made out of each launcher to where the meetings with Darwiche had taken place. Of course, the most important piece of information Abdul-Rahman could give them was how he came to get the weapons in the first place, a story that, by this stage, had already been partially pieced together. Using the serial number left on the rocket fuse, detectives had embarked on a paper trail that led from filing cabinets in Sydney to a mysterious ADF facility near the small town of Muswellbrook, a six-hour drive away, where military weapons go to get destroyed.

It was there that the paper trail ended.

On paper, Shane Malcolm Della-Vedova, a career soldier and technical expert, was the kind of serviceman that would have made Australians proud. He was an honourable man who'd spent twenty-eight of his forty-six years with the Australian Defence Force, reaching the rank of captain and serving in foreign war zones. His service record was impeccable, not a blemish. He'd been an infantry soldier, then an 'ammo tech', the kind of weapons expert who delivered awesome firepower to combat troops and showed them how to use it. If an improvised explosive device was found on the battlefield, it was Della-Vedova's job to do away with it. There wasn't a working component in a rocket launcher, or any other piece of army weaponry, that Della-Vedova wasn't intimately familiar with.

Once Della-Vedova was identified, the Ridgecrop team had a strong lead on the source of the stolen weapons. He was the man who'd last signed out the launchers and handled them. The trail ended with him and picked up again with Taha Abdul-Rahman. But, as Abdul-Rahman told them, he'd never met Della-Vedova and had no idea who he was. His source in the supply chain was a different person altogether, a middleman who sat on the border of the real world and the underworld – his wife and kids on one side and criminal connections on the other. He was a former Rebels bikie; his name was Paul Carter.

The Ridgecrop team started digging into Carter, pulling up his profile and working backwards through his friends and family to figure out his links to Della-Vedova. It was all in the family: Carter's wife, Kathleen, had gone into business with Della-Vedova's sister, Catherine Taylor. The two families were close. Their kids played at each other's houses, the two women were opening a hairdressing salon together, and Catherine's husband, Dean Taylor, had a distinguished career in the army. At some point Dean Taylor introduced Carter to his brother-in-law, Shane Della-Vedova.

Even with this set of connections mapped out and the serial number linking back to Della-Vedova, the Ridgecrop detectives lacked the kind of evidence that could see the army captain placed in a set of handcuffs. They had a good case, but it needed to be better – they needed a confession or an admission of some kind, something to tie Della-Vedova to the actual theft of the weapons. Just because he was the last person to handle them, it didn't mean that he'd supplied them to Paul Carter, the man who sold them to Taha Abdul-Rahman.

Carter, however, was a different story. The detectives had him on toast. Abdul-Rahman had given a statement naming him as the supplier of the launchers and he was willing to give that evidence in court. This presented an opportunity to the Ridgecrop team. Carter meant nothing to them; he was a middleman. It was the army captain they wanted. In early 2007, officers approached the former Rebels bikie with an offer to work co-operatively with them: wear a wire, record Della-Vedova, give evidence in court, and, in exchange, no charges will proceed.

Carter, a criminal who'd already been to prison and didn't want to go back, accepted the deal.

On 21 February 2007, he sat down in front of Detective Inspector Neil Tuckerman, the officer in charge of Strike Force Ridgecrop, and told him everything he could remember, casting his mind back six years to when everything began at Long Bay Correctional Centre.

It was visiting day, he said, a Saturday morning in early July 2001. At the time, Carter was about halfway through serving out a sentence for drug supply. When his wife arrived she brought her new business partner and her husband along. It was a meet-and-greet, a chance for the two families to get to know each other. Back then, Carter hadn't met either Catherine or Dean Taylor and considering the two women were opening a salon together it was seen as good business for everyone to get to know each other.

Carter told Tuckerman that his conversation with Taylor had started out in the usual way, mostly with banter. Taylor then told him about his background in the army and how he'd left on medical grounds, but that his brother-in-law Shane Della-Vedova was still serving.

According to Carter, the conversation then veered into unexpected territory. A question came up about military weapons. Taylor asked if he was interested in buying some rocket launchers, grenades, bulletproof vests and night vision goggles. 'He offered me other military stuff but I can't remember it all,' Carter said. Taylor made it obvious that his brother-in-law could divert these weapons from the army.

Carter told Tuckerman that about two months later he was on work release from prison when Taylor arrived on his doorstep with a shopping list of illegal weapons written on a sheet of paper. At the top of the page were the words '10 x 66mm ready to rock': ten rocket launchers for sale.

'Dean told me that Shane's job involved the disposal of rocket launchers after their shelf life had expired,' Carter said. 'Shane would write the rocket launchers off as destroyed but actually took them home.'

Carter took the first launcher just before Christmas. He said that Taylor showed up with a black garbage bag and told him the '66' was inside. When he opened the bag, Carter saw a tube about one metre long. It looked like it had been sprayed with an aerosol can.

Taylor denied all this at his criminal trial, telling the court he never had any conversations with Carter about the sale of military weapons at Long Bay Correctional Centre and certainly never handed over a rocket launcher at his house that day. He conceded he had been at the house, and had passed on a bag from Della-Vedova, but was unaware of what was inside it.

With the rocket launcher in his hands, Carter said he began shopping it around to underworld figures to see who might be interested in buying. He called up Milad Sande, a drug dealer he knew, and offered him the weapon for $20,000. Sande was a connected underworld figure, well known and linked to several major organised crime families. Carter thought he'd make a great middleman and cut a deal with him. When Sande picked up the launcher he asked Carter if he could get more. Carter said yes. Within days he had secured a second weapon from Taylor, he told the detectives. But by then Sande had reneged on the deal. He'd already called Carter and asked for his money back on the first launcher – it turned out that whoever Sande was representing wasn't happy with the weapon once they had seen it. 'They didn't realise it was only a single-shot weapon,' Carter said to Tuckerman.

Stuck with two rocket launchers, Carter wrapped both the weapons in plastic and left them in his garage. Months passed. He didn't hear anything. One New Year's Day rolled into another. Suddenly it was August 2003. Carter couldn't remember the reason why, but he told Tuckerman that he'd decided to contact Taha Abdul-Rahman, another old criminal contact, who expressed interest and said he'd find a buyer. Deals between them soon followed.

The first launcher was traded for $15,000 on 30 September 2003 (Abdul-Rahman's cut was $1000). A month later another seven rocket launchers followed, this time moving directly from Della-Vedova to Carter. Taylor was bypassed because by then, two years on, he was mostly out of the picture; he'd been caught up in a messy divorce with his wife, Della-Vedova's sister Catherine, and had fallen out of touch with everyone. Carter told Tuckerman that the payment for the seven weapons was in a box that Abdul-Rahman handed over, roughly $70,000. In Abdul-Rahman's account of the deal, it was $50,000.

This was something of a minor inconsistency, but it goes to the difficulty of determining the absolute truth of the matter. But there were other more important contradictions between their statements. For example, Adnan Darwiche had told Wakeham and Adams that he had bought six rocket launchers and then sold five to the Sydney terror-cell leader Mohamed Ali Elomar. Assuming this was true, it would have left one launcher remaining in his possession, and that would have been the one he had traded with police as a goodwill gesture. Except, there was one problem. Carter and Abdul-Rahman might have contradicted each other on the money, but they were in agreement about the weapons sold to Darwiche. According to both men, Darwiche had bought eight rocket launchers in total, not six – one at first, and then seven afterwards. If Darwiche was telling the truth about having sold five weapons to Elomar, then basic maths would suggest he had three launchers left and had only given one back to police. This meant at least another two were still out there in his control.

On 27 March 2007, Carter was wired up with a listening device and sent in to interact with both Dean Taylor and Shane Della-Vedova, neither of whom he had seen for years. The meeting was timed to capitalise on recent headlines revealing that a cache of rocket launchers had been stolen from the army, sold into the underworld, and that an investigation was continuing to find the culprits behind the mess. These media revelations presented an opportunity for the Ridgecrop detectives; it was a good excuse for their informant – Paul Carter – to call a meeting and, with any luck, get incriminating statements from Della-Vedova and Dean Taylor on a tape recorder.

Carter was told to call Della-Vedova and ask him to set up a three-way meeting with Taylor. His cover story was to accuse Taylor of mouthing off at the pub about the rocket launchers after getting cut out of their lucrative deal. This, of course, was all a fabrication.

On the drive out to Taylor's house, Carter pretended to be nervous. He told Della-Vedova: 'I told youse from the start, he's the weakest link, this bloke.'

They arrived a few minutes later and walked up a gravel path towards the front door. Taylor was surprised to see them.

'I just wanted to talk to you,' Carter began before launching into a string of accusations, telling Taylor that word had filtered back through the hairdressing salon that he'd been 'down at the pub' telling people about the rocket launchers Della-Vedova had stolen.

Taylor couldn't understand what Carter was talking about. He said he hadn't been to any pub in years, didn't drink alcohol, and had barely left the house in recent times. More importantly, he hadn't breathed a word about Carter or the rocket launchers; as far as he knew there was only one weapon he'd seen and it was the device he'd been duped into handing over.

'I gave up all this shit,' Taylor said.

Carter called him a liar.

'Mate, it's you that's been down there,' he said. 'The information, you're the only one who knows.'

But why, Taylor asked, would he want to spread rumours that would implicate himself? 'As if I want me fucking arse in a fucking sling!' he said.

Della-Vedova could see the situation escalating. He tried to calm things down and said they had only turned up on his doorstep because of the newspaper articles and television coverage.

'Mate, my fucking heart stopped when that fucking showed up,' Taylor said.

Carter nodded. 'Tell me about it.'

Della-Vedova said, 'You're not the only one.'

The arguing continued, with Taylor and Carter at a stalemate. Taylor said his new wife would get suspicious if they kept talking for too long.

Eight days later the Ridgecrop detectives knocked on Taylor's front door, handing him a warrant to search his property and putting him in handcuffs. At the same time, a separate team appeared on Della-Vedova's doorstep at his house in Wattle Grove. They drove him back to Surry Hills Police Station where he was introduced to Detective Inspector Neil Tuckerman, who sat him down for an interview. Della-Vedova made admissions immediately, offering lengthy and emotional explanations about why he stole the weapons and the rationale behind it. He also gave candid demonstrations of how to use the rocket launcher when asked by Tuckerman; he had brought one into the room in a sealed evidence bag.

The army captain's version of what had happened put the whole situation down to an innocent mistake, a stuff-up of almighty proportions. He said it all started with a routine assignment to destroy some rocket launchers at the ammunition depository in the town of Muswellbrook. The weapons were nearing their use-by date of twelve years. He took them up in a purpose-built trunk and, once at the depository, made a courtesy offer to destroy any additional weapons for the depot staff. It was just something you did, he said to Tuckerman. As it turned out, the depot was housing a few surplus rocket warheads, the same kind Della-Vedova had brought with him to destroy.

On the ammunition range he set up the demolitions required, blew up each of the expired launchers, and then hopped on the truck for the drive back to Sydney. It was only when he returned to Holsworthy Barracks that he realised he had somehow completely forgotten to destroy the rocket launchers he'd taken up with him. They were still sitting in the back of his truck. The only warheads he'd blown up were the ones given to him by the depot staff.

The rest of the story played out in the same way as most downward spirals: he panicked and tried to cover his tracks. He hid the weapons away, spray painting them and removing their external markings. He dismissed any thoughts of admitting to the mistake. All he could think about was how, if he owned up to it, he'd be ruled out of a promotion he was angling for, to be an ammunition technician to the Special Air Service Regiment.

With the weapons hidden, Della-Vedova considered several options, including burying them in a remote location. But in the end, as he told Tuckerman, he took the weapons home to his garage in the same plastic trunk they were stored in and set about trying to quietly sell them to a collector, figuring they could pass as trophies, a centrepiece in an enthusiast's gun cabinet, or something to show off to friends. 'I thought they would be gone, as I said, in somebody's bloody trophy cabinet, sitting in their shed somewhere out in the middle of [the] boonies by some cow cocky or someone who maybe wanted the damned thing for his trophy cabinet,' Della-Vedova said. 'Never in my deepest regrets and fears would I think that they would come back because of some fools, and some idiots linked to terrorists and shit like that. And that's the truth. I just stuffed up.'

It spiralled from there with Carter's arrival into the frame. He walked into the salon one morning while Della-Vedova and Taylor were doing renovation work. By then he already knew Taylor, but hadn't met Della-Vedova. The conversation between the three men eventually worked its way around to the rocket launchers and Carter offered to get rid of them.

'It just compounded,' he told Tuckerman. 'I was like, what am I going to do with these damn things and then it just ... How it come about – it was mentioned or whatever. It just come about – and I was stupid enough to do it.'

Tuckerman asked how much money he made off the sale of each launcher. Della-Vedova said it was virtually nothing. He'd been ripped off, he said, receiving only about $5000 for all ten of the weapons he sold, so $50,000 in total.

Tuckerman was surprised. 'If we had received information that it was seventy thousand dollars ... you'd remember that?' he asked, referring to the amount quoted by Carter in his statement.

Della-Vedova almost laughed. He assured Tuckerman the money he made was nowhere near as good as that.

The interview went on like this for another two hours. At one point Tuckerman held up the launcher that had been brought to the police station in a sealed bag and asked Della-Vedova to briefly identify its components. Della-Vedova took the weapon and explained its mechanics, how the firing worked and the propulsion it created to send the warhead flying. As he spoke, Tuckerman listened and then abruptly cut him off, asking him what would happen if the device was used on a car or a group of people.

'It would be terrible,' Della-Vedova said softly.

Before the interview ended, Della-Vedova said that years earlier he'd given some thought to coming clean and working with the police. The idea had eaten him up inside. 'I thought maybe that I could come and say something or do something about it,' he said. But the big reason he didn't was Carter. In the back of his mind he wondered whether by agreeing to some kind of formal co-operation with the authorities he'd be putting his family at risk. 'Sydney's a nasty place,' he said. 'I thought about it so many times and worried over it. But in the end I didn't, did I? You know, and that's ... Honestly, sir, I didn't do it, you know? I'm here now talking to you. I fucked up.'

Shane Della-Vedova pleaded guilty to one count of possessing a prohibited weapon and one count of theft of Commonwealth property when his case went to court in 2007. During sentencing, the judge hearing Della-Vedova's matter cast serious doubt on most of his story, particularly his claims that the rocket launchers had come into his possession through oversight, and that he had only made $5000 from the sale of each weapon. Della-Vedova's thoughts, or hopes, that the launchers would end up in 'some cow-cockies' trophy cabinet' were also 'wholly unbelievable', the judge remarked. The former army captain was sentenced to seven years in prison for the crimes and lost an appeal in 2009. Today he is out on parole.

Taha Abdul-Rahman, who pleaded guilty to buying prohibited weapons without authority and receiving stolen Defence goods, received a maximum sentence of three and a half years in prison.

Dean Taylor, who argued that he had been set up by Paul Carter and went to trial alleging that he had nothing to do with the sale of the rocket launchers, was found not guilty on all charges of supplying the weapons, the jury taking just two hours to reach the verdict. He wiped away tears as they delivered their decision. He left court telling the waiting media only that he was glad to be going home.

Paul Carter, who was given the code name 'Harrington' by the police, received a full indemnity for his co-operation with their investigation. In 2009 he was sent back to prison after being convicted of drug supply offences and was caught in yet another sting not long after his release, this time an undercover drug operation, according to a February 2016 report in the *Sydney Morning Herald*. At the time of writing, Carter was awaiting a decision on whether he would be deported to the United Kingdom, where he was born.

In April 2007, not long after the arrests, Wakeham and Adams were pulled off Strike Force Torpy and put in charge of new cases. The way McKay saw it, their investigation was over; the MEOCS brief had been to work on Darwiche and he was out of the picture. The Della-Vedova side of the equation was a matter for the army or counter terror police.

Of course, neither Wakeham nor Adams saw it that way. In their minds, there were still too many loose ends; the intelligence suggested Darwiche still had one, possibly two, rocket launchers hidden somewhere in Sydney. For months they had been thrashing out methods to try and track them down, ways of outsmarting the inmate to get the weapons back without his co-operation. Neither of them could walk away from that. It was during one of their long drives to visit the inmate at Lithgow that they'd coined a new way of recovering the devices. When they ran the concept past McKay he thought it was worthwhile and provided the green light. It was kept top secret and given the codename Strike Force Seawater. It revolved around Adnan's older brother, Abdul. He was an authority figure in the family and was the most likely to know where the stash of weapons would be hidden. The plan went like this: if Wakeham and Adams could get a rocket launcher from the army, make it inert, and then discreetly sell it back to Abdul, they could follow it to its hiding spot which, most probably, would be the in the same place as the rest of the missing rocket launchers. All they needed to make it work was an informant, an Abdul-Rahman-type figure, someone who could approach Abdul Darwiche with an offer to sell a rocket launcher without twigging any fears that he was being caught in a setup.

The guy they had in mind was a drug dealer who had recently decided to quit the business, selling his run for $70,000 and committing himself to a fresh start. The proceeds of the sale had kept him going for a few months, but the demands of an expensive lifestyle and a difficult girlfriend soon left him cashless and looking for ways to make money again. Becoming a police asset wasn't what he had in mind, but he reluctantly accepted Wakeham and Adams's offer.

With that side of the equation settled, they moved to the more complicated phase of their mission: dealing with Canberra's bloated, slow-moving bureaucracy. In order to release the rocket launcher for use in an undercover operation the detectives needed the blessing of several state and federal government departments and high-ranking officials, a process that soon became bogged down in tricky legalities and obscure jurisdictional protocols that defied common sense. One of these rules said that a rocket launcher couldn't be released for a state-based investigation because it, technically, was Commonwealth equipment.

As these kinks were ironed out, politicians and top Defence brass were assured that nothing was going to go wrong. Briefings for this operation went all the way to the top of every department: the chief of defence, Angus Houston; the defence minister, Brendan Nelson; even the prime minister, John Howard, was kept informed of the matter. The rocket launcher would be completely deactivated, the detectives said; even if it somehow got lost, it would be inoperable, nothing more than a powerful-looking ornament.

Every step of the operation demanded signatures and assurances in writing. Each time a hurdle was cleared another would come up. Just as the weapon was cleared for release, someone demanded it be test-fired to ensure it definitely didn't work. Just when they thought the final sign-off had been given, another signature was suddenly required.

As these backroom processes played out, the street asset at the centre of the mission's success started becoming wary. He was back on drugs, paranoid about getting caught out, and had become a constant liability; the delays had given him too much time to mull over the risks and he was threatening to pull out of the deal. Wakeham and Adams assured him he would be kept safe, but his wavering had made everyone nervous.

Tensions also simmered in the police ranks. One night Wakeham sat with McKay by the fax machine waiting for a final signature from one of their superiors. Several minutes had already passed. McKay looked at his watch; the delay was infuriating him. He picked up the phone and demanded to know what the hold-up was. He couldn't understand all the hysteria over the operation; the launcher had already been made inert. A fierce doorstop it may have been, but a deadly threat? Hardly.

His boss, the assistant commissioner, answered the phone and said he was having second thoughts.

'Just fucking sign it!' McKay said. 'It's a piece of metal!'

The signature came through a few minutes later, but within days the operation was put to bed. The asset's behaviour and drug use had made him too erratic for the pressures of an undercover operation. McKay decided it wasn't worth the risk. Wakeham and Adams hated to admit it, but they felt the same way. Within a few months both officers left the Middle Eastern Organised Crime Squad, transferring to Local Area Commands, mostly for personal reasons. Adams had grown weary of major organised crime investigations. He'd seen enough death to last him a few lifetimes. He went to a rural command for a while and then retired in 2010.

Wakeham still works as a detective sergeant in the NSW Police Force and is now a team leader himself at a busy command somewhere in metropolitan Sydney. He and Adams were belatedly recognised with commendations for their effort recovering one of the state's missing rocket launchers. The certificates arrived nearly a decade after the weapon was handed to McKay on 30 September 2006. Nagle's acknowledgement was lost in the mail. At the time of writing, she was yet to receive any recognition for her involvement in Strike Force Torpy.

The only other clues to the whereabouts of the nine remaining rocket launchers stolen from the army emerged during Operation Pendennis, the landmark terrorism investigation that culminated with arrests in November 2005. The cell was led by the now-imprisoned Mohamed Ali Elomar, who had allegedly bought five launchers from Darwiche in 2003.

One indication of their possible hiding spot emerged during a police raid on the home of Victorian man Aimen Joud, which happened on the same day that Elomar was arrested. Joud was part of a Victorian cell working within the same terrorist conspiracy as Elomar. Analysts trawling through Joud's computer found a document containing explicit instructions on how to cache weapons for long-term storage. It recommended using a stormwater pipe with slip-on caps and various other solvents, epoxy and PVC cement to seal the tube, which would allow the safe storage of a weapon for many years. Raids conducted on Sydney members of the same terror network uncovered a completed pipe that had been assembled according to these instructions. Investigators opened the pipe but found no weapon inside.

The only other hint emerged during the criminal trials of Mirsad Mulahalilovic and Omar Baladjam, both of whom were members of the Sydney cell and were targets in the same operation. In the four days leading up to their arrests, both were seen by surveillance operatives in Sydney moving a set of PVC pipes between two vehicles – four pipes in total. It was never determined what was inside the pipes. Their whereabouts remains unknown.

Today, there are still nine stolen rocket launchers missing somewhere in the community.

CHAPTER FIVE

TELOPEA STREET

PUNCHBOWL, 2006

Telopea Street: the days of open-air drug dealing are over, but the vestiges of the old era remain. Cocaine is still available. So is ice. But if you want to buy them there's an implicit discretion, a text message or call in advance. The days of turning up in a car and buying through the window are long gone. That was the 1990s. Back then, Telopea Street was like a supermarket. If you wanted cocaine or heroin you stopped at the house with the palm tree out the front; a runner would come to your window and hand you a film canister – black for heroin, clear for cocaine. If you wanted cannabis it was the house with the carport, a few doors up.

Telopea Street in the late 1990s was a no-go zone for police: it was 500 straight metres of single-storey brick and fibro, a place where a squad car was once shot at and the local gang, the Telopea Street Boys, ruled. On one infamous night sometime in the late 1990s, Shadi Derbas, a pioneer of the local drug trade, noticed two officers in a police car creeping through on patrol and expelled them, using a loudspeaker to order them out. The scene was caught on videotape. Derbas is still around between stints in prison. For a while his bedroom was encased in steel to keep out the bullets from drive-by shootings.

These were the badlands. This was the street where in October 1998 fourteen-year-old Edward Lee had been stabbed in the chest on his way to a birthday party, a crime that resonated across the community and became a symbol of the anarchy taking hold of the area. Other murders also found their way back to here, including the death of Anita Vrzina – she was killed in a drive-by shooting, an attack that police said was targeting her partner, a witness to the Edward Lee murder. The man responsible for Edward Lee's death, Mustapha Dib, was a leader of the Telopea Street Boys. He served nine years for the crime. Then he served a few more over Anita Vrzina's death until his conviction for that murder was quashed on appeal in 2015. A panel of judges found that an eyewitness's account naming Dib as the shooter was unreliable.

By 2006 the street had undergone something of a transformation. The Telopea Street Boys were a spent force. The street runners had been arrested and the masterminds locked up. Undercover police had put covert cameras on telephone poles and the roofs of houses to record the buying taking place. They got council permission to lop down trees so that they could have uninterrupted views of more than 400 cars that turned up to score each day. After that, Telopea Street had faded back into obscurity, becoming like any other stretch of road in the rabbit warren of Punchbowl. Then Blackie Fahda showed up and police took notice again.

Mohammed 'Blackie' Fahda, a nineteen-year-old with tattoos and a distinctive mullet that went to his shoulders, had come down to Telopea Street to have it out with his cousin Mohamad 'Bruce' Fahda. It was 17 July 2006. Tensions between Blackie and Bruce had gone back some years, but when they came together on that day they went off like a match strike to a tinderbox. Shots were fired on both sides, there was a gunfight in the middle of the road.

It was only luck that no one was injured. In the aftermath, Bruce and members of his crew – seven men in total, remnants of the Telopea Street Boys – drove out in a convoy looking for Blackie, each wearing bulletproof vests, their cars loaded with an arsenal of weapons – handguns, a Mac-10, an automatic shotgun. They didn't find Blackie that night, but the match pieces had been set. As one informant told police: 'Everyone in the area knows that the war is going to happen and is just waiting for it to start.' Blackie's shoot-out with his cousin wasn't just a bold move. It was a declaration of war, one that could expect a swift response.

The genesis for all this had been the murder of Blackie's older brother, Ahmad Fahda, back in October 2003. People called Ahmad 'the shark' because of his standover tactics. 'He'll take a bite out of you,' that's what people said. He died in an ambush, his 25-year-old body taking twenty bullets from two Glock pistols as he was standing outside the AP Service Station in Punchbowl a short walk from Telopea Street. Ahmad's death sent sixteen-year-old Blackie into a depression spiral. He had bouts of uncontrollable rage. He quit school, drank until he blacked out and snorted up to seven grams of cocaine each day. His weight fluctuated from 80 kilograms to 110 kilograms and back again. Psychologists call this a 'severe grief reaction'. It wasn't the first time Blackie had been faced with violence in his family. When he was eight his father had nearly killed his mother during a domestic dispute, stabbing her at least three times in the neck with a carving knife and breaking a frying pan on the back of her head.

Following his brother's death, Blackie sat up each night clutching a gun, checking the doors and windows of the family's home to keep guard against more attacks. He was convinced that whoever killed his brother would come for his family next. Homicide detectives lay the blame with Adnan Darwiche and two members of his crew – Ramzi Aouad and Naseam El-Zeyat. Both were charged with Ahmad's murder. Darwiche went on trial for ordering Fahda's assassination, the victim's close ties to the Razzak family a possible motive. Darwiche was acquitted while Aouad and El-Zeyat had their convictions quashed on appeal. To Blackie, it didn't matter what the courts ruled; he was convinced that Darwiche had ordered his brother's death. As far as he was concerned, Adnan Darwiche was the source of all his problems.

Unable to get to him while he was in prison serving life sentences for the Lawford Street murders, Blackie's mission became a manhunt to get anyone even remotely linked to Ahmad's murder. No one was spared in this campaign. The first victim was Bassam Said who turned up at Canterbury Hospital one night clutching a gunshot wound – he'd been the guy who had driven Ahmad Fahda to the petrol station where the attack had taken place. Then there was Tony Haddad, the professional conman, who was badly beaten up in the days after the murder merely because he'd planned to meet Fahda on the day of his death. Even Blackie's own family members weren't spared. A close relative was kidnapped and tortured; not only was he considered to be too close with Adnan Darwiche, it was suspected that he'd helped set up Ahmad on the day of his slaying.

To police, the acrimony between Blackie and Bruce was another extension of this conflict. Bruce and members of the Telopea Street Boys had aligned themselves with Adnan Darwiche in the drug trade, creating bad blood between the two Fahda cousins. With open warfare looming, everyone watched and waited as Blackie and Bruce circled each other, trying to see which cousin could find the other first.

This hunting peaked on 30 July 2006, a Sunday night, nearly two weeks after the cousins' gunfight on Telopea Street. Blackie had been given a tip-off that Adnan Darwiche's younger brother, Michael, would be sitting inside the Titanic Café in Bankstown. This was to be the sweet revenge he'd been waiting for.

His car stopped at the edge of Raymond Street, its engine left idling as Blackie stepped out, walked along the footpath and approached the entrance to the café. It was busy inside; a fog of noise and competing aromas hit him as he walked through the door – scented tobacco from the shisha pipes, charred meat from the grill, burnt dough from the wood-fire oven. He scanned the room and spotted a table where associates of Darwiche sat around like mafia dons, sipping black coffee. There was no sign of Michael.

With a gun tucked into the back of his pants, Blackie made his way over to the table. If he couldn't shoot Michael, his plan was to shoot one of his allies – it all sent the same message. When he got to the table an argument started. 'What are you doing here? Get the fuck out!' Other customers turned around to observe the fracas. Blackie wouldn't budge. He reached for his gun and fired once at the man closest to him, Bilal Fatrouni, hitting him in leg. The bullet sent him to the floor.

Amid the rush to help Fatrouni and the frantic shouts for an ambulance, Blackie slipped out of the restaurant and back to the car waiting at the corner, disappearing into the night.

Blackie went into hiding that night, lying low as gunmen circled for him. A carload of men pulled up outside his mother's house in Birrong with plans to shoot it up. There was talk of a contract out on his life. At Liverpool Hospital, where Fatrouni was taken, his associates stood outside armed with pistols, on edge for battle.

Local police found it all too complex to manage. They didn't understand the history. The Darwiche-Razzak feuds, the warring that led to the murders on Lawford Street and even Ahmad Fahda's murder, were still fresh in everyone's minds. Police feared that the shooting of Fatrouni at the Titanic Café threatened to repeat that bloody history. For these reasons, the case was sent to MEOCS CI, the Squad's criminal investigation branch.

Strike Force Kirban, as the investigation into the shooting of Fatrouni became known, was picked up by Mick Ryan and thrown to Steve Patton, a detective sergeant on his team. Patton had transferred into MEOCS from Strike Force Enogerra, the investigation launched into the Cronulla Riots. His last case had been a stabbing that had occurred during the riots in the suburb of Woolooware, a young man out on a date. When McKay was given MEOCS, he told Patton to come as well.

Strike Force Kirban was his first assignment, a tricky case with dual objectives: its first task was to solve the Fatrouni shooting. Its second and more immediate priority was to prevent an outbreak of war – MEOCS informants were insisting that more violence was about to blow up.

In Patton's mind, the best way to end the feuding was to get Blackie off the streets. There was little doubt he was behind the shooting at the Titanic Café, as a number of informants were suggesting, but the evidence was weak. Patton wanted to breathe life into the case but the scene gave him little: there was no CCTV footage of the incident, the weapon hadn't been located, and the dozen or so witnesses who saw what happened wouldn't talk. Even the victim, Fatrouni, wasn't saying a word. A man with his own rapsheet, each time Patton asked Fatrouni for a statement he politely refused. It wasn't that Fatrouni was being obstructive; he just didn't want the hassle. In phone calls and visits to his house, Fatrouni continued giving Patton the same response until the detective broke things down in more sobering terms. In a last-ditch effort Patton said that, without a statement, Blackie would walk. It would be as though the shooting never happened. 'You need to do the right thing,' he said to Fatrouni, 'because we've got nothing.' Somehow, this tactic seemed to resonate.

A couple of days later, Patton walked into Mick Ryan's office. It was glass-walled with corkboards, one of the few perks given to MEOCS team leaders. In his hand was a witness statement that ran for several pages and had Fatrouni's name at the top: he'd finally agreed to go on paper. There was no motive supplied, but his statement named his assailant as one Mohammed 'Blackie' Fahda, which was good enough to get him off the street. Patton said he was ready to move and make an arrest, but it was Ryan's call as detective inspector to approve.

'You need to get more,' Ryan said. He'd worked scores of gangland shootings and had seen what could often happen to victims in the witness box. Some recanted, others were paid off and made sensational assertions about police coercion. Besides, he said, Fatrouni was a gangland figure; a good lawyer would shred his statement to pieces.

Patton thought that keeping Blackie on the streets was an invitation for trouble. It was too much of a risk; he was either going to attack again or end up dead himself. And, he told Ryan, the investigation was going nowhere. 'Let's get him off the street and see what happens. Either the brief will get better or it won't, but right now it's going nowhere,' Patton said.

Ryan was unconvinced. He wanted to keep Blackie in the field and see where he could lead them. Follow him around a bit longer and keep listening to his phone calls, Ryan said.

'Fine,' Patton said. 'We'll do it your way.'

Two weeks later, with the case still having gone no further, Blackie was arrested on the front lawn of his home at Kingsgrove and taken back to Hurstville Police Station. Patton and his primary detective, Aaron Phillips, spent the afternoon grilling him, throwing out questions and pressure-testing his denials. According to Blackie's statement, he was nowhere near the Titanic Café on the night of the shooting. After four hours, Patton and Phillips laid two charges over the shooting and took him into custody.

With Blackie off the streets and no longer a threat, Patton prepared to move on to the next stage of the Kirban investigation.

But the victory with Blackie was short-lived. Not long after his arrest, Fatrouni recanted on his evidence. It all played out just as Mick Ryan had forewarned. At the committal hearing, Fatrouni got into the witness box and denied everything in his statement, telling Sutherland Local Court that he had no idea who shot him and that he had been coerced into going on paper by the two detectives in charge of the matter – Patton and Phillips. The remarks crippled the case. It was tossed out of court that day and Blackie walked free for a while longer.

By then, however, Strike Force Kirban had evolved into a new investigation. Blackie had only been one side of the equation. The other had become his cousin, the cocaine dealer: Mohamad 'Bruce' Fahda.

Detective Sergeant Steve Patton's theory on drug dealers is that they live in a kind of mutual, unspoken understanding with police. There are thousands of them out there in the community, too many for the police to investigate all at once; some of them are known, many of them aren't. In that sense, they have an advantage – anonymity is longevity. Staying low key means living another day. The dealers that police can't see, can't hear, will never be a priority. 'It's the ones that shoot each other who go straight to the top of the list,' Patton tells people, especially drug dealers, but only after he's caught them.

That's how it went down for Mohamad 'Bruce' Fahda. Had it not been for the shoot-out with his cousin Blackie, it's unlikely Patton would have taken an interest in the cocaine sales from his house on Telopea Street.

In a career spanning two decades, Patton had worked many shooting investigations. But drug jobs were a passion, a recurring motif in his career that had started with the Drug and Organised Crime Strike Force Program of the late 1990s and then the Gangs Squad in the early 2000s. These cases revolved around biker gangs, but drugs were always beneath the surface, each investigation riffing on the same themes of clandestine laboratories, kilogram imports, turf wars and distribution rights. Drug investigations were a faster, more pragmatic way of putting criminals in prison. They were the tax dodging charges that landed Al Capone in Alcatraz. Why spend months working the unsolvable drive-by shooting with no witnesses, and victims who refuse to talk, when you know the guy behind it is running drugs from his apartment?

A drug job, in Patton's view, is a world of weak links, its supply chain littered with vulnerabilities – the dealer that gets ripped off, the supplier who doesn't get his money on time, the runner who gets arrested and wants to make a deal. And the weakest link of all is the customer, the end user that drives it all; they are the flaw built into the business model. They're sloppy, careless, loose on the phone, often stoned, usually broke. They're the first to turn informant on arrest, keen to avoid the hassle of court appearances and the burden of a criminal record. It's true: whatever loyalty a customer might feel towards their supplier will evaporate fast once a deal is offered as questions fly at them about the dealer's name, the drugs they're selling, the quantities available and, most importantly, the number of the drug phone, which, once received, paves the way for warrants to be drafted and the line tapping to begin.

Enter Bruce Fahda.

Patton set up a surveillance detail on Telopea Street where Bruce was known to be selling, watching as customers approached his parents' house to buy cocaine by the gram each day. From what Patton could gather, Bruce had two mobile phones: one for text messages and the other for phone calls. He did most of his business on the former, telling customers to meet him at home or at the nearby petrol station. The latter he used for everyday business, social calls and the like; he spoke to his parole officer on this number, identifying his movements and reporting in as required. He had only been out of jail a few months, cut loose after getting caught carrying a gun.

Bruce didn't work alone. His business partner was a seventeen-year-old boy who lived in the neighbourhood. Even at such a tender age, he was already known to police as a significant MEOC identity.

The third target of Patton's case was Khoder Katrib, twenty-two, a street-dealer since the age of fourteen and a member of the Telopea Street Boys, even though he lived in the separate suburb of Greenacre. Fahda and Katrib were tight. One intelligence report kept on file about them stated that earlier that year, on 8 March 2006, both Katrib and Bruce had walked into the Arab Bank of Australia in Bankstown and tried to deposit $20,080 into Katrib's account. They had wanted the bank staff to send the money to Lebanon once the deposit was through. But there was a problem with the cash itself. When the bank teller had picked it up, the bundle felt unusually cold. The staff had been trained to watch out for these types of situations – frozen cash, wet bills, cash movements over $10,000. Suspicions were raised. In the end, the boys had walked out and tried their luck later that afternoon at another branch. The same thing happened there. The staff refused to bank the money, believing it to be the proceeds of crime. No charges were laid, and technically nothing illegal had occurred, but both incidents were reported to AUSTRAC – the federal agency that monitors suspicious movements of currency – and stored on law enforcement databases.

It was Detective Aaron Phillips who had typed up the warrant application for Bruce's drug phone. He'd done the checks and discovered that it was registered to John Daoud, a fictional identity living on Fredrick Street in Campsie. The tap on Bruce's phone meant the Strike Force Kirban team had a back door into his whole operation. From what they could gather by intercepting his calls and texts, Bruce had a customer base of about fifty regulars. Police followed some of these people from his door after they'd done a deal, and then arrested them, a tactic known as a 'takeaway', a routine move to seize drugs and glean intelligence.

It's almost standard for a drug investigation to pick up a celebrity buyer within the general mix of customers. Usually it's a football player, sometimes it's an actor. Occasionally it's a politician. In Bruce Fahda's case it was a high-profile employee of the NSW Attorney-General's Department. She was a personality known to the public, especially the Muslim community, and was a fixture on radio and television. Newspapers devoted lengthy column space to profiles about her after she was nominated to win a prestigious state award: NSW Young Australian of the Year. Her name was Iktimal Hage-Ali.

She was twenty-three years old and striking, ambitious and beautiful, a western Sydney success story: a rising star in political circles. A mentor to young people, she cut through the hackneyed stereotypes – the dour sheikh, the old-world preacher, the silent, burqa-clad woman. When the Grand Mufti of Australia gave a speech at Lakemba mosque in October 2006 comparing immodestly dressed women to 'uncovered meat', Hage-Ali had been one of the first to lambaste him, branding his view as primitive and casting herself as the new voice of young Muslims. She rejected his message and said most of her peers felt the same, calling his views 'garbage' in a newspaper interview. She was a fresh take on a misunderstood religion. In Hage-Ali, the public saw the meeting point between the respected Muslim, the sharp feminist, the political mover and the proud Australian; a woman who sipped champagne, loved beach barbecues, backed a footy team and didn't wear a hijab. When Prime Minister John Howard set up a Muslim advisory group following the Cronulla Riots, the London bombings, and the Skaf gang rape trials – all of which had been flashpoints in an ongoing, racially charged debate about Islam in Australia – he invited Hage-Ali to join as one of twelve representatives from the Muslim community, making her the youngest person in the room by at least a decade. Around the same time, news broke that she was a NSW finalist for the Young Australian of the Year Award and was firming as a frontrunner for the national title, an accolade that would put her name alongside luminaries such as swimming legend Ian Thorpe and the army general, now Governor-General, Peter Cosgrove.

But all of this jarred with the profile emerging during Patton's investigation of Bruce Fahda. As it turned out Hage-Ali and Bruce were old friends. Her coded text messages to him were among the first to be read by investigators when their interception of his phone began. 'I'd return the dress if I were you, babe,' she wrote. 'No good … first dress was heaps better.'

Even though it seemed Hage-Ali was living a double life – her private world at war with her public persona – neither Patton nor Phillips paid much attention to her cocaine purchases. They weren't interested in arresting end users and, even if they were, she appeared to be buying only very minor amounts from Bruce – half a gram, a gram tops. At times she wasn't even buying cocaine but actually getting it for free.

She had been a classmate of Bruce's at Greenacre Public School, a more innocent time for both of them. Back when they were in Year Three, Bruce had cast a vote to help Hage-Ali get nominated onto the school's Student Representative Council.

It was only when they moved to high school that their pathways went in opposite directions. By the age of twenty-two, Hage-Ali was well known and mixing in important government circles. She sat on community boards, had been elected to prestigious government posts, and journalists wanted to include her opinions in newspaper articles. Around Punchbowl, few could believe how far she had come.

She had become prominent; Bruce had become infamous. By twenty-two, he'd been shot at, jailed and placed on parole. The only profile he'd attained was with police, his mugshot photo revealing a man with stubble on his chin, a receding hairline and a perennial smirk on his face. 'May carry firearm,' stated one of his police database warnings. 'Has threatened to kill police,' said another. When officers approached him it was usually with one hand floating near their capsicum spray.

Bruce and Hage-Ali had rarely crossed paths during their teenage years and beyond, except a couple of times at Punchbowl train station. By then Bruce was already street-hardened. When they bumped into each other he'd walk with her and act as a shield, protecting her against the deadbeats who hung out at the station and cat-called after her. They wouldn't dare do that while he was with her.

Beyond the train station, they went their separate ways again – Bruce to prison and Hage-Ali to university. As adults, they were only reunited by chance through an old primary school friend, Gordon, who suggested the three of them catch up for coffee in the winter of 2006. It was like old times: joking around and reminiscing, then giving each other dot-point highlights of their last decade. They stayed in touch this time and met again for coffee without Gordon, the conversation becoming deeper, for Hage-Ali especially. She was struggling with the pitfalls of success, the gossip and envy, troubles with her parents. Cocaine, she confided, had been a solace. There was a world of expectation on her shoulders, she said. And everyone was doing it – just take a stroll through any bathroom in a Kings Cross nightclub. As she told Bruce, 'All you can hear is the percussion of all the women sniffing.'

Bruce told her cocaine was a dirty drug. He warned her to stay away from it, but at the same time, and after a bit of convincing, conceded that he knew where to get her some. A few hours later, her green BMW appeared at the petrol station around the corner from his house on Telopea Street. Bruce walked up to the window and dropped a rock of cocaine onto the passenger seat. A free sample, he said. It was half a gram.

From then on he became her dealer, taking up to four calls a week from her. Patton and Phillips monitored these calls, but they still weren't of much interest; she was still just an end user to them. It was Bruce Fahda they wanted.

It was around this time that a tip-off came into the Target Action Group that demanded immediate action. Dave Roberts had learned that a machine gun and a sawn-off shotgun were being hidden beneath 1 Telopea Street, an empty investment property across the road from Bruce Fahda's property.

The owners had been trying to rent out the house for months without success. Each time the house was opened for a viewing, a dozen men would stand outside the property and make it seem like a very unattractive place to live. These men, naturally, had an interest in keeping it empty – it had become their very own makeshift weapons storage facility. The owners had tried everything to lease out the property, even lowering the rent substantially. They came to police in tears.

The TAG office's work rarely overlapped with the MEOCS CI team's, but this case was an exception and the matter was compounded by sensitivity. Normally Roberts would have just put a team together and stormed the property that afternoon, but that wasn't possible while Patton's case was running. Everything had to be handled delicately. Mick Ryan had asked local commanders to keep their officers away from Telopea Street while the investigation into Bruce Fahda played out. The last thing either he or Patton wanted was for Bruce to get spooked and change his phone number because he'd seen a police car on the block. A raid, therefore, was out of the question – everyone would know the street was under surveillance. On the other hand, leaving the guns alone wasn't possible either – wait too long and they might be sold, or used in a crime.

Roberts went to Dave Adney, his commander at the TAG, to try to gin up a solution. He explained the background. They needed a way to get the guns out of the property without revealing to anyone that Telopea Street was being closely monitored. A covert removal was tossed up, but rejected – it was dangerous and risked tipping off everybody in the same way; suspicions would be levelled at police if the guns disappeared.

Adney's other plan was experimental and elaborate. Something similar had never been tested before, but he figured if it was done correctly it might stand a chance at success. Instead of going in covert, Adney's idea was to go in *overt*. He wanted to create a scene: lots of noise and spectacle, something that would work as a diversion. Adney wanted screeching cars, wailing sirens, cops running down the road; the more attention the better.

Adney's plan was to stage a mock pursuit through the streets of Punchbowl, a fake car chase that would end on Telopea Street and draw every curious resident out of their house. With the chase as a cover, they would be able to extract the guns in full view of everybody.

He and Roberts went to work immediately. They borrowed a bombed-out 'stripper car' from an obliging car dealer and signed up two undercover officers to play the driver and passenger. They were cast as joyriding thieves who'd stolen the car, each one styled in a bad haircut and tattered clothes to appear as pathetic as possible.

The plan was put into motion on Friday, 29 September, a steamy morning that began with the usual din of traffic from Punchbowl Road. Jet-fuel seemed to evaporate off the roads, a faint smell of diesel in the air.

Suddenly, there was a squeal of tyres, and a bombed-out car accelerated hard into Telopea Street, fish-tailing from Koala Road, with half a dozen police cars chasing it down. Sirens blared and wheels lost traction. Residents peered out their windows and saw a police helicopter circling low overhead.

It was over in a matter of seconds. The car lost control coming out of the fish tail and hit a kerb, mounting the footpath and nearly crashing into the front fence of the house on the corner: 1 Telopea Street. The driver jumped out and disappeared down the side of the house, leaving his companion in the car.

All at once came the sound of more screeching tyres, doors opening and boots hitting the ground. An officer threw open the passenger side door of the 'stripper car' and wrenched out the undercover officer, pushing his face into the ground and cuffing his hands, all part of the script. The driver was dragged from his hiding spot shortly after and frog-marched back onto the street. The officers who caught him emerged carrying a pump-action shotgun with them. It was wrapped in a towel and found in a crawl space where the driver had attempted to hide. To everyone watching, the weapon looked like an incidental find, an accidental bonus that had come with the arrest.

Everything had gone exactly as planned.

But the real test was back at MEOCS HQ, where Patton and Phillips were waiting for movement on Bruce Fahda's phone line. They were trying to gauge his reaction to the mock pursuit: if his line went dead then it meant the operation had failed and blown the Kirban investigation. If it was active, then it meant everything had worked as planned.

His phone stayed silent for the rest of that day and they waited nervously for a result. The break came the following morning when intercepted text messages showed he was back in business, telling customers to either meet him at his house or the petrol station around the corner.

*

Three weeks later, Patton was in the office one night when Phillips asked him to come over and take a look at something. They had a training day scheduled the next morning at North Cronulla Surf Club, a mandatory cultural awareness event for all MEOCS staff. For McKay this was again about the battle for hearts and minds, a way to engage with the Middle Eastern community and get some perspective from its leaders. The speakers were organised by the NSW Police Force's Education and Training Command, which had no input or knowledge of ongoing investigations. Phillips had the speaker list in front of him. One of them was a young man who had risen to prominence as a youth representative in the aftermath of the Cronulla Riots. He'd been an advocate for a non-violent response to the riots, emerging as a mentor to troubled young people by channelling them into boxing instruction and religious study.

But it was another speaker on the list that Phillips wanted to show Patton. He tapped a finger against the name: Iktimal Hage-Ali.

Patton's immediate thought was to have her pulled from the speaking program. Since the investigation started he'd been watching her buying habits and was beginning to suspect a change in her behaviour. Her text messages said things like 'have an order for half' and 'friend didn't like it'. Patton had seen this kind of thing before – the sample comes in for free, there's no 'friend' at all, and the whole exchange is just a ruse to get some free cocaine. On the other hand, Patton thought Hage-Ali might be supplying. The texts were suggestive, but unclear. He couldn't be sure.

Regardless, he didn't think it was appropriate that she give a lecture to police when she'd come up on the periphery of a Middle Eastern Organised Crime investigation, which was the precise topic she was due to speak about in the morning. He called McKay.

'Boss, it's above my pay scale, but this girl you've got speaking tomorrow has been coming up on our intercepts,' he said.

McKay was stunned. It didn't make sense.

'What do you mean?' he asked.

'I mean, this speaker is one of our targets!'

'Well, how the fuck did this happen!' he said, nearly shouting. McKay found it hard not to be impressed by the coincidence.

Patton pressed his point to dump her from the program. What if, he said, a decision was made to shift the investigation in her direction? Surveillance could be compromised. 'She might recognise our faces,' he said.

McKay disagreed. He wanted to keep her there; it might raise suspicions if she was suddenly told not to come. He asked Patton how much was known about her. Patton said not much; she was a buyer on the periphery. Good, McKay said. He told Patton to use the opportunity; his detectives could take advantage of the chance to collect basic corroborating details: the car she drives, her phone number. Did he have solid confirmation that it was really her voice, or her text messages, getting picked up on the intercept? The answer was no: as unlikely as it was, someone could have plausibly registered a SIM card in her name, just like Bruce had done with his own phone.

The next morning, two of Patton's detectives waited in the car park of the North Cronulla Surf Club. As Hage-Ali's green BMW pulled into one of the vacant spaces, they noted down her licence plate. Once she was inside the surf club, business cards were exchanged. Her name and phone number matched the digits coming up on the intercept.

A few speakers preceded Hage-Ali, one of whom famously suggested that MEOCS officers, as a courtesy, remove their shoes before conducting search warrants. This prompted eye rolls from some in the audience; it was precisely the kind of impractical and dangerous advice that made officers skeptical of well-meaning cultural training days. There wasn't a police officer on the planet who would take off their shoes before running into a house where the risks weren't known.

When it was Hage-Ali's turn to stand up in front of the officers, she spoke about the southwestern Sydney that she knew best, telling the officers about the good people in the community who wanted something done about crime, the youths who felt angry and isolated by racism, and the mistrust of officers which had led to a breakdown in communication. McKay, who was listening, thought she spoke well. Aside from the handful of people on Patton's team, few people knew about her peripheral role in the Strike Force Kirban investigation.

After another month of listening to Bruce Fahda's phone calls and making takeaway arrests, Patton's team was ready to move on the Fahda syndicate. On 21 November the operational orders for several search warrants were drafted and included four targets: Mohamad 'Bruce' Fahda; his seventeen-year-old business partner; Khoder Katrib; and Iktimal Hage-Ali. She was to be arrested and questioned not for buying but on the suspicion of drug supply.

Hage-Ali was still asleep when Detective Sergeant Belinda Dyson knocked on the front door of her parents' house at 7am on 22 November. Her father answered the door, greeting Dyson and two officers flanking her in the doorway. Iktimal's mother and brother arrived as well to see what was going on. As they all spoke, Iktimal walked out of her room dressed in pyjamas.

Dyson asked her to step outside, but Hage-Ali refused. 'What's all this about?' she asked.

'Do you know Mohamad Fahda?' asked Dyson.

'Yeah,' Hage-Ali said. 'He's a friend.'

'Well, you have him to thank for this.'

Hage-Ali's mother tried explaining to Dyson that whatever was happening must be a misunderstanding. They couldn't possibly want to arrest her daughter. 'Not Iktimal,' she said. 'She's the good one.'

For Hage-Ali it had become obvious that this was over the cocaine she'd been buying, but even she had the presence of mind to remember some of the texts she'd sent asking for some free samples to help out her friends. 'If you had his phone tapped, I can explain,' she said. 'The drugs were for me. I owed him money, so I told him they were for a friend.'

Inside the station, Hage-Ali was escorted past a grim procession of holding cells. She was petrified, uninitiated to the bleak, miserable world of custody at a busy, metropolitan police station.

Patton and Phillips waited for her in an interview room. It was a windowless pod with a table and some recording equipment. When she sat down, Phillips pressed a button to start recording.

'Time commenced is 9:00am. Also present is Detective Sergeant Patton,' he said. 'Iktimal, do you agree there are no other persons in the room other than those I just introduced?'

'Yeah,' Hage-Ali replied.

She had already agreed to provide full co-operation, telling both detectives she would make a statement, provide an interview and, if necessary, give evidence against Mohamad 'Bruce' Fahda in court. Once they got through her basic personal details, Phillips informed her that she'd been arrested on suspicion of supplying cocaine.

'I didn't supply cocaine to anyone,' she said. 'The cocaine was for my own personal use. I never bought it for anyone, never gave it to anyone. It was solely for my purposes.'

'All right,' Phillips said.

Hage-Ali continued her explanation, telling both detectives that she constantly lied to Fahda – all of the cocaine that she told him would be bought for her friends was really for herself. There were no friends asking for samples of his product; it was just her way of getting free tasters. Apart from free cocaine, the other reason she had lied to Fahda, she said, was to cover up her use of the drug, particularly during Ramadan – she just didn't want him to know she was using during the holy month.

Patton was intrigued. He'd been looking out for the telltale signs of a liar, watching out for inconsistencies, bad eye contact and claims of poor memory. Hage-Ali didn't fit the profile. She never stumbled, she remained emphatic about her version of events, and she made full, uncomfortable admissions about everything else the investigation had captured about her cocaine use. He also knew that outside the text messages, he had no corroborating evidence. And apart from anything else, Patton believed her story.

It was Patton's call on whether to lay charges or not. He was the officer in charge and had an opportunity to use his discretion. She was a drug user, not a supplier, he thought. But his view clashed with his superiors'.

Over the next two hours he fielded calls from both Mick Ryan and Ken McKay seeking updates on the arrests and charges being laid. Ryan applied no pressure and told Patton it was his call to make. But McKay was confused by his stance; so she hadn't supplied cocaine, he said, we should still charge her with something. He wanted to insulate the police from a wrongful arrest or defamation suit. 'Just charge her with use/possess,' he said. The way he saw things, it was up to the courts to decide on a person's innocence, not the police. Patton dug in his heels. He saw a morality issue.

To the hierarchy, she was a name, but to him she was just another drug user, one who was prepared to give evidence in court against the main target of his investigation. On that basis alone, Patton was happy to let her walk free – you don't charge rollovers on minor drug offences; it defeats the purpose of their co-operation.

She was let go within the hour without any charges hanging over her head. News of her arrest wasn't made public. Patton told her there wouldn't be any media release about what had happened, but advised her to resign from her position with the NSW Attorney-General's Department and, painful as it might be, to pull out as a finalist for NSW Young Australian of the Year, which was being announced within the week. As Hage-Ali walked away she gave him an assurance she would think about it.

Even though McKay didn't agree with Patton's decision not to charge Hage-Ali, he supported him internally as the police hierarchy fired off lengthy memos seeking explanations for what had happened. For Peter Dein, the Operations Manager at the State Crime Command, the lack of charges meant that, legally, the NSW Police Force couldn't inform Hage-Ali's bosses about the arrest. It had been nearly a week and she was still working in her role with the NSW Attorney-General's Department and, despite what she told Patton, appeared to be a sure thing to win the NSW Young Australian of the Year Award.

Dein had commissioned some legal advice about how to handle the situation. It suggested that if anyone tried to tell Hage-Ali's boss about the arrest it could leave the NSW Police Force open to a compensation payout in the neighbourhood of $40,000.

McKay shielded Patton during these exchanges of legal letters, providing the cover fire he needed to keep working on the loose ends of his investigation. That was his command style: back your troops, even if you disagree with them sometimes. 'It is my belief as an experienced illicit drug investigator,' McKay wrote to Dein, 'that it was an appropriate use of discretion.'

The following week, Hage-Ali was named NSW Young Australian of the Year, accepting her award from the state's governor-general, Marie Bashir, at a formal ceremony. News about Hage-Ali's arrest hadn't broken in the media, but the prevailing view among MEOCS detectives was that she'd been wrong and audacious to accept the award. By contrast, Hage-Ali saw nothing wrong with accepting the accolade and remaining in contention for the national finals. In her mind she had given eight years of service to the community as a Muslim youth representative – why should that be voided based on her personal lifestyle choices?

A few days after receiving her award she was contacted by a journalist at Sydney's *Daily Telegraph* newspaper. The journalist told her he'd received a tip-off about her involvement in a drug arrest. Hage-Ali calmly deflected the journalist's questions, denying the allegation and putting it down to rumour mongering in her community.

'I am a high-profile person,' she said. 'I have no idea why people would be saying this.'

Without her confirmation, the story fell over. But a week later, having somehow received new information, the newspaper ran a front-page story that triggered days of follow-up coverage and national debate. 'PM'S ADVISER IN DRUG BUST' ran the headline. Hage-Ali resigned from her job immediately and relinquished her title as NSW Young Australian of the Year. She left Australia that week, flying out to Dubai amid the storm of coverage and vowing to sue the NSW Police Force over her treatment. Three years later, after months of hearings in the District Court, a verdict was handed down in her favour in the case she'd brought against the authorities over wrongful arrest.

During those hearings, the judge found that Hage-Ali should not have been arrested in the first place. Legally and morally, Patton still felt he had done the right thing – he had had genuine suspicions that she might be supplying drugs, but had let her go almost immediately when he realised it was not the case. He's since privately wondered whether or not he should have charged her with a 'use/possess' offence, per McKay's instructions, which might have prevented the ugly lawsuit.

For the wrongful arrest, the judge awarded Hage-Ali a payout of $18,705. It was a vindication of sorts; the judge ruled the police had reasonable cause, but because her role was so minor she should have been issued with a summons. The decision was handed down in late 2009 and, by then, each of the Kirban targets had already been sentenced and released on parole. Mohamad 'Bruce' Fahda and Khoder Katrib, the syndicate's runner, had done just under two years for drug supply while their business partner, the teenager, received a far lesser sentence because he was a juvenile at the time. All three men to this day remain firmly on the police radar.

CHAPTER SIX

MEOCS TAG: THE RISK

WETHERILL PARK, WEDNESDAY, 15 MARCH 2007

At the far end of an outdoor car park, at the back of an IGA supermarket, in a corner where nobody was watching, an undercover officer stood by the hood of his car steadying himself for a drop-off. For the last six months he'd been posing as a high-level drug dealer, worming his way into a ruthless syndicate starting at the very bottom. He'd started with a ring of street dealers and moved onto their bosses, infiltrated their suppliers, and then shook hands with the wholesalers – the men with links to the pill presses. And now he was here, the penthouse above the top floor, about to meet the 'upline suppliers', men who were both mysterious and rarely seen. In the boot of the car was $28,000 in crisp bills, neatly stacked in a bundle and tied with rubber bands, the money earmarked to purchase 2000 MDMA pills.

Cloaked in the background were a dozen sets of eyes, teams of police involved in the operation, watching or listening using hidden cameras and sensitive microphones. Each man had a role. A supervisor was wired directly into the undercover, his earpiece picking up every sound the officer made. Brian Jeffries, the primary eye, a MEOCS detective, sat in a surveillance vehicle controlling a camera. It had been planted in the car park that day and gave him a clean view of everything. Close by were tactical officers sitting in an armoured truck. Dressed in assault gear, they were waiting for their signal to move in case of an emergency. And in a covert sedan was Dave Adney, the operation's commander. The big decisions – to wait, to move, to abort – were his to make. Next to him was Mark Spice, the officer in charge of the investigation, a suburban detective who had come to MEOCS after stumbling on a group of small-time dealers with big-time friends, the tail of a rattlesnake.

Adney's command car sat near the car park on Rosetti Street where the undercover officer was waiting but he had no view of the scene itself. Both he and Spice relied on Jeffries, the primary eye, for their updates.

A few minutes past 2pm, Jeffries's voice squawked over the radio. He'd picked up something on the screen in front of him.

'Car arriving,' he reported. Adney put the word out to everyone: look alive, people. Then he sat back and waited, taking in the radio silence and the fading afternoon light on Rosetti Street, a pleasant part of the world: the view in front of him included neat houses lined up on one side of the road, a shopping centre on the other, and a spacious reserve the size of a few football fields – all of it a world away from where this investigation first started.

It's a good forty-minute drive from the car park on Rosetti Street to the Castle Hill Tavern, a bustling pub on the northwest of Sydney, the kind of place heaving with beer gardens, football players, and singles looking to pick up on a Friday night. It was also crawling with drug dealers from outside the area. Ecstasy was a favourite at the tavern, selling for about $25 a pill to each of the young buyers. Spice cottoned onto this and set up a drug operation using sniffer dogs and officers in uniform to needle the customers into giving up their dealers.

What followed were two dozen arrests – buyers and sellers – the majority of whom had no real value. They were the dregs, small-time peddlers with no one heavy in the trade behind them. But eventually Spice found two runners with potential, white kids from the suburbs, cleanskins with no criminal records. They said the Tavern was 'theirs' and gave an undercover officer a business card. Things moved quickly. Five days later, in the Tavern's car park, the undercover met the suppliers and bought fifty pills. They were the next link in the chain. One was the son of a prison officer. The other, Alen Muschulu, had cousins on the MEOCS radar, organised crime identities working with the DLASTHR street gang. These were men of Assyrian heritage, migrants hailing from Iraqi, Iranian, Syrian and Turkish families. Through Muschulu, Spice saw his next move forming, a slipstream into the upline suppliers, the guys dealing in batches.

It was around this time, September 2006, that Dave Adney received a phone call from Spice's commander offering to hand over the case to MEOCS. It had become too big, the commander said. This was no longer an investigation into a few pills being passed around a suburban pub. Spice had transcended a hierarchy – he'd thrown a grappling hook into the middle tiers of a syndicate and had another one ready to stab into the mountain. What he needed was a much bigger team behind him, experienced organised crime detectives who could handle the job full time, without the distraction of important but less complex local priorities.

Within days, Spice walked into the MEOCS TAG office and dumped the case files onto his new desk. By February his investigation – Strike Force Tapiola – using an unwitting Muschulu, had deployed more undercover officers and locked onto a new collection of targets, the chief distributors or 'upline', as police call it, all of whom had links to the DLASTHR street gang. There was Hormis Baytoon, one of the main men. He met with undercover officers numerous times, selling them thousands of pills, with Superman and Mickey Mouse logos embossed on both sides. Circling Baytoon was a cohort: Hayati 'Harry' Cevik was a nominee for the Rebels outlaw motorcycle gang; Amar Kettule was a suspect in a 2006 homicide; and Phelmon Shemoon appeared to be a shot-caller in their hierarchy, a man who Spice believed was the next link up in the chain.

They were a hot-headed crew, marauders who rampaged through the underworld and spawned their own offshoot investigations. They ripped off buyers and stood over rivals, bashing down doors and pointing guns in their faces. Spice's team watched with growing concern; someone was going to get killed, they thought. The gang's MO was to cut the power to a house and wait at the fuse box. In the most serious incident a man living at Toongabbie went to check why his lights weren't working and found three men waiting for him around the side of his house. One had a shotgun. Another had a taser. They forced the homeowner inside and ransacked the property, demanding drugs and cash in front of his family, convinced he was a dealer with a hidden stash – that was what they'd been told, anyway.

The victim insisted it wasn't true, but they didn't believe him. He was tasered as a show of their will: it was a warning to show they meant business. When his denials persisted they pointed the shotgun at one of his children. One of the attackers checked the address a second time and discovered they were standing in the wrong house. At least half a dozen other similar home invasions were thought to be linked to the men.

There were other problems emerging. A recent batch of pills bought by Spice's undercover had returned positive readings for the substance known as PMA, a volatile and deadly amphetamine that had recently killed young dance teacher Annabel Catt at the Good Vibrations music festival. Her death was hitting headlines as the lab tests came back.

Adney and Spice discussed their options. Those pills needed to be taken out of circulation before more users were killed. The decision they agreed upon was to keep buying the tablets off Baytoon and his distributors to try to identify the manufacturer – the engineer with a hand on the pill press.

They arranged their next buy for 15 March 2007, a Wednesday afternoon. The scene was the IGA supermarket on Rosetti Street at Wetherill Park with Adney and Spice in the command car, Jeffries watching from the surveillance vehicle, tactical police on standby, and the undercover officer mic'd up and breathing slowly as a car pulled up alongside him.

Hormis Baytoon stepped out of the passenger seat and walked around the bonnet. Hayati Cevik stayed in the driver's seat. In the back was Ano Edison, another member of their crew; he'd also turned up to a couple of earlier deals. Baytoon took the cash from the undercover and started counting it, flicking fast through chunky layers of twenty, fifty and hundred dollar notes to make sure all $28,000 was there. When he neared the end of the bundle he turned back to his car and shouted out to Edison. 'Bring it to him, cuz!'

The front seat rolled forward and Edison stepped out, a Nike hat over his head and a shotgun in his hands. It was rusted and sawn off, its barrel hanging open like it had been freshly loaded. He snapped the weapon shut and moved fast around the bonnet. The undercover saw the gun and threw his hands up, surrendering and talking fast like he had been trained.

'Oh god, this is just like what happened to me that time in Wagga Wagga,' he said, weaving in a distress code.

All Edison heard was babble, but the tactical team and undercover supervisor heard the code word. Officers swarmed through the car park, running hard at the vehicle and firing gas canisters through the windshield as Baytoon dived back into Cevik's car with the money.

Adney saw none of this from his command car. He'd grabbed his radio and authorised the assault team to move the moment Brian Jeffries, his primary eye, sighted the shotgun and said the words, 'Gun, gun, gun!' Seconds passed, and then Jeffries came back over the radio: 'Shots fired!'

To Adney, it sounded like the undercover officer had been shot, possibly killed. He braced for the worst as the results of the arrest were radioed through: all targets arrested. The undercover officer, who'd been taken down too for dramatic effect, had been placed into a police car uninjured – the only shots fired had been the ferret rounds let off by the tactical team, which filled Cevik's car with smoke.

The situation still ranks among one of the more tense moments in recent policing history – a gunpoint robbery of an undercover officer. For MEOCS TAG, the Tapiola case marked the first of many high-risk operations and near misses to follow.

By 2007, the end of its first year in operation, the MEOCS Target Action Group had reached a tempo that dwarfed any other command in the NSW Police Force. Search warrants were the benchmark of this achievement. Not a week went by without at least one house, sometimes more, getting raided for drugs and weapons; these were fast, high-impact and dangerous jobs where on paper the risk was known, but in practice they were fluid and vague. The sudden appearance of a shotgun during the arrest phase of Strike Force Tapiola was proof of that.

Every shift in the TAG office had great potential to become a shoot-out. Catastrophes lurked and disasters loomed. The targets hated police and walked around armed with weapons. With a nose full of cocaine, anything was possible. To survive, officers found it best to compartmentalise the risk, worry about it later and hug the kids a bit tighter at night.

Close calls became something of a theme during 2007. Tapiola was one case, but there were others, the jobs rooted in memory by address and suburb. Everyone who worked there then remembers Kay Street, Guildford – the time when officers bashed down the door of an active drug lab and inhaled plumes of toxic smoke spilling out. The warrant was supposed to be a quick raid to recover some drugs, but no one was aware of the cooking going on inside the premises. Medical teams arrived and faces were flushed, but the follow up was hopeless. Dave Roberts broke open the door and copped most of the fumes. No one ever told him or any other officer what they had inhaled that day. They spent years wondering whether cancer, or some other disease, would suddenly manifest in their bodies.

Hydrae Street, Revesby was another one they all remembered, a raid on a drug den. It happened on 7 August 2007. Roberts had heard there were bags of cannabis and ice on the premises, mounds of the stuff. Like most TAG jobs, the warrant moved quickly. He got the information that afternoon and by nightfall he had a team forming up around the property ready to move. The owner of the house, 22-year-old Riad Taha, was already under investigation, a person of interest in a kidnapping.

They drove fast into his driveway, speeding down the side of the house towards the back door. A second team waited at the front, in case anyone tried to run.

Taha saw them coming from the back. He was smoking a cigarette when the car pulled up and four cops jumped out. One was Roberts, hefting up a battering ram. Taha's eyes widened. He flicked away the cigarette and hurried inside, slamming the door behind him as Roberts got close. A moment later the door was flung open and officers spilled inside screaming, 'Police! Get down on the ground!'

The TAG objective was to contain the situation, get everyone on the floor and ask questions later. They turned right into the living room, dodging a coffee table and lounge chairs. On the table was a bong, its cone packed with cannabis. A man on a couch stood up and adopted a fighting stance. In the struggle that followed, his head went through a gyprock wall, right next to a money counting machine.

Taha was still at large, running through the house. Its rooms were connected in a circuit and he was heading towards the laundry when Detective Peter Butcher spotted him. A former Bulldogs front-rower, Butcher brought him down in a dive-tackle that ended right next to the washing machine. When Butcher looked inside the machine he found a Colt .45 handgun wrapped in a towel, its serial number was scratched off. To everyone standing there it looked as though Taha was heading for the gun – why else was he running to the laundry, they asked.

Taha denied all knowledge of the gun during his interview at Bankstown Police Station. The place was just a flophouse, he told detectives Alan Walsh and Nick Glover, somewhere to take his girlfriend and smoke some weed after work. Taking her home wasn't an option, he said. 'It's very disrespectful to my parents.'

Walsh and Glover weren't buying it. So far he'd told them he didn't own the house, had no idea about the gun, and definitely had no idea about drugs that were found in the bedroom. In a locked safe was a half-kilogram of cannabis and five ounces of crystal methamphetamine, or ice, worth about $40,000 alone. Taha's fingerprints had been found inside the safe. The money counter as well.

Yes, yes, fine, Taha said, but he still had no idea how the prints got there. It was the same story with the rest of the evidence. If the place was a flophouse, the detectives asked him, why was there a doctor's note in the kitchen with his name on it, a set of keys in his possession that worked on the front door, and letters in his car addressed to the property?

'I wouldn't have a clue,' he said. 'I don't know what was in the place, mate.'

It was a short interview, fourteen minutes, but the case ran long. Two years later it was still going, dragging out as Taha denied his charges and won small victories along the way. The jury was deadlocked on the gun possession charge due to the lack of evidence and the charge was dismissed. It was the same old story – without fingerprints or DNA linking him to the weapon, 'exclusive possession' as it was known, anyone could have put the gun in the washing machine. In the end he was convicted for the drugs in the safe and on charges of using the house as a drug den. He was out of prison within fourteen months.

The risks went beyond search warrants. Every facet of the TAG detectives' work seemed to edge them closer to a shoot-out, the blue of the flame – their fingers passing close to the tip each time. After Hydrae Street came a vehicle stop, a routine late-night patrol. At the wheel was Vlad Mijok, another detective in the TAG office. Dave Roberts sat next to him. In the back was Tom Howes, a gun-recruit who had been handpicked to join the TAG office.

As the detectives cruised the M5 motorway, a pack of Comanchero bikies came into view, roaring past them in formation and weaving in and out of traffic. Their leader was riding up front in a West Coast Choppers jumper. Without a radar it was impossible to tell how fast the bikies were travelling, but based on the speeds recorded in their own car, trying to keep up with them, Roberts estimated it was somewhere in the neighbourhood of 150km/h.

The Comancheros veered off the highway onto Bexley Road, ignoring the sirens. The next seven minutes were a steady pursuit. Petrol stations and parks zoomed by. Calls for backup went unanswered, the radio operator apologising each time as Roberts unsuccessfully repeated his requests for assistance. The Comancheros were in the middle of a turf war with the Hells Angels over a patch of southern Sydney and, in that climate, backup was necessary. Members on both sides were aggressive and armed up for protection.

As the bikies approached the border of Rockdale, the next suburb, their leader turned off into Watkin Street and finally pulled over by the side of the road. Around them was a quaint suburb hedged by busy intersections and a commercial district. To the north were houses, churches and a kindergarten. To the south was a train station, glass buildings, banks and coffee shops. The remaining bikies circled the block, parked a short distance behind and watched their leader's interaction with the cops.

Roberts kept a hand near his gun as he approached the rider. He was already off his bike, a Harley Davidson. He had a bumbag slung across his shoulder and a cloth mask covering his face, the jaw replaced with a rictus of bones and sharp teeth. He took off the mask and handed over his licence without any trouble. Roberts looked at the name: Joshua Tutawake Johns, twenty years old. He had an uncanny resemblance to Sonny Bill Williams, the football player.

Back at the car, Mijok called the radio operator and waited for any intelligence reports to be read out. There were five on Johns, the operator said, warnings and intelligence summaries about gang links and gun possession. Roberts listened over Mijok's shoulder and then walked back to the bikie where Howes had been standing guard. Johns seemed to know what was coming. When Roberts told him he was going to be searched for weapons, Johns replied: 'No, you're not.' Roberts saw the bikie reach into his pants and pull out a handgun, the weapon flashing past both himself and Howes as Johns threw out his arm.

Johns hesitated for a moment, giving both officers a chance to snap to their holsters. By the time they had their Glocks out he was already sprinting towards the corner of Fredrick Street. The gun was still in his hand and it swung out as he took the corner, the barrel shaking and aimed back at them. Roberts considered the options as he aimed at Johns – was he about to shoot? Was it just a threat? He had a split second to decide and then fired twice at the moving target – blau! blau! – both shots missing as Johns ran down Fredrick Street.

Roberts and Howes chased him hard along the footpath, guns at their side. His arm bounced up every few seconds seemingly in a threat to point the weapon back at them again. People walking out of a 7/11 convenience store and lining up at a pizza shop watched them all running down Frederick Street with guns in their hands. Someone called Triple 0 to report the shooting. As Johns reached the train station, he rounded a second corner, turning right into an alleyway of cars and apartment blocks. By the time Roberts and Howes got there he'd vanished into the backstreet.

Within minutes, the full force of the law arrived. Ten minutes earlier they were nowhere for backup. Now a police helicopter was hovering overhead, illuminating the street with a spotlight. Patrol cars clogged up the road and more were arriving, the radio operator struggling to communicate with them all. Riot Squad officers and sniffer dogs went on a manhunt, finding Johns's facemask and leather jacket behind a parked truck in the alley. His handgun, a Chinese-made Norinco loaded with thirteen bullets, was there as well, fingerprints all over it.

Dave Adney came up to the police station that night. He was on annual leave but there was no way he couldn't be there. For Johns to have pulled a gun, as Roberts and Howes described, was a big deal. It's rare that an officer will fire shots on the job; some cops go their entire career without pulling out their gun. When it happens, it means the danger is extreme. At the station, routine protocols kicked in. All three officers involved in the chase were separated and told not to speak to each other. Roberts's gun was seized. This was all standard stuff, but the process still made everyone feel like they'd done something wrong. Earlier, in the seconds after the shots had been fired, an officer got on the radio to remind everyone about their obligations under the organisation's newly enforced Critical Incident Guidelines. They didn't ask whether anyone was injured.

Roberts and Howes were back at work the next day figuring it was pointless to dwell on what happened. Joshua Johns was still at large, but intelligence had come in suggesting fellow gang members were hiding him. McKay called Mick Hawi to end the standoff, arranging to meet him at a café in Brighton-Le-Sands. Hawi, president of the Comanchero gang, was a big man with neatly cut hair and gold rings on each hand. He symbolised the modern-day bikie boss: designer suits, big house, a civil manner with police. It didn't make sense to him to have the police offside, and McKay felt the same – the way he saw things, both sides could be useful to each other. But at this meeting, McKay laid down the law. Pulling a gun on a cop was a big no-no, he told Hawi. If Johns didn't show his face, the Comancheros would pay for it – clubhouse raids, vehicle stops, gang members locked up for minor offences. He said life would become very uncomfortable for the Comancheros of Sydney.

A few days later Johns appeared at Hurstville Police Station with Hawi and a solicitor at his side. He joked about what happened during his interview, telling Roberts he'd heard the bullets whizzing past his head.

But he disputed the most serious charge he was facing – that he pointed the gun at the detectives. He repeated this during his pre-trial hearings a few months later, telling the court that he carried the gun for protection – his newly purchased Harley Davidson was his 'pride and joy' and he feared it could be carjacked.

In his version of what happened he never pulled out a gun at all. Instead – and even the judge found this recollection dubious – he left the weapon in his pants the whole time. When Roberts had said he'd be searched, Johns told the court that he'd pointed to the ground and shouted, 'There's Tom Cruise!' to buy himself a few seconds, sprinting away as the officers tried to catch a glimpse of the Hollywood actor. As for carrying the weapon, Johns said he threw it into a spot where police would easily find it and had never aimed the gun back at Roberts and Howes during the chase.

Unfortunately, the true merits of this story never had a chance to be properly tested by a jury because just as his trial was due to begin the crown prosecutor representing the police secretly accepted a plea deal from Johns's lawyers, a move that would see Johns confess to the gun possession charge, but not the more serious offences of pulling out a gun or aiming it at police that would have attracted a higher sentence. Roberts, Howes and Mijok were dead against this move, but the wheels had already been put in motion without their knowledge. They were only told about it at court – the paperwork had been finalised. As a result, Johns was sentenced to a year and eight months in prison, a sentence that was calculated on the gun possession charge alone.

From that day forward, neither Roberts nor Howes ever left the office without a bulletproof vest.

One of the more memorable arrests for the TAG office from 2007 revolved around a serial offender by the name of Hussein Taoube, a wily fugitive who'd made robberies his forte. His targets were mum and dad convenience stores, soft targets with few security cameras that could be easily held up with a knife. He did enough of them that he even coined a passable opening catchphrase: 'Don't do anything stupid!'

For a brief period, Taoube became notorious. He'd become skilled at lying low, had eight warrants out for his arrest, and officers across several commands were coming up empty trying to find him. At MEOCS he'd earned his way into fifth spot on the Squad's Most Wanted List, somehow surpassing some of the biggest names in organised crime.

The job of finding him had been tasked to the MEOCS Uniform branch who sat outside his parents' house and searched cheap motels looking for him. While this was happening he carried out another two robberies, both with a knife: one in Tempe and another in the CBD. The need to catch him increased.

The mere fact he was still committing crime while also being the subject of a manhunt became something of an embarrassment. With the Uniform branch struggling, Roberts and Mitchell – the Breaker Brothers – offered to take over the search, figuring they might succeed where others had failed. One advantage they had was Taoube's mobile phone number, which they had managed to get, somehow.

It was Taoube's private line, a number he'd handed out only to a trusted few. In the Bourne movies that would be enough to triangulate a location, but at MEOCS that kind of technology wasn't available. Instead, they came up with a cover story, a plan to end the chase and make him come to them. Policing might be a world of policy and rules, but tricking a fugitive into handing himself in is not one of them. Their idea, devastatingly simple and slightly unorthodox, was to grab a couple of women, book a hotel room, and invite Taoube to a cocaine party.

There weren't many women working in the office that night and generally they formed a small contingent in the TAG office. Samantha Alam and 'Jenny' (a pseudonym) were both officers in the MEOCS Uniform branch and agreed to play starring roles in the plot, casting themselves as the honeytraps to lure Taoube to police. Their cover story was to tell the fugitive that he'd given them his number while out in a city bar. Intelligence had recently placed him around the Hilton Hotel a week earlier, which gave the cover some plausibility. With the phone on speaker and mood music playing in the background, Jenny and Alam started dialling. Text messages had already gone back and forth to get the conversation going.

They kept him on the line with flirty banter, giggling and peppering their conversation with a bit of Arabic. This was uncharted territory for Roberts and Mitchell listening in the background. Both of them only half-expected the ruse to work.

When Taoube asked where they were staying, the women made their move, telling him they were having a party. 'We've got a room at the Novotel,' one of them said. 'Why don't you come over?' Taoube seemed interested, but sounded skeptical. His answer was yes, but who could be sure? It was after midnight. Mitchell and Roberts put a team together with half a dozen officers and drove to Brighton-Le-Sands to try to find a hotel room.

They hurried through the lobby of the Novotel Hotel and introduced themselves to the duty manager at the front desk. He was an adventurous type, obliging and curious about what they were doing. He gave them two sets of keys and sent them to the top floor where a pair of suites was waiting. Roberts and Mitchell took one room with Jenny and Alam while the rest of the team piled into the second room and blocked off the staircase – the plan was to wait for Taoube to arrive and then spill out into the hallway.

Taoube pulled into the car park in his Mercedes-Benz just after 3:30am. He had already committed yet another armed robbery that night. At the front desk the night manager handed him a key and pointed towards the elevator. Then he reached for the phone. 'He's coming up,' the manager said.

Roberts stood by the door. Mitchell was next to him, waiting by the peephole – he was the only person who knew what Taoube looked like, having arrested him a year earlier. Jenny was behind them, dressed in a bathrobe for effect. When the knock came, Mitchell looked through the sight expecting to see a decoy, someone Taoube had sent up to ensure the invitation wasn't a trap. But there was Taoube, his face distorted and bulbous, miserable-looking and anxious in the warped view. Mitchell turned to Jenny and gave a thumbs up: it was him.

'Just a second,' she called, opening the door a few inches until it caught in the latch. It was just enough of a gap for Taoube to see her and be lulled into a false sense of security. 'I'll just unlock it,' she said, smiling and closing the door. When it opened again ... *bang!* Taoube's worst nightmare. Guns drawn, muzzles at his head, cops filling the hallway screaming at him to get on the ground. He actually jumped in fright, nearly hitting his head on the ceiling. Later, he told Roberts that some criminals had been looking for him and he'd been relieved to find out it was only cops who'd set the trap.

The arrest was celebrated widely, receiving all kinds of praise from across the organisation. One of the best parts was notifying the investigators who'd been looking for him in relation to his string of armed hold-ups, letting them know where they could find him. When McKay found out what had happened he was delighted, impressed by the ingenuity of it. The job took on a kind of legendary status as word spread through the police force.

But not everyone was pleased with how the operation was handled. When the commander of the Undercover branch learned of the arrest he reported several flagrant breaches to McKay, citing broken protocols and errors of policy. In giving fake names to the two female officers, everyone involved had technically broken some rules.

McKay dealt with the complaint by phone, patiently at first, but these after-the-fact arguments always infuriated him. Of course, the commander had a point, but here was a violent criminal who had been running amok across Sydney, who was now finally off the streets – and yet the hairsplitting about policy had somehow become the priority. Minutes passed with the conversation going nowhere. McKay got bored. He held the phone away from his ear and looked at it.

'Just fuck off!' he said, slamming down the receiver. That was the end of it.

But it wasn't all success stories. There were also disappointments, investigations that aimed high and fell short. Targets who had been to prison and learned from their mistakes, emerging as much smarter criminals. Walid Chami was one of them. An old hand in the drug trade, he'd spent five years inside for his role in the 'Dice syndicate', a group of dealers who controlled several drug runs around the inner-western suburbs of Sydney, areas like Marrickville, Canterbury and Hurlstone Park, between 1999 and 2000. Chami was the leader. He used his time inside to study how undercover officers and telephone intercepts had brought him undone. He walked out of prison a much smarter criminal, hardened to police methodology. From there he became something of an untouchable.

In the latter part of 2007 intelligence had come in to the TAG office suggesting Chami was heading up a new syndicate in the same area of inner-western Sydney. It was a slick enterprise with a team of runners working in shifts from 10am to 10pm, delivering cocaine direct to the customers' doorsteps. One trick his dealers pulled was to ride around with a water bottle stored in the passenger well of their car for emergencies – if they were pulled over by police they could swallow the drugs and avoid any charges.

Chami became the principal target of Strike Force Stoneware, a TAG investigation run by five detectives. Within three months they'd mapped the syndicate's hierarchy and placed Chami at the head. He had a run manager beneath him and four dealers below that, among them a seventeen-year-old boy.

A tracking device planted on a car uncovered a safe house at Revesby and the syndicate's dealing patterns, which allowed undercover operatives to move in and start buying. They stuck with small amounts, grams of cocaine. Lab testing had the coke coming back with purity levels as low as seven per cent pure on some days. It was nasty stuff. Each buy gave the Stoneware team more promising evidence on most of the players, but not enough on Chami. He remained elusive, rarely on the phones and never near the drugs. His hands were clean. There was little evidence linking him to what was going on. There was talk of introducing an undercover detective, but it never worked out. The case became sluggish as the months progressed, chewing up staff and resources – buy money, listening devices, lost hours of transcribing – with nothing new against Chami to show for it.

For these reasons, a decision was made to start wrapping up the investigation. The detectives couldn't continue chasing Chami forever. They got moving on 8 December 2007, pulling over a run car and arresting two street dealers inside, one of whom was the seventeen-year-old boy working for the syndicate. He'd done as instructed, swallowing the balloons of cocaine using the bottled water to avoid being caught with the product. The situation produced a tricky legal quagmire for police. Because he was a minor, they needed his parents' permission to legally allow doctors to administer a laxative at the hospital. Thankfully, the parents agreed.

The unenviable job of collecting the balloons was left to Ryan Jeffcoat, a TAG detective who'd cut open his arm during the arrest. He'd punched a hole in the run car's window, sending blood everywhere.

Jeffcoat stood outside the bathroom at the hospital with a bandage around his arm. Inside was the kid with a bedpan. Next to Jeffcoat were two colleagues, Nick Glover and Paul O'Neill.

Jeffcoat thought the bandage around his arm gave him a free pass from going anywhere near the bedpan, but he was mistaken. When he asked who would have to do the dirty work, O'Neill and Glover gave him a knowing look.

'Highest registered number, bro,' one of them said, a reference to the shield number given to every officer who joins the NSW Police Force – the higher the number, the more junior the officer, the shorter the straw. Most unenviable tasks are settled in this way.

'Oh what?' Jeffcoat said. His number was highest.

The kid laughed as Jeffcoat went through his bedpan. It was full because of the laxative and Jeffcoat dry-retched the whole time, his hand going in to the knuckles.

The hope had been that Chami would hear about the arrests and somehow expose himself – maybe pick up the deliveries or deal directly with the customers, or even get on the phone and try to hire new people – but it never happened. Instead he did nothing. It was like he had nothing to do with the syndicate in the first place; and maybe he didn't. A month later, Glover and Jeffcoat knocked on the door of his apartment in Erskineville on a whim, hoping to find something – a drug ledger, a packet of cocaine … anything.

Chami answered the door stark naked, slurring his words and clearly high on something. Glover and Jeffcoat stood in the doorway – they'd arrived under the guise of a noise complaint and didn't have a search warrant but Chami let them inside and invited them to go for their lives with a search, which they did, turning up nothing.

With few options left they charged him with breaching his bail. The result was a quick court hearing a few days later, a Section 9 bond with no conviction recorded and he walked free immediately. The case against him was shelved after that.

The next time Chami emerged was in 2010 when he was shot at a park in Greenacre, getting injured but surviving the attack. After that he moved to Western Australia where intelligence linked him to a new chapter of the Rock Machine, an outlaw motorcycle gang prominent in the United States. Apparently he was attempting to bring the gang to Australia.

Not long afterwards he was charged by the Australian Federal Police with four other men over a conspiracy to import large amounts of drugs from Tanzania. When the case went to court, a magistrate found the officers had moved too early. The evidence suggested there was something suspicious in the behaviour of the five men, but the evidence didn't quite stack up. Reluctantly, the magistrate let the case go. Chami, once again, slipped away.

CHAPTER SEVEN

ALL IN THE FAMILY

Just before Christmas 2007, Angelo 'Ange' Memmolo, the detective inspector in charge of Team 3 at MEOCS CI, walked into Ken McKay's office and shut the door behind him. Memmolo's team was just coming off a job and McKay wanted to sound him out for a fresh investigation, an ambitious new assignment for his twelve-man crew: McKay asked Memmolo to build a case against the Kalache family.

Over the years, countless intelligence profiles, reports and informant-generated tip-offs had given the Kalaches a reputation as one of the most entrenched organised crime families in Sydney. They were a clan of twelve – six brothers and four sisters plus the parents – immigrants from Lebanon who had fled the civil crisis in the 1970s and settled in Auburn. Police attention had mainly focused on the brothers – Nasser, Gadir, Bilal, Khaled, Rabii and Hassan.

Nasser, the eldest brother in his late forties, was considered by police to be the frontman. Fewer people had been the subject of more intense surveillance and intelligence profiling over the years, his police file spilling over with details of his extensive family network, his psychological profile, his business ventures, and cars he was known to drive. One report noted his awareness of police techniques and his unorthodox style of violence. As of 2007 his only stint in prison had been during the early 1990s over an incident where a teenager was doused in petrol outside a hotel and set on fire. He emerged a handful of years later, starting up tow truck companies, a money-lending business and a debt-collecting agency. Since then his rap sheet had been filled with words like 'charges dismissed' or 'withdrawn'. There was also a pizza shop that detectives watched with great interest. It had unusual opening hours and a low customer base, but used several delivery vans, each one with a catchy decal on the back window: 'Drivers wanted, enquire at your nearest outlet.' Detectives noted these ads with suspicion – the business, as one intelligence report said, only had one outlet.

Rabii Kalache, the middle brother, had been jailed along with Nasser over the burning of that teenage boy in the 1990s, except his sentence was far longer: a minimum fifteen years with most of it spent in maximum security. He went inside aged nineteen, when two-cent coins were still in circulation, and he came out in 2007 to a new era: the internet, smartphones, hybrid cars. In prison he was kept in isolation and classified 'Extreme High Risk' on account of his family's name. He was punished for bad behaviour and had a year added over a stabbing. Life inside became an endurance test against the four walls, a contest to stave off insanity.

The youngest brother, Hassan, was still in prison serving a 22-year sentence for a shooting murder in July 2000 – what had caused the altercation between him and the victim, Wassim Chehade, was never fully established. In the hours after the murder, Hassan had driven from Sydney to Melbourne and planned to disappear overseas. Short on funds, he lay low with an uncle and convinced his girlfriend, based in Sydney, to bring 200 ecstasy pills south of the border for him to sell. He was arrested eleven days later, before he could step onto a plane. During sentencing he expressed some regret, but little remorse, about what had happened. Intercepted phone calls to his girlfriend were tendered during the hearings, providing further insight into his mindset at the time. He told her: 'The hustler had to do what he had to do.'

McKay's rationale for the job was simple: Nasser's name was not only at the top of the MEOCS Most Wanted List, but he was also at the centre of three separate strike force investigations. Not only that, his brother Gadir was listed directly beneath him on the same register. And now with Rabii fresh out of prison after a fifteen-year stint, McKay wanted someone to take a look at them.

'So, what do you think?' he said to Memmolo. As well as work colleagues the two men were friends, the kind who argued often and robustly.

'Fuck,' Memmolo said, thinking about it for a moment. 'I'm happy to do it, but they're a tough crew.'

McKay was prepared to give him a blank cheque. 'What would you need?' he asked.

'A bigger team for sure.'

'OK, you've got it,' McKay said.

And, just like that, Memmolo had his own mini-squad at his fingertips, Strike Force Skelton: a team of twelve plus another eight officers on loan, each one with their own specialty. There was a Drug Squad officer who knew the name of every major supplier in southwestern Sydney; a Gangs Squad detective who knew the big shots of Auburn; a Fraud Squad officer who could unpick Byzantine company structures; and an officer from the Robbery and Serious Crime Squad who'd already been building a brief on Nasser. Their plan was to work slowly and take their time to gradually build up an intelligence profile on each member of the family. It was a fact-finding mission to pick apart their financial arrangements, property holdings and sources of income, and look for evidence of illegality. Detectives call this a 'cold start' – the type of case that hasn't got an informant in the camp or a back channel of information.

When the case launched two months later it kicked off as a slow-moving proactive job, in many ways mirroring the work done by the TAG detectives. Low-level players were rounded up – drug dealers, shonks, strongmen; anyone loosely linked or vaguely affiliated with the Kalache family – and leaned on for information. The COPS database was filled with varying grades of intelligence about what each of the six Kalache brothers were up to, but the information was old. Memmolo needed something new.

All kinds of useful leads emerged during this period, even tips that had nothing to do with the original purpose of the investigation. One informant told detectives about a drug syndicate in Bankstown, based on Carmen Street, that was moving half kilograms of cocaine, huge amounts worth $125,000. Because it fell outside the immediate investigation and had nothing to do with the Kalache family, it was put on the back burner for later.

But, more pertinently, information had come in about Hassan Kalache, the youngest brother in the family, which was somewhat surprising given he was being housed in isolation at unit 5.1 of Lithgow Correctional Centre, a segregated section of the prison known as the STG-IP, or Security Threat Group Intervention Program. This is where gang leaders and influential inmates are taken to break up their powerbase. They spend most of their days in isolation, each one locked down in a cell with a caged yard opening up out the back where they can feel the air against their skin and see the sky through a small steel cage. On the other side of their cell doors is an empty corridor, patrolled only occasionally by guards; they mostly keep tabs on the facility through CCTV cameras.

Still, even in this realm of intense isolation, alliances can be made through the wiring of the cage yards and 15-millimetre cracks at the bottom of each cell door. And in late 2007, one of the alliances rumoured to be forming was between Hassan Kalache and another inmate, Bassam Hamzy.

A former resident of the Supermax prison in Goulburn, one of the most secure jail facilities in the southern hemisphere, Hamzy was what corrective services officials termed an 'Extreme High Risk' prisoner, one who was both influential and manipulative. Memmolo had heard rumours through street intelligence that Hamzy had smuggled a phone into the prison, or that he had access to one, but he didn't take them seriously. The STG-IP was a place where inmates were strip-searched and had their food X-rayed every day. The idea that Hamzy had a phone inside one of the country's most secure facilities outside of Supermax was, in Memmolo's mind, basically laughable.

In the background to the Skelton case, the Australian Crime Commission (ACC) was running an unrelated investigation into a drug run between Sydney and Adelaide owned by the Finks outlaw motorcycle gang.

The ACC is not a police force and therefore has no enforcement arm. Its investigators do not make arrests or go on street patrols like ordinary cops. Their focus is high-level organised crime, from transnational drug rings to sex trafficking. Its offices around the country are staffed with surveillance officers, analysts, technical experts and source handlers with informants in every state. Its biggest advantage over ordinary police forces has always been its coercive powers — its agents can summon people to give evidence about a crime and those who refuse to co-operate face imprisonment.

These hearings usually generate valuable intelligence which gets disseminated to state police forces for their interest and follow-up.

Several months of taps on phones belonging to the Finks had revealed its members were routinely sending kilograms of cannabis between NSW and South Australia; truckloads were dispatched along the Mallee, Sturt and Hume Highways for the fifteen-hour journey. The commission had nearly fifty phones 'off', or under interception, almost all of them belonging to members of the gang.

One day in April a new voice was overheard on one of the intercepted phone lines. It was familiar to many in law enforcement – articulate and relaxed with a slight Middle Eastern accent.

As a standard procedure, the phone number underwent a subscriber check, a process that threw up several red flags. Firstly, it was subscribed to a Stacy Ridggio living in Casula, NSW, and follow-up checks revealed the name was a fake; Ms Ridggio didn't exist. That was red flag #1. Next, the cell site data was pulled up, revealing that each of the calls were passing through Lithgow 2, a phone tower covering the Lithgow Correctional Centre. That was red flag #2. The clincher came in a follow-up call: the ACC's target, whose phone was being intercepted, referred to the man as 'Bassam'– red flag #3.

The ACC analyst took the information to her bosses and showed them the call charge records, an itemised list of the date, time and length of each conversation linked to the phone number. They were astounded – hundreds of calls each day going to Sydney, Melbourne and Adelaide. It was almost too many for a single person to make. By this point the ACC officials had accepted that Bassam Hamzy was the person most likely to be using the phone. An investigator familiar with his voice had already listened back to the recorded conversations and confirmed the belief that it was him. But how was this possible? How was he even keeping the battery charged? The STG-IP was supposed to be an isolated maximum-security facility. Most inmates were lucky to have a toaster and yet here was Hamzy with a personal phone line to the outside world.

In late April 2007 an email landed in Memmolo's inbox from an official at the ACC, asking him to come in for a meeting. There'd been a development in one of their cases they wanted to discuss, the official said. Memmolo had spent three years on secondment there and knew the staff well, everyone from the analysts to the translators to the surveillance branch. The only reason he'd left the ACC was to come work at MEOCS with Ken McKay.

Strike Force Skelton was still very much active and Memmolo and his team were chipping away at their investigation into the Kalache family – but after nearly three months they were struggling to get traction. There were a few leads, a couple of bits and pieces, but nothing to the standard of what McKay was looking for; in his mind the case was churning through resources and he'd already signalled to Memmolo that it was probably time to move on. In that sense, the ACC's timing was perfect.

At a briefing room in the commission's Sydney office Memmolo was given a rundown about Operation Tutoko, their ongoing investigation into the Finks, and informed about the developments with Bassam Hamzy. So the rumours were true, Memmolo thought. The officials showed him the charge records of the inmate's phone activity, the hundreds of calls between the inmate and certain high-profile criminal characters. These weren't social calls either, they said; Hamzy appeared to have his hands deep in several unfolding plots to shoot people, and plans to either buy, sell or act as a middleman in a number of wholesale drug deals, too many to keep track of at once.

The job was getting too big, the ACC officials said, and was outside their charter. They didn't have the capacity to investigate these fast-moving crimes. Their plan was to inform corrective services officials so they could remove the phone immediately. Unless, they said to Memmolo, you want to take the job over to MEOCS?

Memmolo didn't need any time to think about it. Were they kidding? That smuggled phone was a honeypot of intelligence. It was a chance for law enforcement to eavesdrop on the best organised crime figures in the country and get in front of mass movements of drugs. The potential in that phone dwarfed the fact-finding mission of the Kalache investigation. Some of the biggest names in the underworld would be calling Hamzy and talking to him at length over that line in the false belief it was untapped and secure. Would he take over the job? Of course he'd take over the job!

The next step was to convince the Commissioner of Corrective Services NSW to let Hamzy keep the phone. All it would take was one ramp search of his cell and it'd be gone forever – either seized by guards or flushed down the toilet, the latter being more likely. The commissioner, Ron Woodham, was a tough old screw who hated Hamzy almost as much as Hamzy hated him. Both men were locked in a legal stoush over Hamzy's incarceration at Supermax – he was personally suing Woodham for leaving him too long in isolation, denying him basic privileges, namely visitors, and violating his human rights.

At a meeting over tea and sandwiches, Woodham told Memmolo and McKay that it pained him to let Hamzy keep the phone. The fact he had the device at all was something of an embarrassment. But on the other hand, he said, listening to Hamzy's calls could lift the lid on an incredible amount of criminality. In the end he gave them the green light they sought. The only rider attached was that if any threats were picked up against either himself or his staff then they had to be reported immediately.

Of course, both officers agreed.

Outside of the Skelton team at MEOCS and a few high-ranking police brass, Woodham was one of the few law enforcement officials who'd been made aware of the phone. Even the prison guards at the STG-IP at Lithgow were kept in the dark about it.

It took two days to complete an affidavit for a tribunal judge. Detective Senior Constable Ian Wright, an investigator on Memmolo's team, filled out the paperwork, cramming in every last detail known about Hamzy and his phone to get the intercept approved.

On 1 May 2008, around 3pm, the first calls coming to and from Hamzy's phone were intercepted at listening posts in the MEOCS office. Unlike at the ACC, the police staff who were listening were not bilingual in English and Arabic, so translators were put on standby to decipher the calls.

Within minutes, however, there was a serious problem. The number of calls being picked up by the intercept was far in excess of what the small team of eavesdroppers and translators could manage. They were inundated with phone calls, back-to-back conversations that were out of context and coded. Each one had to be transcribed, translated and sometimes deciphered of codes making vague references to places, people, drug quantities and shootings Hamzy wanted carried out. 'Green like the colour you're wearing,' they heard in one call. 'Get a toy' was another code. As these calls were dissected, more piled up in the background, creating a backlog of conversations that had to be played back later. Trying to keep up and listen to the conversations live became impossible. It was like running on a treadmill that wouldn't stop speeding up.

What quickly became clear was that Hamzy had a small army of men at his disposal outside prison, seemingly willing to do his bidding; somehow, even from jail, Hamzy held power over these people. With a phone call he could dispatch a person to drive from Sydney to Melbourne, find a gun, have someone kidnapped, or even carry out a shooting. This all became apparent within the initial batch of recorded phone calls when detectives overheard what sounded like a plot to harm someone who had seemingly done wrong by Hamzy's standards. As the notional head of his family, Hamzy saw himself as somewhat of a mafia figure, a respected don who needed to dole out face-saving discipline when necessary to maintain order.

'In the mafia,' Hamzy said, 'if you disrespect the head of the family they cut your fuckin' head off.'

Detectives continued listening to the calls, trying to piece together who the intended target of this ire would be. Soon, the pieces fell into place: he was organising a kneecapping of his younger brother, Haysam.

It was a matter of discipline, Hamzy said. Haysam had been secretly undercutting the family in their drug supply business, sourcing his own drugs and then selling them at an inflated cost to regular customers. Buyers were being ripped off and the family was losing face. 'If he gets away with it, everyone is gunna think they can get away with it,' Hamzy said over the phone.

The Skelton detectives couldn't believe what they were hearing – admissions of a drug syndicate, family members implicated, a possible lead on the supplier, and plans to shoot his own brother. It was this sort of intelligence that detectives worked for months, sometimes years, to uncover.

In a bizarre way, Hamzy even tried to be scrupulous about what he was doing and claim the moral high ground. He didn't want his little brother killed, he said, but he had to be hurt. His instructions to his henchmen were specific: the shooting had to be carried out with a .22-calibre gun, a 'two-two' as he called it, which would fire a bullet small enough to cause searing pain, but not permanent damage. A second condition was that it had to be in the leg. The third and final condition was that Haysam would have to present himself to the gunman rather than be chased around.

He spent all of that day, the first of the phone being intercepted by police, trying to organise the hit, making dozens of phone calls and micromanaging the process. He needed a gun, a getaway vehicle – preferably a motorbike – and a hitman to carry out the deed. In between pulling these various levers came the pleading calls from his family members who had learned of the plot. They wanted the shooting called off.

'Listen, shut the fuck up,' he said to his brother Ghassan, who was given the job of sourcing the firearm. 'Don't question me,' he threatened, 'or I swear to God I'll shoot you too.'

Hamzy vowed not to sleep until the job had been completed. In a separate call a bit later, once tempers had cooled, Ghassan tried again to appeal to his brother's reason – this was family, Ghassan said. Surely there was another way to work things out?

Hamzy was unmoved. 'I don't give a fuck, Ghassan. I don't give a fuck who he is, bro. No one fucks with me, bro.'

It appeared that people rarely said no to Hamzy, but still it was proving difficult to secure a gunman, even with a slew of loyal footsoldiers at his disposal. Whenever someone learned the target was Hamzy's own brother Haysam, they backed out. Take, for instance, a trusted friend and significant MEOCS identity who turned the job down almost immediately. Mustapha 'Wak' Assoum, another lackey, managed to secure the .22 but then backflipped and refused to supply the gun to the triggerman when he heard the target was Haysam. Quite boldly, he too tried to talk Hamzy out of his plan, without success.

The only person willing to take the contract was Hamzy's cousin Mohammed Hamze. At first he'd been asked to find a suitable gunman, but by 8:55pm, with options running out, he accepted the job himself at Hamzy's request.

Three minutes later, in between his calls with Mohammed, Hamzy's phone rang. It was Haysam, angry and full of bravado. He'd learned of the plot to shoot him and laughed off his brother's demand to present himself for the punishment. He said the shooter could come to the 7/11 in Burwood where he was waiting. 'Let 'em come shoot me,' Haysam said. 'I'm fuckin' waiting. See ya. I'm waiting here for ya.'

The rest of the night played out with a wild goose chase. One minute Haysam was at a 7/11 in Burwood, the next he was driving off in a car, saying he was on his way to Progress Park – never turning up, of course. After several hours he switched off his phone to ignore his brother's calls, laying low until the morning.

Hamzy wasn't the bluffing type. If he made a threat, he followed through. The fact that Haysam hadn't been shot yet left him fuming in his prison cell and he had stayed up all night stewing about it; he'd told people his brother would be punished and now feared that he looked inept – like a 'dog weak cunt' – because he hadn't lived up to the commitment. To save face he upped the ante, telling anyone who asked that Haysam would now not just be kneecapped, but killed for his insolence. A source of solace was that he knew his brother had bail obligations. It meant he could easily be found: 'At the end of the day I know where he signs on … If he doesn't come and face the music I'm going to be waiting for him in front of the cop shop,' he said during a recorded call to one of Haysam's friends who was working with Hamzy to try to find Haysam.

As these threats continued to fly and it became clear the problem wouldn't go away, Haysam disregarded his bail conditions, booked a plane ticket and flew out of the country. When he returned a week later he was arrested at the airport and thrown in jail for breaching his bail conditions. The police had taken out a warrant for his arrest while he was gone. While it wasn't ideal, he was technically safer in jail than on the streets of Auburn, his brother unable to get to him as easily.

By then, Hamzy had already moved on from trying to have his brother killed and was putting the bulk of his attention back into the drug trade. In the underworld, they didn't rank much higher than Hamzy, and as a drug supplier he had the money and clout to source huge amounts of virtually any type of product. He bought cannabis by the kilogram and ice by the bagful, the crystals sparkling and pure, virtually untouched by cutting agents, coming almost straight from the manufacturer, barely changing hands. Detectives overheard him calling his brother Ghassan in the midst of one of these deals. His instructions were to take half a kilogram of ice from the family's supplier and, using their dedicated courier, get it down to Melbourne where a buyer was waiting. It was a lucrative deal, worth about $120,000.

Reluctantly, Ghassan went along with it.

Hamzy used the phone through the night. By day the phone stayed with Tekotia Wiperi, a New Zealand-born inmate housed across the corridor from Hamzy's cell. Wiperi was a huge man, angry and aggressive, a Muslim-convert serving out the last few months of a thirteen-year sentence. Imprisoned for armed robberies, he'd joined a prison gang while inside and changed his name to Abu Bakr. His calls were social mostly, to his family and a girlfriend back in New Zealand. At 3pm each day he would tie the phone to a thin, metal disc using a piece of dental floss and then slide it across the corridor and under the 15-millimetre gap at the bottom of Hamzy's cell door, where it stayed with him until the following morning. Detectives adjusted their shifts to work around the phone's schedule. It was worth the effort; Hamzy was running the device hot, averaging about 460 calls a day. At times he told people that he had to put the phone down for a minute because it needed to cool and was burning his ear.

Memmolo could only speculate how the phone had got inside the prison in the first place, but he suspected it had been smuggled into the jail internally by an inmate transferred from a minimum-security centre, where contraband phones, steroids and other drugs are routinely found. As for charging the battery, the suspicion was that Hamzy had a cord, but not a wall plug. As long as he was prepared to throw the bare wires into the socket, the phone's battery would continually replenish.

When he was still a teenager, Bassam Hamzy had put one of his cousins in a bathtub, filled it with water and scored him with a clothes iron. Afterwards he cracked his cousin's leg with a stick, breaking a bone. It was all to punish him for stealing some money from one of their aunt's houses. Sadistic back then, these actions are a snapshot of his early years, long before he walked a pathway to murder.

Over time, Bassam Hamzy had come to be an archetypal criminal figure, a mastermind with superior abilities. As he prepared to enter the prison system in 2000, a psychologist warned of his abilities in scheming and influence, his veneer of charm. 'A guiding principle for him may be to outwit others, exploiting them before they exploit him,' she noted.

Never the strongest or toughest man in prison, he showed a capacity for bending people to his will – he could tame dangerous people and psychopaths to act on his behalf. It was behind the walls of Goulburn Supermax prison, the impenetrable fortress, where he developed his notoriety, allegedly amassing a small army of Islamic converts, each one shaving their heads, growing out their beards and kneeling before him to kiss his hand.

Prison life had turned him into a devout Muslim. He taught himself to read and write in Arabic, he listened to Koranic tapes and studied religious texts, and encouraged other inmates to do the same regardless of their colour or creed. Prison authorities watched with concern as Anglo-Saxon and Indigenous inmates began reciting the Koran each day and praying loudly to Allah from their cells, demonstrating their piety by sleeping on concrete and rejecting television. When money began mysteriously turning up in inmates' accounts, officers took action, moving Hamzy to a different prison and accusing him of orchestrating an escape plot. He has always denied that this was the case, telling whoever will listen that the charges were trumped up by the commissioner, Ron Woodham, due to personal issues between them. His next stop after Supermax was Lithgow's segregated unit, where he had somehow managed to procure the smuggled mobile phone enabling his sphere of influence to extend outside of prison.

Bassam was the complicated middle child of the Hamzy family, a clan of cousins and extended family that set down roots in southwestern Sydney with the arrival of his father, Khaled. A soldier in the Lebanese Army, Khaled, like many other of his compatriots, left Lebanon for Australia during the early 1970s, just prior to the outbreak of the country's civil crisis. At the time, he had been living in the foothills of Mount Lebanon, near the port city of Tripoli, and had just married his wife, Lola. They came to Sydney, where he had previously spent some time as a younger man, and settled in a house on Albert Street, Auburn, ready to start a family. First was a boy, Mejid, then a girl, Mejida. In 1979 Bassam was born, followed by the twins, Ghassan and Haysam, eight years later.

Life was stable in those early years. The kids were enrolled in school and Khaled began a short working life. But a car accident threw everything into doubt, forcing him out of work and into a long period of recuperation where the family lived off a large compensation payout. In 1989 he bounced back and took up part-time work as a leather cutter. Soon after he started a company with a friend exporting powdered milk to Lebanon, a short-lived venture that ended two years later with a police raid and charges of supplying heroin in kilogram quantities. It was 1992. Bassam was eleven. His father was given a thirteen-year prison term.

The biggest shift in Bassam's life can be traced back to this point. He left home at thirteen and moved to Kings Cross where he lived with two prostitutes, both friends of his father. He sold drugs to make money, but then started using them as well to regulate his moods – if he wanted to be happy, he took ecstasy; if he wanted a quick rush, he reached for coke; if he needed to forget, he shot himself with heroin. There was a drug for every occasion. Pot calmed him down, speed gave him energy, and LSD was a trip – a drug for the good times.

He stayed in school but was shunted around as his aggression increased. It was an unstable period of chopping and changing each year. There were fights, weapons and threats to schoolteachers. He was expelled from Year 7 at Granville Boys High School, then Birrong Boys High School less than a year later. He got his School Certificate from Granville South High School before being expelled a year later for verbally abusing a teacher.

Jobs were flicked and crushed out like half-smoked cigarettes. He gave two months to a carpentry apprenticeship before calling it quits. Then he tried labouring on construction sites – getting up early and shovelling soil, digging holes and dragging bags of cement in the hot sun – but he eventually grew tired of being ordered around and dropped that job too.

In his spare time he showed a talent for alternative trades: rebirthing cars, extortion and low-level drug supply. He grew his own pot, then started buying harder drugs from a Vietnamese contact, dealing around Auburn and gathering the attention of police. At sixteen he was charged with resisting arrest. At seventeen it was stolen property, then assault, then weaponry, larceny, driving with a cancelled licence and cultivating drugs. By then it was 1998. He was nineteen. That year, on a brisk night in May, he got his first taste of murder.

In the shadow of a streetlight, on the corner of Oxford and West streets in Paddington, just outside the Ardino Hairdressing Salon, Bassam stood silently, gripping a 9-millimetre pistol in his jacket pocket. Across the street, dozens of people were spilling out of the Mr Goodbar nightclub and milling about on the footpath, waiting for friends to come outside and jump into taxis to go home. It was closing time, 3am.

An argument that had started inside the venue migrated onto the street. There were two groups of men, something about a girl. On one side were Bassam's friends, Nedhal Hammoud and Kader

Chakaik. They were trying to goad the other group into a fight, throwing taunts and shoving them. A little older, and with a slightly greater number – five versus two – the others resisted the urge and made a decision to walk away. Their designated driver, Arthur Kazas, tried defusing the situation.

'Mate,' he said to Hammoud, 'we don't want anything to do with what you want.' With that, Kazas and his four friends – Kris Toumazis, Nick Lambos and two others – started back to their car, a Ford Capri, parked a short distance down the street. As they piled inside, Chakaik ran over and kicked the passenger side door, reigniting the situation. He dashed across the street with Kazas, Toumazis and Lambos chasing him on foot.

Hamzy watched from the shadows as they came in his direction. As they neared him, he pulled the gun from his jacket pocket, aimed at the trio chasing Chakaik, and let off three shots.

One bullet went through Lambos's shoulder. Another struck Toumazis in the chest – he had seen the gun and made a run at Hamzy with his arms outstretched, getting shot from about one metre away. Kazas, who'd made it past Hamzy, turned back at the sound of gunfire. Screams came from the crowd as Toumazis collapsed on the concrete outside the hairdressing salon.

What Kazas witnessed next stayed with him: he saw Hamzy plant a foot on a low brick wall for balance, aim his gun down towards the ground and put a final bullet into Toumazis's prone body. Toumazis died in hospital later that morning.

Hamzy turned back to the crowd. They were watching him. He fired three more shots in their direction and made a run for it, catching up to Chakaik and Hammoud down West Street just as two police officers appeared. They had been sitting in traffic outside the Mr Goodbar nightclub when they'd heard the gunshots.

'Freeze!' they shouted. All three men turned around. One officer was aiming his gun. Hamzy raised his own and saw the muzzle flash from the officer's weapon, sending out a gunshot that missed; the distance was too great.

Hamzy, Hammoud and Chakaik turned into Holdsworth Lane and started running, managing to shake the cops. They hid out in a motel for the night, and two days later Hamzy and Hammoud flew from Melbourne to Lebanon. Chakaik stayed behind. An anonymous tip-off to police named Hamzy as the gunman a few days later. His brother's car had been left at the scene too, giving the tip some plausibility. Not long after he became the investigators' number one suspect.

Detectives figured they had time on their side – they knew Hamzy was out of the country, meaning they could work slowly and methodically to track down witnesses and build their case. There had been 120 people inside the nightclub and most of them had scrambled when the first gunshots were let off. Each one of them had to be tracked down, interviewed and shown photos and video footage to establish with certainty whether Hamzy was the culprit.

One problem, however, was how to bring Bassam Hamzy home once charges were ready to be laid. In choosing Lebanon, Hamzy knew he was outside the reach of any extradition treaty, posing a huge problem for investigators. On the other hand, he didn't know he was a suspect in the shooting, and investigators wanted to keep it that way. They gathered their evidence quietly in the background to avoid tipping off his friends and family. The strategy was simple: build a case, issue an international warrant for his arrest, and then hope he might be lulled into a false sense of security, and make a trip to Vegas or some other hedonistic wonderland where he could be arrested at the border.

What detectives didn't know was that tensions were building between Hamzy and Hammoud in Lebanon. Cabin fever had set in. They argued regularly, about what had happened that night, blaming each other. Hammoud's brother was secretly urging him in phone calls to come home; he'd confided that he'd become a Crown witness – mainly to help Hammoud cut a deal.

Hammoud felt swayed by his brother's words and, tiring of the fighting with Hamzy, he quietly made plans to return to Sydney. Within a month he was back in Australia and co-operating with the police investigation. Whether Hamzy was aware of this co-operation or not isn't certain, though he was also on the move.

Towards the end of 1998, about six months after the murder, detectives in Sydney received an Interpol advisory document indicating that Bassam Hamzy had departed Lebanon and was currently in the Central American nation of Belize, staying with an uncle. Within weeks he was neck-deep in mischief, capitalising on the low cost of cocaine and arranging exports to Sydney. His method was to have the drug mules come to him, and then send them home with a kilogram each in their luggage. Of course, this was 1998. Email was in its infancy, phone tapping wasn't a widely acknowledged police methodology, and everyone was using landlines to communicate quickly with people overseas. Detectives had nine different phone lines under surveillance, each one belonging to members of the Hamzy, Hammoud or Chakaik families. By eavesdropping on the phones they had become aware of the cocaine importation Hamzy was attempting to pull off. The need to intercept the couriers was high, but it had to be done carefully – the detectives didn't want Hamzy knowing his phone was being tapped. At that stage, it appeared as though he was still unaware how closely police were scrutinising him. Strategies were put in place. When he eventually found out that both mules had been caught at Sydney and Brisbane airports, he put the failure of the mission down to bad luck. Then he moved on, unperturbed, to his next plot: busting his father out of prison.

It was the same story: detectives overheard the plan via the intercepted phones and passed on the details to their colleagues at Corrective Services. The next day prison guards tossed Khaled Hamzy's cell. He was six years into his thirteen-year sentence. They found wire cutters strong enough to cut through the steel fencing at his minimum-security jail in Sydney. Within twenty-four hours he was moved to a high-security prison. Again, for all his nous, Bassam suspected nothing. In the meantime, the criminal case against him had built steam.

Detectives felt they had a case, but their problem hadn't changed. Australia had no extradition treaty with Belize, meaning as long as he stayed there he was safe: he couldn't be arrested, flown home and tried for murder. But Belize was close to Miami – a gangster's paradise of beach resorts, fast cars, white powder and loose women – and detectives banked on its power of temptation. It was a long shot, but worth the paperwork. On 3 December, a warrant for Hamzy's arrest was issued in the United States over the murder of Kris Toumazis and the wounding of Nicholas Lambos. Unfortunately, by then, Hamzy had already become well aware that he was suspected of the murder and had been overheard on a phone call telling a relative he would 'do thirty years' if captured. With this in mind, the expectation was he'd stay in Belize.

But barely two months later, on 30 January 1999, Hamzy stepped off a flight from Belize into Miami, Florida, picked up his suitcase and walked into a set of handcuffs. At the time he was on his way back to Lebanon, travelling through Miami for a connecting flight. Three months later he was brought home, tried and convicted of the Toumazis murder. He denied the murder during his trial but eventually told a psychologist: 'I shot two blokes … one died, one didn't.' Bassam Hamzy's punishment had been a minimum twenty-four years in prison, which would have made him eligible for release on parole sometime around 2017.

Due to the Strike Force Skelton investigation, the length of his prison time has since been significantly revised.

Bassam Hamzy's drug empire, the one he ran from prison, was largely a family affair, relying on his father, his siblings, several cousins and friends, who would physically purchase the drugs and deliver them to buyers in Sydney or Melbourne. It was a flat structure, a dictatorship, with Bassam on top and everyone else beneath him. He was the quintessential despotic ruler: he ruled by fear, exerted cruelty on those who crossed him, and – except in the case of shooting his brother – few dared to refuse his instructions.

Key to Bassam's success were several people. Khaled Hamzy, his father, who by 2008 was out of prison, was the financial controller of the syndicate. He was also his son's proxy on the outside. In some calls, Bassam referred to him as 'the godfather'. His role was mostly to handle the profits of the syndicate and oversee each transaction for quality control. Occasionally, he also did the buying from the supplier, an Asian man living in Campsie, calling Bassam to quote prices and give an appraisal of the drug's quality.

Ghassan Amoun, Hamzy's younger brother, a twin, was twenty-one years old and a middleman and gofer to the syndicate. Tired of the police attention associated with being a Hamzy, he changed his surname to try and go straight. After school he did a TAFE course and then a painting apprenticeship. He even earned a modest salary.

But Bassam wouldn't have it. He disapproved of the low wage and ordered him to quit painting, threatening to kill him if he didn't obey. Mostly Ghassan was a go-between who often sourced drugs for his brother, met with buyers, collected cash and worked closely with the courier to ensure everything ran smoothly.

Mohammed Hamze, Bassam's cousin, was the man who had taken on the contract to shoot Bassam's brother Haysam. Mohammed's role mirrored Ghassan's in some ways; he stepped in at times to either find drugs or get them to the courier. Every family, every business, is rife with politics and the drug world is no different. Bassam didn't trust Mohammed as much as his brother Ghassan, or others working for him in the syndicate, and believed he was diluting or 'jumping on' the drugs before they reached the buyers. What this meant was that he was effectively ripping off both Bassam and his customers. Because of these suspicions, the relationship between the two cousins eventually broke down.

The courier, 'OS1' (a court-ordered pseudonym), was the odd one out in the syndicate. He was a failing businessman who had transformed his cash-starved refrigerated trucking business into a thriving drug delivery service, getting paid up to $5000 a pop to take kilos of drugs to Melbourne or, occasionally, South Australia. Over time he became a trusted lieutenant of the Hamzy family, liaising closely with buyers, learning about drug purity and the process involved in diluting. He became so good that, after a while, he only had to look at a kilogram of meth to know whether it was quality stuff.

OS1's entry into the Hamzy inner circle began with one of his drivers, who happened to know Mohammed Hamze – Bassam's cousin – and made an introduction to the big man himself on the smuggled phone. Bassam needed a courier and OS1 needed an angel

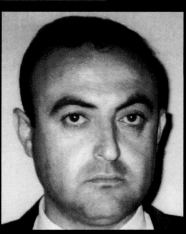

TOP: The house at 5 Lawford Street, Greenacre, where Ziad 'Ziggy' Razzak and Mervat 'Melissa' Nemra were murdered on 14 October 2003. They were killed when gunmen fired ninety-nine bullets at the house. Police later determined that seventy-five rounds struck or penetrated the front wall, windows and awnings of the property.

ABOVE LEFT: A mugshot photograph of Ziad 'Ziggy' Razzak. He and his brother Gehad were former drug runners for Adnan 'Eddie' Darwiche during the late 1990s. Both fell out with him and went on to start their own syndicate based at Hurstville.

ABOVE CENTRE: A rare mugshot photograph of Adnan 'Eddie' Darwiche, the man serving twin life sentences over the Lawford Street murders. It was Darwiche's on-and-off feud with the Razzak family between 1998 and 2003 that became pivotal to the formation of Task Force Gain.

ABOVE RIGHT: Ali Abdul-Razzak (pictured) married Adnan Darwiche's sister, Khadije, in 1990. Following years of abuse, their divorce was confirmed under Islamic law in 2002. According to police, this abusive marriage was one of several key factors driving the animosity between Adnan Darwiche and the Razzak family. Ali was murdered outside Lakemba Mosque on 29 August 2003. Adnan was charged over the murder, but the jury was deadlocked on a verdict and he was later discharged.

ABOVE LEFT: Dave 'Robbo' Roberts, one of the most feared and respected detectives to work at the Middle Eastern Organised Crime Squad. A keen fighter, he took up professional boxing while off-duty from police work.

TOP RIGHT: MEOCS TAG Detective Ryan Jeffcoat arresting Telopea Street kingpin Shadi Derbas, a pioneer of the local drug trade, on 23 November 2008. *(Gordon McComiskie/Newspix)*

BOTTOM RIGHT: Detective Inspector Mick Ryan, best known by the nickname 'Dirty Harry', scrutinising a piece of bagged evidence found during a search of Telopea Street in March 2000. Ryan was one of several experts on organised crime recruited to MEOCS CI in its earliest days. In 2009, he was the commander of the Squad's Target Action Group. *(Noel Kessel/Newspix)*

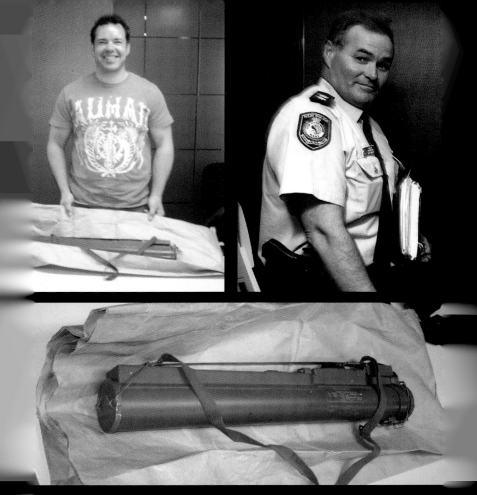

T: Detective Senior Constable Mark Wakeham standing proudly with the M72 rocket launc
is colleagues secretly recovered from Adnan Darwiche in September 2006 as part of Stri
e MEOCS detectives had entered into confidential negotiations with Darwiche over the w
awaited sentence over the 2003 Lawford Street murders.

HT: Ken 'Slasher' McKay, the inaugural commander of MEOCS. McKay was a man of the o
problem solver who ran his Squad like a football team — combining strategy with flair.
ne position after commanding the police response to the Cronulla Riots, and was in cha
6 until December 2008. *(Marc McCormack/Newspix)*

. A close-up of the rocket launcher, a 'white whale' that most cops thought would never
elpfully printed on the far right-hand side of the rocket launcher are instructions and sn

TOP: Telopea Street, Punchbowl, was a no-go zone for police during the late 1990s.
(Marc McCormack/Newspix)

BOTTOM LEFT: Mohamad 'Bruce' Fahda was a primary target of Strike Force Kirban, an investigation into drug supply on Telopea Street, Punchbowl. Already on parole, he was found guilty of drug supply and sentenced to a minimum twenty-two months in prison. The investigation was prompted by a shoot-out between Fahda and his cousin Mohammed 'Blackie' Fahda.

BOTTOM MIDDLE: A mugshot photograph of Bassam Hamzy, the criminal mastermind who led a drug empire from his segregated, maximum security cell at Lithgow Correctional Centre.

BOTTOM RIGHT: Detective Inspector Angelo Memmolo, the team leader at MEOCS Criminal Investigation (CI) who led the enormous investigation into Bassam Hamzy and his family. *(Stephen Cooper/Newspix)*

TOP LEFT: The Hungarian-made handgun found in a washing machine by MEOCS TAG detectives at a drug den linked to crime figure Riad Taha.

The shotgun (TOP RIGHT) used by Ano Edison to rip off $28,000 in police buy-money (TOP CENTRE) from an undercover operative during a controlled operation to buy 2000 MDMA pills. A still from a covert police camera (MIDDLE RIGHT) shows tactical police surrounding the getaway car.

MIDDLE LEFT: A bag of 1000 PMA pills bought by undercover detectives during Strike Force Tapiola in February 2007. Only days earlier a young dance teacher, Annabel Catt, had died after taking a PMA pill at a music festival.

BOTTOM LEFT: A police photograph of a major MEOCS target who had two of the Squad's Highway Patrol cars tattooed onto his legs. When officers told him one of the cars was now yellow in colour, the criminal said he'd have it added. 'There's still space on my right leg,' he reportedly said.

BOTTOM RIGHT: Omar Ajaj, a cousin of Bassam Hamzy, photographed during a vehicle stop in May 2016 sporting a 'MEOC' tattoo on his neck. When asked by a reporter why he had the acronym inked onto him so prominently, Ajaj laughed and said, 'Cos they're my buddies!' *(Gary Ramage/Newspix)*

TOP LEFT: Mohammed 'Blackie' Fahda being led back to prison after pleading not guilty to the murder of Abdul Darwiche on 14 March 2009. Fahda had encountered Darwiche by chance at a service station in Bass Hill, then fled to Tonga as a stowaway on a cargo ship. He was captured there six months later and extradited to Australia, where he was subsequently found guilty of the murder. *(John Grainger/Newspix)*

TOP MIDDLE: A mugshot of Mohammed 'Blackie' Fahda released by police on 19 March 2009, five days after the murder of Abdul Darwiche.

TOP RIGHT: Ahmad Fahda, known as 'The Shark', was Mohammed 'Blackie' Fahda's older brother. A close associate of the Razzak family, Ahmad was shot dead by two gunmen on the afternoon of 30 October 2003.

Fadi Ibrahim (MIDDLE RIGHT) being rushed into surgery on 5 June 2009. He was shot five times by an unknown would-be assassin while he was sitting in his Lamborghini (BOTTOM RIGHT). Ibrahim said later that he was grateful he was wearing decent underwear at the time.

Middle right, Seven News, Channel Seven. Bottom right, Gordon McComiskie/Newspix)

LEFT: Philip Nguyen (left) during his walk-through interview with Homicide Squad detectives following his shoot-out with MEOCS TAG officers at Cairds Avenue, Bankstown. Standing with him is homicide detective Tony Williams, a member of Mick Sheehy's Critical Incident Investigation Team.

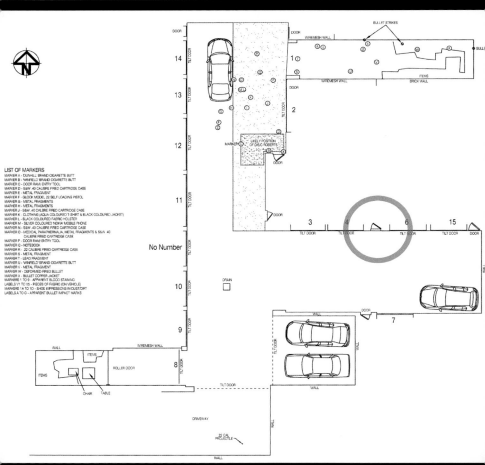

LIST OF MARKERS

MARKER A - DUNHILL BRAND CIGARETTE BUTT
MARKER B - WINFIELD BRAND CIGARETTE BUTT
MARKER C - DOOR RAM ENTRY TOOL
MARKER D - S&W 40 CALIBRE FIRED CARTRIDGE CASE
MARKER E - METAL FRAGMENT
MARKER F - GLOCK MODEL 22 SELF LOADING PISTOL
MARKER G - METAL FRAGMENTS
MARKER H - METAL FRAGMENTS
MARKER J - S&W 40 CALIBRE FIRED CARTRIDGE CASE
MARKER K - CLOTHING (AQUA COLOURED T-SHIRT & BLACK COLOURED JACKET)
MARKER L - BLACK COLOURED FABRIC HOLSTER
MARKER M - SILVER COLOURED NOKIA MOBILE PHONE
MARKER N - S&W 40 CALIBRE FIRED CARTRIDGE CASE
MARKER O - MEDICAL PARAPHERNALIA, METAL FRAGMENTS & S&W 40
              CALIBRE FIRED CARTRIDGE CASE
MARKER P - DOOR RAM ENTRY TOOL
MARKER Q - NOTEBOOK
MARKER R - 22 CALIBRE FIRED CARTRIDGE CASE
MARKER S - METAL FRAGMENT
MARKER T - LEAD FRAGMENT
MARKER U - WINFIELD BRAND CIGARETTE BUTT
MARKER V - METAL FRAGMENT
MARKER W - DEFORMED FIRED BULLET
MARKER X - BULLET COPPER JACKET
MARKERS 1 TO 9 - APPARENT BLOOD STAINING
LABELS V1 TO V5 - PIECES OF FABRIC (ON VEHICLE)
MARKERS 1A TO 1D - SHOE IMPRESSIONS IN DUST/DIRT
LABELS A TO G - APPARENT BULLET IMPACT MARKS

ABOVE: A police rendering of the basement car park layout at Cairds Avenue. The officers entered through the door opposite garage number 7 (circled), unaware of the second door next to garage

LEFT: A portrait of Detective Constable William Crews which now hangs at the entrance to the MEOCS office. Crews, a promising young officer, was shot and killed during the raid at Cairds Avenue, Bankstown. His death prompted an overhaul of search warrant procedures in NSW.

RIGHT: Detective Superintendent Deb Wallace was appointed commander of MEOCS following the departure of Ken McKay in late 2008. Wallace had experience dealing with gangs; some key members of an Asian crime gang had nicknamed her 'the smiling assassin'. She said Middle Eastern criminals treated their crimes like a trade skill, something passed on from father to son, brother to brother, or cousin to cousin. *(Anthony Reginato/Newspix)*

investor to save his business, Parcdel Pty Ltd. When he eventually spoke to Bassam on 8 May they came to an agreement: Bassam would provide OS1 with a financial injection for his company, and OS1 would let the business become a front for other family pursuits.

With Parcdel in his back pocket, Bassam started looking at much loftier goals – drug supply was just the start of his empire building. Included in these ambitions were plans to start a new street gang, a crew who would take its lead from the mafia structures of North America. It would be just like the outlaw motorcycle gangs of Sydney, but for Muslims only. Instead of motorcycles, they would cruise Sydney in a fleet of stately black Chrysler vehicles, a hat-tip to the Cadillac and Lincoln town cars famously used by members of the Bonannos, the Gambinos and the rest of the Five Families. Overheard conversations suggested plans to set up chapters across Sydney with captains and lieutenants in their charge to draw in recruits.

Bassam even designed a logo for this group with one of his many cousins, Khaled Hamze, and used stolen credit card numbers to order t-shirts, hoodies, patches and leather jackets bearing the insignia: two AK-47 assault rifles crossed in the middle with the name printed above – Brothers 4 Life, or B4L. The drug dealing was the foundation for this project, a means of raising funds for weapons, cars and a factory clubhouse in which to base the gang's operations. Their mission would be to hunt in packs, muscle into drug territory, create their own turf and stand over legitimate businesses.

Bassam's father was tasked with scouting around for a factory with a cheap lease to use as a clubhouse. When they spoke about it, Bassam reasoned that if thirty people paid a membership fee of $30 a week they would be able to raise enough money to fund the venture. Another idea was to borrow money from a bank, using OS1's home as collateral, but this didn't proceed.

Vigorous discussions took place between Bassam and his cousin, Khaled Hamze, about putting his name on the lease. He'd be perfect, Bassam thought: he had no criminal record and would, therefore, make the perfect 'cleanskin' to put on the documents. Khaled, however, didn't love the idea; he had never worked a day in his life or paid a dollar in tax. He thought a sudden leasing arrangement would garner some heat. 'They are gonna look that up,' he said. Undeterred, each day Bassam rifled through newspapers, raiding the classified sections and looking at vehicles for sale, properties on the market, to cut out and analyse.

The first drug deal Bassam Hamzy brokered from prison – the first one picked up by Skelton detectives in any case – was for seven kilograms of cannabis leaf sitting in Melbourne for $37,500. A deal like that created havoc on the listening posts at MEOCS HQ. Hamzy went into overdrive with phone calls, settling the deal, organising the pick-up, cold-calling buyers. That's how he worked – he invested, he sold, he retained a small balance, and then he moved on to his next big venture. His courier, OS1, retrieved the cannabis from Melbourne mostly without a hitch – his truck broke down along the way and a separate car had to be organised to finish the journey. Again, more phone calls, more micro-management, more screaming fits when things didn't go his way. Police watched the truck the whole time and took notes.

Selling the cannabis wasn't so easy. It took another week to get rid of it all, by which time Hamzy was already brokering his next play.

This time it was crystal methamphetamine, the drug known as ice. With the profits from the cannabis sales, he put a down-payment on $120,000 worth of ice and found a buyer in Con Bodiotis, a Melbourne supplier and soon-to-be one of his regular customers. Bodiotis told Hamzy he'd make an upfront payment of $25,000 and then the rest would come two days later. Hamzy agreed to the deal and put Ghassan on standby to fly to Melbourne for the $95,000 pick-up.

That night OS1 drove his ten-pallet Nissan truck to a McDonald's restaurant in the suburb of Granville where Mohammed Hamze was waiting for him. He had a sealed plastic bag packed tight with ice crystals. Together they lifted the dashboard console and pushed the bag deep down until it hit the air vents. Hours glided by as OS1 drove through the night to Melbourne, only stopping once he'd reached Bodiotis's unit in the suburb of Carlton the next morning.

The first thing Bodiotis did was take the bag, open it up and prepare for a crude cookback – the street method of testing a drug's purity. He measured out one gram of ice crystals and put them in a saucepan with water, boiling the product and then weighing it again once the water had evaporated, taking any cutting agents with it. OS1 was sitting down and didn't see the cookback's results, but Bodiotis was impressed, telling him the delivery was tip-top. Part ritual, part necessity, he smoked some of the drug vapour, inhaling it through a glass pipe about the length of a biro. High and satisfied, he then handed over the $25,000 as promised. Bassam's net profit from the deal, once all the cash had arrived, was about $30,000.

Despite his reputation, Hamzy was not immune to the pitfalls of the drug industry. The supply game has always been high stakes, a realm where product is provided on loan, stashes are jumped, and obscene interest rates are applied on late payments. While the Bodiotis deal went smoothly, Hamzy soon found himself caught out when some of his own customers fell short on their payments.

It wasn't just about face-saving; he, too, often borrowed from his supplier. When customers didn't pay, this pressure built and violence followed.

On 18 May 2008, OS1 arrived in Melbourne with 370 grams of ice destined for Imran Allouche, a local dealer with a drug habit of his own. Allouche lived in the suburb of Fawkner on the outskirts of the city. Like the Bodiotis deal, OS1 drove to Allouche's house so he could examine the crystal meth and hand over the cash. Both men took a seat in his bedroom while the ice was weighed and a sample cooked with water. Allouche had been around a while and could tell just by looking at the bag that the product had been jumped. It was already a mix of crystals and powder before he'd even touched it, probably more powder than crystals. He told OS1 he wasn't happy with the way it looked. When OS1 called Hamzy to discuss their options even he conceded that Allouche was being ripped off.

'It's been jumped to the max, bro,' he said. Hamzy asked who'd touched the drugs before the delivery. OS1 said it'd been only himself and Ghassan. Allouche, standing there listening, said he no longer wanted the product at all, which put Hamzy in a bind. He really needed to sell it to make good on his own debts.

'I don't know how much the car is going to cost you to repair,' Hamzy said, speaking in code, trying to be accommodating. The 'car' was the bag of ice. The 'repair' was whatever their new sale price would be. 'I don't want to put no pressure on you. If I tell you I want this much for the car and the car gives you headaches ... all I can do is penalise the auctioneers and next time make it up to you,' he said.

Allouche said he would take the drugs, but only if Hamzy agreed to a much better price. Their original deal was for $120,000. After several minutes of negotiation and a few mathematical calculations, the two men agreed to a new price of $6700 per 28 grams, or a total of $87,100 for thirteen ounces. Hamzy did all the calculations in his head.

Allouche took the drugs on loan and began selling it off in chunks to his downline suppliers. When they paid him, he'd pay Hamzy – this was the standard supply routine. He had two main customers: 'Wayne' and 'Harry' (both pseudonyms), dealers working independently of each other. They, in turn, took the drugs on loan and promised to pay Allouche once they'd sold their share. In this way the supply chain relied on numerous compounding consignments, meaning that it would only take one broken link to ruin everything.

Four days later Hamzy called his cousin Omar Ajaj to ask him a favour. The money he was expecting from Allouche hadn't arrived and too much time had elapsed. He was starting to lose face. Allouche had insisted that it wasn't his fault: his buyers had refused to pay up their share and he himself had been left out of pocket.

Normally, Hamzy would just punish Allouche. He would have known of these risks when he signed up for the drugs. But in this case, Hamzy saw him as a potentially useful ally, someone who could assist him with handguns and other weapons for the B4L gang he was creating. Hamzy wanted these types of cross-border connections, so shooting Allouche was not in his best interests, he thought. Instead, he told Allouche that he would take on the debts himself and use his own men to collect the money. He instructed Ajaj to fly to Melbourne, meet with Allouche, and then call him immediately. 'You're gonna sit him down and I'm gonna work out everyone that owes him money, and then we're gonna go and pick up all the money,' he said. 'We're not gonna let him pick it up, we just want addresses, names, everything.'

The next afternoon, Ajaj stepped off a Virgin Blue flight with two henchmen, Hamed Ajaj – his cousin, another member of

Hamzy's extended family – and Abdulgini Klink, a young friend, aged eighteen, who lived in the Auburn area. Hamzy asked Ajaj several times whether his sidekicks were up to the task. The people they were looking for had guns, Hamzy said. 'So if your boys are not one hundred per cent, I don't want you going.'

Ajaj assured him they were fine.

The trio were collected at Tullamarine airport by Khaled Chkhaidem, Allouche's right-hand man. They dropped off their bags at the Novotel Hotel on Collins Street, in the heart of the city, and then drove to Allouche's house in Fawkner on the outskirts. They walked in to find a stash of guns on show, ready for them to take their pick. Ajaj called Hamzy and described each one. 'There's a short nine. It's wonderful,' he said. Another was a 0.40-calibre. 'Like, you know, the one the police carry.'

The plan was to visit the drug dealer known as Wayne first and try to collect the money amicably. He owed the most money, $45,000, and Allouche already had his address. If he didn't pay up, the back-up plan was to shoot his house. Harry, the second dealer, owed Allouche about half as much as Wayne but his address had been harder to track down. Calls were being made to pinpoint his location and Hamzy had decided he wanted him kidnapped.

Back at the MEOCS office in Sydney, the Skelton officers scrambled to establish where this apparent shooting and kidnapping were going to take place. They were listening live to each call but all they had to work with were the nicknames Wayne and Harry. Firmer details about their locations and the timings of each hit weren't being discussed over the line, and if they were, those calls were getting lost in the deluge already being monitored. The job of translating each call had already put the detectives behind on what was happening, like watching a live sporting event on television with a few minutes of delay, sometimes more. With the little information they had there wasn't much they could do except keep listening, keep reading the translated transcripts, and hope for someone to slip up and drop a key detail over the line.

About 9:35pm on 24 May, Ajaj called Hamzy and gave him an update on the situation. He was ready to go to Wayne's address but still had had no luck finding Harry. 'All right,' Hamzy said. 'Go to this … go to this fuckin' Aussie cocksucker's house.'

Wayne, aged twenty-one, wasn't around when Ajaj and the others arrived at his family's home in Meadow Heights, a suburb of low incomes, high crime and fibro homes with cars parked on the front lawns. Wayne's parents answered the door, telling Ajaj that he wasn't home and there was nothing to pay. No one owed anyone any money. An argument broke out and Ajaj walked away, unsure what to do.

'He's a liar, hey?' Hamzy said when Ajaj called him, riling himself up for a response. He told Ajaj to 'go bang the house' with a shooting.

'Spray the house?' Ajaj asked.

'Yeah, go and empty everything on the house. Stay in the car and fuckin' do it and then burn the car,' Hamzy said.

Allouche hadn't joined Ajaj and the others when they visited Wayne's parents. He was nervous about the Sydney crew. They'd flown down and were running around picking fights with people when these disputes could be solved much more diplomatically, he thought. Shooting houses and kidnapping people, he said in one phone call to Hamzy, was an unnecessary extreme. In Melbourne, money can take a little longer to kick back up the food chain, he said. He pleaded for more time to broker a peaceful solution.

There was one guy, he said, a mutual friend, who could go and talk to Wayne's family to straighten this all out. 'He can get the money off them, because he knows his dad,' he said. Hamzy wasn't interested. He wanted to make a point and flex his muscle.

'You got to scare them,' Hamzy told Allouche. 'After I spray, we'll send your mate there and he'll say, "Listen, this is the first warning. The second warning is gonna be the actual people." All right? So spray, then send your mate to them.'

By now it was after 11pm and Allouche was becoming more desperate to avoid a shooting. He knew that drive-by shootings were common in Sydney, but in Melbourne the drug business was very different. Shooting a house, he said, would send everything out of hand.

'Don't give a fuck if they get out of hand, bro,' Hamzy said, assuring Allouche that he had a powerful ally on his side. 'We were born for things to get out of hand, bro ... We are Arabs. We are Muslims. We love war ... If he wants to know who I am, tell him go and google Bassam Hamzy on the internet.'

An hour later, a few minutes after midnight, a white ute with its lights switched off and four men inside slowly turned into Wayne's street and stopped near his house. His parents were in the living room, watching television. They heard noises outside but weren't sure what it was – they didn't realise twelve bullets had just been fired at their home. Witnesses heard gunfire and a car tearing off at high speed. Bullet casings from a Glock pistol – the kind used by police – and another handgun, a .45-calibre, were found on the road outside.

Ajaj and the others flew back to Sydney the next afternoon and waited another week to return and deal with the drug dealer known as Harry. By then, he had been in regular contact with Hamzy by phone, negotiating a payment plan for the $20,000 he owed. Harry assured him the payment would follow; he just needed more time.

Hamzy was open to negotiation and flexible about payment. He put it to Harry that he could pay off his debt by handing over his BMW, worth $5000, pay the remaining $15,000 a week later, and then continue furnishing the remaining $50,000 loan owed on the car.

'I don't want to get nasty,' Hamzy warned, 'I just want my money.' Harry made a counter-offer: what if, in exchange for an extra week, he paid $25,000 instead of $20,000? Hamzy agreed to the deal, but watched Harry closely, contacting him regularly as the deadline loomed. When it passed and Harry's phone suddenly became disconnected, Hamzy called in his cousin Omar Ajaj to go take care of the matter. It was just after midnight on 3 June when he asked Ajaj to fly back to Melbourne.

Ajaj found Harry on a street corner, bundled him into a car and drove him back to his own apartment, where they tied him up and wrapped a blindfold around his head. Ajaj, who had come down with his cousin Hamed, demanded the $25,000 Harry said he would pay Hamzy, plus the BMW. Also brought into the negotiations were Harry's family members, who were given a deadline of 11am the following morning to come up with the money. 'If you don't get the money and car he's not going to come back,' Ajaj said to Harry's brother.

Harry was kept under guard all night to ensure he couldn't move, even though he was bound so tightly that his hands turned purple, as Ajaj said in a phone call to Hamzy later that morning. By then they'd changed colour again. 'His hands turned green,' Ajaj reported. 'His mouth smell is foul … I haven't fed him nothing.'

'Get this motherfucker some food,' Hamzy responded. 'In Islam you have to give the captive some food.'

As the deadline approached Harry's brother dealt directly with Hamzy by phone, telling him he could come up with $5000, but could get the rest of the money owed in another two weeks. Hamzy wasn't interested and threats of torture followed; he told Harry's brother that he'd start cutting off his fingers if the demand wasn't met.

Harry's brother asked for more time. Even though Hamzy took a hard line, he let the negotiations continue past the 11am deadline. By 3:40pm a deal had been reached: $5000 upfront, the rest of the cash in eight weeks, and the BMW thrown in as a bonus.

'He's gunna continue to pay the finance off on the car,' Hamzy said to Ajaj, instructing him to stand down.

By 7:30pm, once the cash and the car's papers had been brought over to the apartment, Harry was cut loose and handed back to his family. Ajaj drove the BMW back to Sydney.

In between his calls to shoot up houses and kidnap a drug supplier, Hamzy was still brokering drug deals. In one, sealed just after Wayne's house was peppered with bullets, he arranged to buy 6.6 kilograms of cannabis from Allouche and Chkhaidem in Melbourne, to be brought back to Sydney by his regular courier OS1. The Skelton detectives had been listening to these discussions and tried to jump ahead of this drug movement. It was an opportunity to follow the truck and capture live evidence that corroborated the conversations on the intercepts.

On 27 May, as OS1 prepared to head down to Melbourne, the Skelton team mounted an operation to plant a tracking device on his truck. The tracker would act as a safety net if their surveillance detail got burned. Recently, OS1 had wisened up and become adept at spotting a tail. He'd be driving down a highway and suddenly pull a U-turn, or double up on a roundabout to check who did the loop with him. For the operation to track his truck, the Australian Crime Commission loaned out two of its officers to assist, a pair of its best spies who'd been in the surveillance game many years.

They set up an observation post on Mary Street, Auburn, where OS1 had been told to go before departing for Melbourne. The officers parked on opposite sides of the road, facing each other, their cars stopped next to a reserve at the end of the street. Then, something bizarre happened – a case of unfortunate and incredible timing. As the officers sat around waiting for the truck, two groups of men came together on Mary Street at the precise spot where one of the operatives had parked. A fight broke out, part of a pre-arranged scrap to settle some sort of feud between them. It played out in front of the operative's car; his only option to try to stay invisible as the men wrestled before him, throwing punches and grappling with each other all over the road. During the melee one man even rolled across the bonnet of the ACC vehicle. Then guns were drawn, pulled out on both sides. Out of nowhere, a car pulled up and half the men piled inside. Shots were let off in the air as they drove away at high speed.

The ACC's surveillance operative was a very neat individual, proud of his ACC car. He'd happened to have cleaned it that morning before heading out to Auburn, which meant that local police could fingerprint the bonnet and identify the man who rolled across the car. Once they had his name, investigators were able to track down the rest of the people involved in the fight. Some were later charged over the incident.

It was a quirky side story success, but the unexpected melee had meant that the surveillance officers weren't able to get the tracker on OS1's vehicle. Instead detectives followed him to Melbourne and spotted him meeting with Chkhaidem. They saw him picking up a large bag and placing it in the back of his truck. Not willing to show their hand, the detectives left OS1 alone. Arresting him would reveal their investigation, they figured. OS1 returned to Sydney and successfully delivered the cannabis on Hamzy's instructions, avoiding prison for a little while longer.

Within a day of Harry's kidnapping in Melbourne, on 4 June, Hamzy took a phone call from Bassam Darwiche, a relative of Adnan Darwiche. He was having a problem and turned to Hamzy for some help. That was the power Hamzy had – in some ways, people saw him as a godfather type. Bassam Darwiche was in Adelaide trying to collect a $12,000 debt owed by a local drug dealer, John Baroutas. Darwiche told Hamzy that he needed some muscle, some people to recover the money and show Baroutas that he meant business. Darwiche asked Hamzy if he knew anyone who could help. He wanted bikies – a Fink, a Hells Angel and a Rebel.

Hamzy called back an hour later with excitement in his voice. He said 'Goldie' was coming, a towering figure and gun-for-hire with tattoos all over his body. His real name was Rodney Atkinson and his reputation for standover preceded him. They called him Goldie because his mouth was filled with gold teeth. 'He's a mad, mad soldier,' Hamzy said to Darwiche.

They came to an arrangement that once Baroutas had been confronted, Darwiche would take the $12,000 owed to him, but anything else available – cars, cash, drugs – would go to Atkinson. The standover man stepped off a Virgin Blue flight the next evening and headed straight to Baroutas's townhouse, calling Hamzy along the way. Hamzy asked to be live on the phone while the bashing and torture of Baroutas played out. 'It's gonna be a walk in the park,' he said to Atkinson, as if he was almost slapping his hands together.

Bassam Darwiche was waiting outside Baroutas's townhouse for Atkinson with two other men. Getting inside was no problem, and Hamzy was on the line, talking on speaker from prison. He introduced himself to Baroutas and told him he'd assumed control of Darwiche's debt. Baroutas was shaking and told Hamzy he'd already handed over $8000 in an envelope to the men. Hamzy didn't care – he was still $4000 short – and he started taunting Baroutas with threats of torture. He spoke about cutting off his fingers, his ears. He told Atkinson to get a knife and put a sock in his mouth so he couldn't scream.

'I told you I'm going to compensate myself,' Hamzy said. Atkinson was standing by, holding the phone to Baroutas's ear. 'The minute I give him the go ahead,' Hamzy said, meaning Atkinson, 'he's gonna cut your ears off, do you know that?'

Baroutas said he could come up with $20,000 by the morning. He had a friend, he said, Sophie, who would be prepared to help him. For Hamzy, that wasn't good enough either.

For the Skelton detectives listening live in Sydney it became obvious that Baroutas's life was in imminent danger. Unlike the previous kidnapping of the drug dealer known as Harry, this time detectives had a name and address where everything was taking place. The issue now, however, was how to intervene without blowing their cover – move in too suddenly and Hamzy would know his calls were being intercepted; how else would the officers have known to suddenly turn up on Baroutas's doorstep?

The clock was ticking. Someone at MEOCS HQ pulled up Baroutas's offender history and scanned it for a possible cover angle. A First Instance Warrant flashed up indicating he was due to be arrested anyway by Adelaide police. The Skelton detectives made a quick phone call to their South Australian counterparts and asked that officers be dispatched to Baroutas's home. The Hamzy investigation, barely a month old, was still a highly classified matter. These officers weren't told why they were needed there; just that Baroutas was wanted on an outstanding warrant.

They found him standing in the driveway to his garage, which connected to his townhouse. He said nothing about the four men sitting in his lounge room upstairs as he handed over his ID.

Officer Paul Carman studied Baroutas as he paced around in the garage. He looked nervous, Carman thought. Upstairs, the two other officers were inside speaking to the large, tattooed men seated in the apartment. Everything seemed normal – there were no signs of blood on the carpet or upturned furniture; nothing to indicate a kidnapping or home invasion had taken place. There were porn DVDs on the table and a couple of security monitors with a view outside of the road next to the garage; they all would have seen the police cars turning up, the officers thought, which explained why Baroutas was in the garage waiting for them.

Bassam Darwiche called Hamzy while the police were still moving between the apartment and the garage. He was shocked by their arrival, but didn't put two and two together. 'The coppers rocked up to Johnny's house to talk to him and they just walked in,' he said, leaving Hamzy on the line to hear the officers question each of the men. Each one gave a false name and was subjected to a search. The cops found $8000 in Atkinson's pants, money that he said had come from gambling winnings. It was removed and then given back to him later.

Ironically, the only person arrested that night was Baroutas himself. Once his warrant became apparent, he was handcuffed and escorted to one of the police cars, effectively saving him from any further punishment. He refused to say what was going on inside the apartment but appeared at ease about being arrested, even volunteering some information to the officers that if they searched his bedroom they would find a homemade sub-machine gun on the top shelf of a wardrobe.

Far from being suspicious, Hamzy boasted about what happened in his conversations the following afternoon. He was amazed at the coincidence, telling someone, 'The fuckin' detectives and that fuckin' rocked up at the house!' By the time he got the smuggled phone back from Wiperi across the corridor that afternoon he'd already moved on from Bassam Darwiche and Baroutas and had turned his mind back to drug supply, preparing to arrange his biggest deal yet. Through his supplier, he'd bought nearly one kilogram of crystal meth for $191,000, a massive deal that was done almost entirely on loan and needed immediate buyers.

All evening he worked the phones. Some buyers expressed interest and then backed out because of the pricing. Others said yes, but couldn't get the money for weeks. Left holding the can, Hamzy appeared to be in some trouble; it was too much debt to carry. In the end, Con Bodiotis, Hamzy's regular buyer, did Hamzy a solid deal and took the bulk of it from him. Not long after, his phone stopped working.

On the morning of 11 June, the day that the drugs were delivered and the money changed hands, prison officers decided to raid Hamzy's prison cell. It was a spontaneous search, routine in the jail system. The guards were unaware of the ongoing Skelton investigation and no phone was located. The Skelton detectives figured Hamzy must have flushed it down the toilet, rather than secrete it somewhere. Had he hidden it internally, they would have heard his voice again over the intercepted telephone line some time later. But from that day forward, there were no more outgoing calls to his number.

Even though the prison guards' impromptu search of Hamzy's cell effectively stopped the ongoing investigation, the Skelton team were actually experiencing a modicum of relief that it was over. It was a blessing of sorts: partly because of the drugs and shootings that Hamzy was co-ordinating, but mainly because of the sheer volume of calls he'd been making since they had started listening. Detectives counted a total of 19,523 calls over the six-week period, many of which, by the time Hamzy had flushed the phone, were still in a backlog that hadn't yet been heard or transcribed.

With the phone gone, the investigation entered a new phase. The days of capturing the calls, keeping up with the new crimes and scrambling to conduct surveillance operations were over. Those pressures had been tough on some officers; one had already quit the investigation from the stress of consistently listening to Hamzy's calls. Now, with this breathing space, the officers had time to work slowly and methodically to build their case against Hamzy and the slew of others involved in his empire.

In the weeks that followed every crime that had been recorded over the phone was chased up for corroborating evidence. Virgin Blue flight manifestos were gathered along with hotel bookings and cell tower records, which were used to place people at various crime scenes. About three weeks after Hamzy's phone was disconnected, OS1's truck was stopped and searched on the Hume Highway at Casula as he was making another delivery. Having lost his phone contact with Hamzy, he was now taking directions from other family members outside. The cops thought it was most likely that he was dealing with Hamzy's dad, Khaled, though it was difficult to say so with any certainty. In the back of OS1's truck, police found 142 grams of cocaine packaged in five small freezer bags. The arrest marked the end of his courier work for the Hamzy family. He was granted bail, but he'd become too hot.

With the drug courier out of play and Hamzy without a phone, Memmolo's team decided to revisit one of their earlier tip-offs, one that was peripheral to the Hamzy investigation and had been put on the back burner. This was the intelligence gleaned about the cocaine wholesalers and their safe house on Carmen Street, Bankstown, which came to them way back at the very start of the investigation when the Skelton case was solely focused on the Kalache family. Observations of the address suggested these wholesalers were storing and packaging the drugs on the premises for downline supply. And as an informant had suggested, they were moving big amounts – half-kilogram blocks of cocaine at a time.

On 12 August 2008, a team of MEOCS officers stationed outside the safe house watched as an Audi turned up. A man got out and disappeared into the house, staying there for about ten minutes before leaving with something in his hands. Detectives followed the Audi closely for a few minutes and then radioed for uniformed police to pull it over. As officers approached the car on foot, the driver freaked out and hit the accelerator, reversing fast into a police car parked behind him, and then speeding off past a second police car that had been blocking the road. He narrowly missed Angelo Memmolo, the Skelton co-ordinator, and Phil Linkenbagh, another detective on his team. Both had their guns trained on the driver as he took off. A few minutes later they raided the safe house on Carmen Street and found fourteen grams of cocaine, nearly 100 grams of pseudoephedrine and $188,150 in cash. It appeared that their timing was off – had they gone in earlier, or while the man was inside, the drug seizures were likely to have been far higher. This was later confirmed when Memmolo learned the driver had a brick of cocaine in the Audi's console, along with a gun, which explained why he was so determined to escape.

That much cocaine, plus a gun, aggravated by driving at police, could put a man away for ten years.

Khaled Hamzy took a seat in front of his son Bassam in the visiting rooms at Lithgow Correctional Centre. It was 28 August 2008. The Skelton detectives had been told the visit was happening and had planted a listening device in advance to record the conversation. Khaled had been banned from visiting his son since his release on parole three years earlier on account of his conviction for heroin supply. Recently, this ban had been lifted. Both men were in good spirits and settled in for a long catch-up.

'I got you undies,' Khaled said. Previously, Bassam had complained about the standards of prison underwear. They were small and uncomfortable, never fitting him properly. Tired of arguing with the guards, he had stopped wearing them altogether. His father put the issue down to his expensive taste.

'Oh, you just wear Valentino, Boss, and whatever is the name?' he joked.

Their talk soon turned to more serious matters, namely their ongoing plans to lease a factory. On the listening device this came across as sounding like more of a social club, one with card tables, a snooker table and lounge chairs. In reality, it was to be a Brothers 4 Life clubhouse. Bassam had counted about sixty people who would help fund the lease with weekly payments but, to be on the safe side, he told his father they should only count half that number.

'Thirty people paying thirty dollars is nine hundred dollars a week rent,' he said.

Khaled said he would wait for Bassam to send him further details and addresses to inspect, factories around the Auburn and Bankstown areas.

They didn't speak openly about the drugs they'd been moving, but Bassam's mood became bitter and angry as the topic circled some of the people they had been dealing with – those who had undercut their supplies and skimmed off the top. Bassam complained that his father had been too lenient with several people who had lied, and urged him to take a stronger hand. The softly-softly stance would affect the family's honour, he said. 'People are laughing at us, Dad,' Bassam said. 'If this is not affecting your honour, I don't know what's going to affect your honour. I can't work like this. How can you work like this? You leave a question mark on everything.'

His father listened but said nothing as Bassam worked himself into a lather, listing several people – family members and others – who had lapsed in their responsibilities. Bassam vowed to get to these people. In jail, he said, feelings of anger don't dissipate over time; in fact, he continued, jail provides the time to come up with imaginative methods of getting square. One that he fantasised about was taking a knife and puncturing a person's ears, then putting acid in their eyes, cutting out their tongue and severing their spinal cord. It would leave them, he said, unable to hear, see, talk or move. They'll have to rely on someone for the rest of their lives. 'And every day they will be thinking I have done this to them,' he said.

It took another five months before the bulk of the phone calls and text messages, stray pieces of evidence and loose strands of intelligence had been dissected and analysed by the Skelton team.

Finally on 4 December 2008 they were at the point where arrests could be made. By then they had been left astounded by the calls, impressed even – not just at the criminality, but also by the workings and abilities of Bassam Hamzy's brain. Sure, he was a criminal, a thug and a murderer, but what became apparent was his unexpected knack with numbers and his ability to make fast calculations on cumulative deals that he could parlay off each other in a way most well-educated people would struggle to visualise in their minds. Every drug transaction, every gram he controlled, every dollar that changed hands, every phone number he called, was being stored in his memory without a single digit written down. He added interest and calculated complex sums on the fly, factoring his sums according to purity levels, wholesale weights, and street values, along with projected earnings on deals that hadn't happened yet. What was even more astounding was the speed with which he worked. In six weeks he'd personally trafficked more than $1.5 million worth of drugs. Had the ACC never picked up on that telephone call between Bassam Hamzy and a member of the Finks outlaw motorcycle gang who was under investigation, or drawn the links to establish that Bassam had a phone, who knows what would have followed, given another month or more.

The ensuing Skelton arrest phase involved sixteen raids across Sydney and Melbourne, an operation that took in more than 140 officers. They formed up in teams outside each house and then burst inside with warrants to search the properties and make arrests.

At a house in Merrylands officers found an inactive clandestine methamphetamine laboratory. At a unit in Greenacre they recovered a machine pistol. At Condell Park, a chunky freezer bag, fat with ecstasy tablets, was seized. And at the Hamzy family's home on Albert Street, Auburn, they found 152 grams of ice.

Thirteen people were swept up in the raids, including Bassam's father, his brother Ghassan, and his cousin Khaled Hamze. The family's drug courier, OS1, was already out on bail, but he was arrested for a second time, along with several other cousins, friends and associates who had been caught assisting the Hamzy family along the way. Compiling briefs of evidence against so many people – twenty-two all up – for such a vast number of offences – 143 in total – resulted in some targets going months, sometimes years, before they were charged. They included people like Omar Ajaj and Rodney 'Goldie' Atkinson, both of whom were under investigation over kidnappings: Ajaj in Melbourne; Atkinson in Adelaide. They were passed over during the initial phase of the arrests, along with Mohammed Hamze, who was under investigation for drug supply and accepting a contract to shoot Haysam Hamzy. The priority, at least during that initial phase of arrests, was nailing Bassam Hamzy.

His arrest took place on 5 December, a day after the raids. Memmolo led six officers from the Skelton team into Goulburn's Supermax prison where Hamzy had been transferred in advance. He was waiting for them in a holding cage outside his cell and had a copy of that day's newspaper in his hands. He held it up for them to see, his smiling mugshot splashed across the front page. He was delighted by the attention.

Six months had passed since his mobile phone had been disconnected, so the search was mostly procedural – the likelihood of finding any documents or evidence, particularly after he had been moved from Lithgow, was low. The only items of any relevance were newspaper clippings of cars and factories, along with articles that Hamzy had been saving.

With shackles on his wrists and ankles he was taken by armed convoy to Goulburn Police Station, a helicopter flying overhead watching out for any potential ambush.

He made no admissions during his interview, the whole thing lasting just eighteen minutes. The detectives had prepared some charges, but not all of them. The drive-by shooting targeting Wayne, the drug dealer, would only come later. It was the same with the kidnappings of Harry in Melbourne and John Baroutas in South Australia. The evidence was still being collected and analysed for everyone involved in these crimes. The only response detectives Richard Howe and Stephen Hunt were able to elicit from Hamzy was a series of belligerent attacks on Corrective Services Commissioner Ron Woodham. They were still embroiled in their legal battle over Hamzy's incarceration conditions at the time.

'Tell the commissioner to eat my shit,' Hamzy said. He gave the same response to most of the other questions.

Bassam Hamzy sacked his solicitors and represented himself in court, switching between pleas of guilty and not guilty that delayed the outcome of his case by about five years. His proceedings, at times, alternated between novel and farcical. He called his own witnesses, tried his hand at obscure legal defences, and mounted sensational arguments for why he should receive a lighter sentence for his crimes – claiming, for instance, that he was involved in a secret deal with a law enforcement agency that had given him the green light to supply drugs and raise money for his family. The full details of this alleged deal, which was rejected by the judge, have been suppressed and cannot be printed.

Having eventually learned that prosecutors weren't going to seek a life sentence for his crimes, Hamzy agreed to plead guilty to all his charges of commercial drug supply, kidnapping and shooting. There were also fraud offences – he'd been charged with using credit card numbers stolen from Melbourne to book flights for his henchmen and to buy t-shirts for his B4L gang. He used his sentencing hearings to mount the argument that his horrible conditions of incarceration, largely spent in isolation, warranted a reduced prison term. He told the court about 22-hour days in lockdown, his months spent alone without anyone to talk to. He described the tortured sounds of his fellow inmates going mad with desperation; how they set fire to their cells, fastened their lips together with paperclips in protest at their conditions, and bashed their heads against the walls in failed attempts at suicide.

To support his argument he tendered studies showing the long-term effects of isolation on inmates. He even called prisoners from Supermax to give evidence about their experiences in jail: one was Carl Little, an armed robber who had been moved to Supermax after brutally bashing and murdering a prison officer; another was Dudley Aslett, a violent rapist serving thirty years. One of the more unusual moments came when Hamzy subpoenaed the prison's superintendent, Mick Reid, cross-examining him in the witness box and pressing him on how he had denied Hamzy visits and phone calls.

'Every single phone number I've tried to put on has been refused,' Bassam Hamzy asked him in court, referring to a list of authorised phone numbers, 'except for my aunty, which is one aunty. Do you accept that, Mr Reid?'

'Again,' Mick Reid replied from the witness box, 'I'm not sure of the numbers but I know it's not many – but yes.'

'It's no big secret that there's a great animosity towards me from the powers that be, correct?'

'All your applications go through a certain channel, I would agree with that, yes.'

The courtroom acted as a strange and ironic leveller between the two men; the inmate suddenly, for a few brief minutes, had clawed back some control. The judge accepted Hamzy's argument that he had served a substantial portion of his prison time in 'oppressive conditions' that had affected his psychological health. But this ultimately had little impact on his sentence, which was handed down on 10 May 2013, and amounted to another twenty-one years in prison. It will make him eligible for parole in June 2035.

As a footnote to the hearings, Hamzy revealed that he had reconciled his differences with younger brother Haysam, whom he had attempted to kneecap and then kill in 2007. He said Haysam had since named one of his sons after him, telling the court this was proof that their relationship had improved.

Bassam's father, Khaled Hamzy, received a seven-year prison sentence for his role in the supply syndicate, as did OS1, the drug courier and truck driver who had turned informant on the group, receiving a discount on his sentence in exchange for his co-operation. Bassam's younger brother Ghassan Amoun was sentenced to a minimum term of six years and seven months for his role in the syndicate, his sentence partly mitigated by his harsh family upbringing and a professed fear of his older brother, both arguments put forward by his legal team. His earliest date for parole was set at August 2016.

Mohammed Hamze, the cousin recruited to carry out the kneecapping of Haysam Hamzy, pleaded guilty to four counts of drug supply and received a minimum six-year prison term, but was found not guilty over the plot to shoot Haysam. He successfully argued that he never intended to carry out the crime, and only said he would do it because he was afraid of his cousin. This was an argument used by several others arrested by the Skelton detectives, including Omar Ajaj, who escaped a charge over the kidnapping of Harry, the drug dealer in Melbourne. Harry refused to co-operate with police, and detectives were, therefore, unable to proceed with the matter. Omar's cousin Hamed was let off for the same reason.

Ajaj pleaded guilty to the drive-by shooting targeting the drug dealer known as Wayne, and was handed a suspended sentence over the crime. He was frank about his reasons for committing the shooting, telling a court-appointed psychologist that he too had been acting under duress at the time of the shooting. 'My cousin is just a scary bloke man,' he said. 'If you don't do what he says he can send anyone to you. He sent someone to shoot his own brother. I thought, what could he do to me?'

Still a well-known Middle Eastern organised crime identity, Ajaj – recognisable by a large 'MEOC' tattoo on his neck – is regularly stopped and questioned by MEOCS officers. A man on a lucky streak, he survived three shotgun wounds to his legs in 2012, an attempted murder in 2013 and then a serious motorcycle accident in 2014 which briefly crippled him. His most recent police charges, a matter that revolved around the kneecapping of a drug dealer at Yagoona, were dropped in 2015 due to a lack of supporting evidence.

CHAPTER EIGHT

MEOCS TAG: THE INFORMANTS

Confidential informants were the lifeblood of MEOCS TAG, the cogs that kept the engines turning. Almost every TAG investigation could trace its way back to a tip-off from a source. The vast majority of these informants were criminals and came in two distinct classes: 'street assets' and 'rollovers'.

Street assets worked in the field and got paid for their intelligence, receiving modest cash bonuses ranging from $20 to $50 depending on the quality of their information. This money was signed off and paid out from the carefully managed MEOCS 'sustenance fund', a pool of cash that could be dipped into quickly and approved for use by the TAG's commander. But many rewards payments, particularly the larger kind, were slow to be released. Their approval was left to a committee panel – the Reward Evaluation Advisory Committee – that only met once a month, so if a member of this panel was sick, or if a decision wasn't reached, it would take at least another four weeks for the matter to be addressed. Sometimes these rewards would be left in limbo for half a year, or even longer, creating tensions between sources and their handlers. For some TAG officers, these delays prompted threats and killed off relationships and trust.

Rollovers were the other class of informant. Many were in prison and turned grass for several reasons, mostly to get bail or a reduction on their sentence. Remand centres became cultivation yards, a place where officers could quietly make an offer. Unlike a street asset's, a rollover's information tended to be one-off, or specific to their case.

Within a few months of its formation, MEOCS TAG had amassed more informants, or 'gigs' as they're known in cop speak, than any other command across the entire NSW Police Force. The figures are rough, but the widely quoted statistic is that MEOCS TAG controlled fifty-six per cent of all registered informants used across the NSW State Crime Command – that's twenty-two officers controlling about half the sources used by 900 detectives across ten crime squads.

Most informants were highly unreliable, dangerous and difficult to manage. Too conspicuous to take to a coffee shop, they usually met with detectives in secluded parks, and were given a pat-down on arrival. This was standard. When picking up a source, officers sometimes arrived with their guns out, or on their lap in the car, for the added protection – you never knew if the whole meeting was a setup. Some informants were so spaced out on drugs that the meetings were cancelled. Occasionally they made outlandish requests – one guy asked for a large upfront cash payment to get his teeth fixed, a request that was flatly denied.

Turning informant quickly became a hallmark of Middle Eastern organised crime, a distinguishing feature right up there with hot-headedness and extreme violence. As a general rule, no one was considered 'unrollable', not even the staunchest MEOC figures. There were no limits to this treachery. Family members turned on each other to save themselves. The Squad, at one point, had two brothers on its books secretly informing on each other.

Even those who professed the most implacable hatred of police, the ones who threatened the harshest punishments for any associates caught collaborating, would inevitably offer to make a deal. In one instance, a major organised crime identity, was signed up as a registered source over a trivial driving offence – he'd been caught for the third time on a disqualified licence and simply didn't want to risk being thrown back in prison.

Cultivating sources was an artform in itself. The most successful method was to hold a charge over a criminal, even a minor offence, and use it as leverage to work a deal – it's a process that happens in police stations every day across the city. Mostly it takes place uneventfully, but occasionally, as was the case in May 2008, things don't always go as expected.

They came in one car – Nick Glover, Dave Roberts, Ryan Jeffcoat – and arrived on a mission to talk. Their target was a man picked up twice for drug possession, crystal meth each time, and the plan was to surprise him with an unannounced visit and an offer. He was well connected, stuck in a jam with charges over his head, and he was considered to be a prime candidate for recruiting as a confidential source.

His house was an austere-looking fibro on Ashcroft Street at Georges Hall, a suburb near Bankstown Airport. Several security cameras pointed at the front door. Glover, Roberts and Jeffcoat walked up the driveway. By this time, Jeffcoat's role in the TAG office had stepped up dramatically. A year earlier he was a trainee detective picking drug balloons out of a bedpan. Now he'd become formidable: juggling informants, personally generating at least one, sometimes two raids a month. He'd won an award for 'outstanding proactive operational performance' and had become a loveable character in the TAG office, a ballsy detective who sent Christmas cards to criminals he'd put in jail with messages like, 'Thinking of you … love, the Coat.' This brand of humour was lost on some. When a colleague once asked how he'd managed to procure so many informants, Jeffcoat kidded that he just pulled their names out of a communal 'gig bag' each morning that anyone could use. Of course, there was no such thing as a 'gig bag', but that didn't stop the officer putting in a complaint – apparently Jeffcoat had been 'hogging the gig bag' and all its informants.

Back at Georges Hall, Jeffcoat walked around the side of the house while Roberts knocked at the front door and listened for movement inside. He knocked again a few seconds later, bringing someone to the door who opened it up just a crack. It was enough for a stench of chemicals to seep out and hit Roberts in the face. He jammed his foot in the gap and asked to be let inside. The man seemed flustered and said the person he wanted wasn't home.

Around the side of the house Jeffcoat moved carefully towards a large window that gave him a full view of the interior. He could see two men moving between the kitchen and the lounge room, one of them holding a frying pan with thick, white sludge inside it. He was pouring the liquid into a big red bucket sitting next to a bottle of methylated spirits. Jeffcoat's eyes widened; he'd seen this in his clandestine laboratory training course.

'They're doing a cook!' he shouted towards the street. At the sound of his yelling, Roberts and Glover barged through the door and wrestled the man on the other side into a narrow corridor where a second man joined in the struggle. Arms were wrenched and bodies thrown into the wall. Jeffcoat watched as the third man hurried towards the kitchen with the frying pan and stuck it under the tap, filling it with water and creating plumes of smoke. Most of the sludge was gone by the time Roberts and Glover made it to the kitchen and had all three men in handcuffs.

It took two days for the Drug Squad's Chemical Operations Unit to decontaminate the house. They moved through the property with a forensic chemist inspecting the seized items: a twenty-litre drum of methylated spirits, a measuring cylinder, a bowl containing the remains of a white, lumpy liquid. The chemist said the men were attempting a pseudoephedrine extraction, a process used to make methamphetamines like speed and ice.

While most of the sludge had gone down the sink, the cops managed to recover the bulk of it. As it coursed through the drain, the liquid solidified with water and became trapped in the S-bend, allowing the Chemical Operations Unit to dismantle the pipe and let the TAG officers seize it as evidence. The prospective source was never cultivated, but the three men inside the house – Jehad Taha, who answered the door; Gehad Alameddine, the man with the frying pan; and Taha Eldarwich, who caused a ruckus in the hallway – pleaded guilty to their charges. Taha and Alameddine were given less than a year behind bars, but Eldarwich walked away with a good behaviour bond. One of the trio, after being released from prison, called Dave Roberts and thanked him, saying the arrest had given him a shake-up – he was done with crime.

Aside from this type of proactive work, the rest of 2008 in the MEOCS TAG office was taken up by several complex strike force investigations, each one rolling on from the last and all connected through the players involved. The genesis for these investigations had been the work of Strike Force Tapiola, the undercover drug investigation that had started in Castle Hill and ended in spectacular fashion at the IGA in Wetherill Park. Tapiola had unmasked several high-level Assyrian crime figures, prompting a new investigation, Strike Force Kialoa, which narrowed the sights even further on this facet of the underworld.

The Kialoa targets were real pieces of work. One of them – a man who was suspected of a break-and-enter in Bankstown and a carjacking in Granville, and who was wanted by the Kialoa team for commercial drug supply – had managed to get the home phone number of a MEOCS TAG sergeant and rang his wife repeatedly, threatening to rape her. The criminal was finally tracked to the Grandstand Motel in Warwick Farm where officers stormed into a room to bring him under arrest. He was brought out with several bruises and a face full of capsicum spray – the official report of the matter noted he had 'resisted arrest'.

Jeffcoat had been one of several detectives assigned to the Kialoa investigation, a case that steered him to a new informant who guided him towards a drug supplier no one at MEOCS had ever heard of, a man who hadn't previously been noted on any police watch lists. The result was a new investigation into an offshoot syndicate, one that sold ice and ecstasy across a sizeable chunk of the NSW coastline, from Wollongong to Sydney and further up to Newcastle. This was how it happened at MEOCS – jobs never finished, they just kept rolling onto the next one, and the one after that. Strike Force Tapiola opened the door to Kialoa, and Kialoa opened the door to Cartella.

The Cartella investigation centred on an unusual cast of characters: there was a former biochemist who'd left a high-paying job to start cooking methamphetamines; a Wollongong businessman aged in his fifties; and the man who sat above everyone, Adeson 'Eddie' Ayshow, a 33-year-old man billed as an upline supplier who was virtually unknown to police. He'd been convicted of a kidnapping three years earlier, but there was nothing on file linking him to the drug trade. He became the investigation's number one target.

Surveillance of Ayshow led to a house on Ryan Street in the Wollongong suburb of Balgownie. It was hidden down a long driveway and owned by the businessman, Peter Conridge, who had been buying off Ayshow for some time but, from what Jeffcoat had gathered, had paired up with the biochemist and begun tinkering with the manufacturing side of the drug business. When officers crashed through his roller door garage they found a bottle of clear effervescing liquid inside – the first stage of a cook taking place. Conridge would end up serving an eighteen-month jail term because of the warrant, taking him out of the investigative frame.

These liquids could be extremely volatile, posing a huge danger not just to the criminals handling them, but also to police. It wasn't unheard of for houses to catch fire and people to be killed due to unstable clan labs bursting into flames. Not long before the raid at Balgownie, MEOCS TAG officers raided the home of a drug cook in Guildford, seizing an unknown liquid inside his house. The liquid was sent to the Division of Analytical Laboratories for standard testing procedures where it turned out to be hypophosphorous acid, another precursor chemical used to make drugs like speed. It's also an extremely dangerous compound. When the research staff poured a small amount of it into a beaker, alarms started going off and the lab had to be evacuated. The search had uncovered twenty litres of the stuff.

Getting to Ayshow took more time than the Conridge side of the investigation. The Cartella investigation was a strike force of just two detectives – Ryan Jeffcoat and Tom Howes. Progress was slow. Ayshow was a difficult criminal and by July 2008, five months after

Cartella had formed, they were no closer to catching him in the act of a big supply. Months were lost on stakeouts, listening posts and close surveillance of his movements.

But then came the break.

Jeffcoat was back at the office one night listening to Ayshow's calls when a conversation was picked up between him and a buyer in Newcastle. 'Meet at the Twins,' Jeffcoat heard him say. It was code for the twin Caltex service stations on the M1, just north of the Wyong turn-off. It had to be a drop-off, Jeffcoat thought. Why else would Ayshow drive two hours up to Newcastle and then two hours back to Sydney? When TAG commander Dave Adney listened back to the recording he felt the same way and put together an operation.

Most of the MEOCS TAG office wasn't working that week. The reasons varied – some officers were on annual leave, others had been seconded to assist with the drudgework of World Youth Week, the international Catholic event that brought the Pope to Sydney. Jeffcoat and Howes were the only two detectives rostered on that night, having used the Cartella investigation as an excuse to avoid the convergence of half a million young Catholic pilgrims descending on Sydney.

Adney slipped on a set of headphones and told both detectives to run surveillance on Ayshow's house at Mount Pritchard, half an hour's drive away from MEOCS HQ. It was a quaint property located on Elizabeth Drive, an arterial road and trucking route busy with traffic at all hours of the night. The house was newly renovated with bushes running alongside its western border, where Jeffcoat took up an observation position in the dark. From there, lying on his stomach, he had a good view of the front door. He'd tried watching the house from his car, but the traffic was obstructing his view.

A car pulled up and a man stepped out holding a bag. He walked to the front door, knocked, and then walked back to his car and drove off without the bag he was holding. When Ayshow walked outside a few minutes later, Jeffcoat saw him shoving items inside the bag and placing it into a compartment beneath the boot lining of his Ford Falcon. Then, because every Jeffcoat story needs a twist, Ayshow walked over to the bushes, unzipped his pants and started peeing – the stream of urine landing about three feet away from Jeffcoat who was lying perfectly still.

Once in his car, Ayshow started driving north towards Newcastle with Howes following in his unmarked car close behind.

Jeffcoat ran back to his car and started the engine, pulling out fast to try to catch up with them, running red lights, cutting off cars and weaving at speed through the highway traffic. About fifteen minutes passed before he finally spotted Ayshow's Falcon with Howes's vehicle tailing him.

The plan was to have the local police pull over the Falcon on a basic traffic violation and search it for any drugs. The detectives wanted a safety net, a means of preserving their investigation – if the uniformed officers searched the car and didn't find anything then Ayshow would probably keep driving and think nothing of it. It wouldn't occur to him that he had been stopped because he was at the centre of a months-long Middle Eastern Organised Crime Squad investigation.

Jeffcoat radioed Fairfield Local Area Command and described the Ford Falcon, telling them it was heading north along Smithfield Road and needed to be searched thoroughly.

Marked police cars appeared in the rear-view mirror a few minutes later and both Howes and Jeffcoat took that as their cue to pull back. They both parked in a side street, got into one car and waited for a phone call from the local Fairfield officers to report the results of their search; they didn't want to be anywhere near the scene while it was playing out.

On Smithfield Road nearby, a local constable appeared at Ayshow's window and told him he had a tail-light out. That might sound like a lazy cop cliché, but it was true – one of the bulbs had genuinely busted. Ayshow stepped out of the car and watched as two officers went through the vehicle, finding seven ecstasy tablets and a bit of cocaine in the front seat – a small amount of powder, barely enough for a bucks party.

The officers called Jeffcoat. He was positive there would be a substantial amount of drugs in the car – there had to be; there was no way Ayshow, an upline supplier, was driving from Sydney to Newcastle with only seven ecstasy tablets and a small bag of coke. He told them to keep looking.

The officers called him back a few minutes later to report the same result; no further drugs. By then another two marked cars from Fairfield had turned up at the scene and Ayshow was getting suspicious; even he thought the attention – three police cars for a broken tail-light – was a bit unusual. The whole idea of discretion looked like it was on the edge of backfiring.

A decision had to be made quickly. If Jeffcoat and Howes called off the search, then Ayshow would very likely disappear. The balloon was up, they thought. They said to hell with it and drove to the scene, introducing themselves as plain-clothed officers from Fairfield Police Station. Ayshow rolled his eyes. *More cops.* It was a gamble, but there was no going back now. If Jeffcoat's hunch was wrong and there were no drugs in the car then months of police work would be as good as gone – Ayshow would throw away his phone and probably go offline for good. Jeffcoat went to the boot of the car and lifted the lining, reaching in deep and fishing around to try to find the items he'd seen Ayshow place there back at his house. Crevices were probed and compartments checked. He plunged his hand into the wheel well and found nothing except black soot.

Then he hit something. He tugged at it, a bag, and pulled it to the surface: it was 900 MDMA tablets. He put his hand back in and found a loaded 9-millimetre Luger pistol, then $50,000 in cash, then a taser, and then, best of all, a package heavy with ice crystals tinged a pinkish colour, worth about $100,000. Jeffcoat looked back at Ayshow on the side of the road. A minute earlier he'd been laughing. Now he looked broken.

He pleaded guilty to his charges and was handed one of, if not the, highest sentences ever given out as a result of a MEOCS TAG investigation: a minimum eight years on the bottom with a maximum fourteen years on the top. No one else had achieved that kind of result. And it had all been from a hunch on an intercepted phone call.

CHAPTER NINE

A FATEFUL MEETING

BASS HILL, SATURDAY, 14 MARCH 2009

Mohammed 'Blackie' Fahda hated service stations. They reminded him of the one at Punchbowl where his brother, Ahmad, had been murdered back in 2003. This one at Bass Hill where he was standing waiting for a friend, a meeting about a drug deal, was no different. To ease his nerves he'd had a few bumps of cocaine before leaving the house and brought a gun with him too, but that was normal; ever since his release from prison about seven months earlier he'd been walking around strapped for protection.

The man he was meeting, 'David' (a pseudonym), had been one of the people Fahda had met inside the segregation wing of Silverwater prison – the naughty boy wing, as David called it. Fahda had found himself there after he was stabbed eight times by two inmates during his stint, an assault that left him with knife wounds to his head, neck and body. When the guards asked, Blackie said he'd done it himself.

This had all taken place after his charges over the Titanic Café shooting were dismissed back in March 2007. He had walked free from court, but was pinched again a few months later and thrown into prison on remand. It was a short stay, just a few months, but evidently a tough period for him.

David pulled into the car park and got out of his car. He was a big man, muscly, with tattoos on his shoulder. Recently released from jail himself, he'd called Blackie with a proposition that he didn't want to talk about over the phone, something about drugs. They arranged to meet at the Subway restaurant on the Hume Highway at Bass Hill, which shared a car park with the United Petroleum service station, a Turkish restaurant and a discount chemist all in the same complex.

They had only just started talking when Fahda caught sight of someone emerging from the Turkish restaurant on the other side of the car park. He was a large man with a big stomach, balding and heavily bearded, a person who stood out instantly. David noticed an immediate change in Fahda's demeanour. It was obvious the men had a history.

'Who's that?' David asked. 'Is there a problem?'

Fahda said nothing. He brushed past David and walked towards the bearded man, meeting him in the middle of the car park. They had never met, had never even seen each other, yet somehow the penny had just dropped for them both. The bearded man spoke first.

'Is your name Mohammed Fahda?' he asked.

Fahda nodded.

'I'm Abdul Darwiche,' he said.

To Fahda this was no coincidence. This was fate, the hand of god himself. For years he had been promising to avenge his brother Ahmad's murder, which he still firmly believed had been orchestrated by Adnan Darwiche, despite the fact he had been acquitted by a jury of soliciting the muder. Fahda had tried and failed to shoot a member of the Darwiche family at the Titanic Café in Bankstown two and a half years earlier. Now, his thirst for payback still not settled, Fahda saw his destiny before him: he had a gun, he was in front of a Darwiche and, of all the places, he was standing in a petrol station, just like the one where his own brother had been slain.

David was standing next to Fahda's silver Honda CRV and watched as Fahda turned around from the centre of the car park and walked quickly back to where they had been standing.

As he got closer he started speaking to David, warning him. 'Walk away,' he said. 'Get away, walk away.'

'What do you mean?' David asked. 'Where are we going?'

Fahda said nothing as he jumped into the driver's seat of his Honda. Across the car park, where Abdul had been standing, a group of women and children emerged from the Turkish restaurant. Abdul shouted out to them to get back inside. There was an urgency to his voice that his wife, Lisa, couldn't comprehend at first. A few moments earlier everything had been fine; they'd paid for lunch and planned to head home for the afternoon. Now, seemingly from nowhere, he was telling her to get back inside.

'It's a Fahda!' he shouted to her. She looked across the car park and saw a car: inside it was a man with a black mullet. He reached over to the glove compartment and pulled out something that looked like a gun. The kids were running around between the cars, unaware of the imminent danger taking shape. Lisa bundled them inside the Subway restaurant with Abdul's sister-in-law and rushed to the front counter, telling the attendant to call the police.

Witnesses saw Fahda and Darwiche in a stalemate. Both men were in their cars at the exit to the car park, Darwiche's Mitsubishi Triton 4WD in front. Fahda emerged from his car and started walking towards Darwiche's car, pulling a gun from the front of his pants. At Darwiche's passenger side door he started firing through the window, laughing according to some witnesses, and squeezing the trigger, only stopping when the magazine was empty. Twelve cartridge cases lay in the driveway.

At the sound of the gunfire, Lisa ran into the car park from the Subway restaurant, just in time to see her husband's car rolling forward off the driveway. Fahda's car could be seen disappearing down Miller Road, a side street running perpendicular to the Hume Highway. Darwiche's car had picked up a good speed and it looked at first as if he was trying to escape the gunshots. Lisa watched as it continued across the road, hurtling over a median strip, another lane of traffic and then crashing into a tree where it finally stopped. A man rushed over to feel Darwiche's neck for a pulse. Lisa was there too, trying to get inside the car to her husband; his door was jammed shut by the tree. The man said he could feel a heartbeat and Lisa screamed for an ambulance, waving one down on arrival a few minutes later. Police swarmed on the area, blocking off several road lanes with traffic cones and crime scene tape. Officers were given frantic explanations about what happened.

Inside the Subway restaurant, Constable Melina Jeffrey, an officer from Bankstown Local Area Command, rushed to get pieces of paper and pens to the children, asking them to write down and draw what they had seen. The kids had surrounded her, all talking and yelling at the same time. 'He had a gun,' said one child. 'He was laughing when he was shooting my dad,' said another. A series of sad drawings were handed back to her a few minutes later, each one depicting a stick figure holding a gun. In one picture, an arrow pointed from the gun to a sentence written in a child's handwriting: 'I am a bad man.'

The investigation kicked into full swing as more police arrived. A crime scene officer lifted fingerprints from Abdul Darwiche's car as well as from the fridge in the service station, where Blackie Fahda had been looking for an ice cream earlier while waiting for David to arrive. Another officer photographed and bagged the cartridge casings found in the car park driveway. Uniformed officers took statements from people who had been at the service station filling their cars up with petrol, a worker in the discount chemist stocking toilet paper in the window, and waitstaff in the Turkish restaurant who'd just finished serving the Darwiche family.

At 4:09pm, roughly forty minutes after the shooting, the NSW Police Force issued a press release with anodyne details about what had happened. 'A number of shots were discharged in the vicinity of Miller Road, hitting a male driver,' the release said. 'Emergency services attended and a deceased male was located. Police would like to speak with the occupants of a silver Honda CRV seen driving in a northerly direction on Miller Road shortly after the incident.'

The press release seemed to mask the significance of what had happened, but, more importantly, it said nothing about who was involved. The gravity of the situation became slightly clearer when Detective Inspector Ian Pryde, the crime manager at Bankstown Police Station, told a radio station that evening: 'I would call for calm.'

Within an hour of the news breaking, dozens of men converged on the crime scene with some trying to break through the police cordon. Abdul Darwiche's body was still inside his car, which was covered with a tarpaulin. His brothers – Albert, Michael and Mohamed – had been taken to the Banksia Motel a few metres away for a briefing with police. By then, CCTV footage from the service station had been given to the cops: it showed images of an unshaven man with a distinctive black mullet milling about in the area of the car park in the minutes leading up to the attack. An officer took a photograph of the CCTV footage and showed it to several colleagues on his phone – the man was immediately recognised as Mohammed 'Blackie' Fahda. Only two weeks earlier, two officers had pointed capsicum spray in his direction as he approached them with his chest out, aggressively, after having his car pulled over in Lakemba.

Heavy rain began falling just after 7pm as Albert and Michael Darwiche approached the police cordon. An officer wearing a raincoat noted their names in the crime scene log and then lifted the police tape high enough so they could duck underneath it. They were ushered towards their brother Abdul's body, still inside his Mitsubishi Triton. Afterwards they walked back to the Banksia Motel where the rest of the immediate Darwiche family were waiting with police.

Senior officers, having been alerted to the shooting, had gathered with the family to find out why Abdul had been killed. Why now, they wondered. Why like this? What motive was there for his slaying? Their expectation was for a full-scale war to erupt, and complicating matters were the long-standing tensions between the Darwiche family and the police as an organisation.

Abdul's brothers had little information to give them. They had no idea why he'd been targeted so suddenly, and in such a random location. Their fear was the attack had been planned, meaning the assailants might target them, or their young families, next.

Ken McKay was in the motel that evening, listening to the Darwiche family's concerns. He had come to the scene not as the commander of MEOCS but in his new role as the director of organised crime for the NSW Police Force, a position that oversaw not one but six major crime squads, including MEOCS.

McKay's replacement at MEOCS was Detective Superintendent Deborah 'Deb' Wallace, a radiant and breezy personality, a commander who wore heels and bright suits to the office. She had been responsible for dismantling the big Asian street gangs of the mid 1990s, crews like 5T that dominated and fuelled the heroin boom. Top gang figures took a shine to her; she had an ability to charm and disarm with a soft word, a sly wink, and earned herself a nickname from them: 'the Smiling Assassin'.

After McKay was promoted, Wallace had had some reservations about applying for his vacant position at MEOCS. For starters, she'd never worked with Middle Eastern gangs. It was also a male-dominated environment. McKay had left the Squad with a folk-hero status and Wallace was unsure if she was the right fit to fill those shoes.

This is what she told David Hudson, the commander of the State Crime Command, when she asked if he thought she was capable of doing the job. A number of others had already been suggested for the position, experienced hands with the backing of deputy commissioners but with little background in organised crime. Ultimately it was Hudson's decision and he didn't rate any of the suggestions made to him so far – but he considered Wallace one of his most experienced superintendents. Breaking up gangs had been at the centre of her career; they weren't Middle Eastern, but the adjustment would be swift. Hudson's answer chased away any doubts in her mind. 'If you want MEOCS, you've got it,' he said to her.

Wallace began her tenure on 2 December 2008 – three months before Abdul Darwiche's murder – and was immediately struck by the stark cultural differences between the Asian and Middle Eastern crime figures.

The Vietnamese gang members she'd busted had tended to be first-generation criminals. They had come to Australia speaking no English and possessing few skills. The drug dealing and standover was a short-term solution, a way out of poverty. It was never a vocation and they were remarkably philosophical about their circumstances – they didn't blame the police or the system for their criminality. Instead, and this was often repeated to Wallace, they saw their paths playing out in a fatalistic way: either they would be killed, imprisoned or, if they were lucky, grow up and grow out of crime altogether.

The Middle Eastern criminals Wallace was seeing seemed to come at crime from a different mindset. They were stuck in a bleak cycle. Crime wasn't a way out of poverty but rather a career and a trade skill, something handed down from one generation to the next. There were whole families of criminals, parents and children; the kids were Australian-born, had access to schooling, spoke fluent English and, theoretically, had bright futures in front of them. They had opportunities for apprenticeships, TAFE courses and university degrees, and yet these first-world advantages were being routinely squandered, whether by the lure of fast money, or as the result of poor parenting or peer pressure – or maybe all three, Wallace could never be sure. Very few targets appeared to grow up and grow out, as the Vietnamese crims had done, or evolve like the Chinese, who went from stabbings and standover in Chinatown to commercial drug importations; their sophisticated ventures were so slick and well organised that most went largely undetected. In Middle Eastern organised crime Wallace saw flashbacks to that early 1990s era. Petty disputes were still being settled via shootings in public places as well as violence that was so public and obvious that it drew the attention of police. This had gone on for at least a decade. The time for change was due, but by the end of 2008 when she took over the job as MEOCS commander, it still hadn't come and wasn't even close.

It was around this time that another tectonic movement took place within the Squad: David Adney was leaving his role as TAG commander. He took a job as a crime manager working at Kogarah Police Station in the hope of enjoying the slower pace of suburban police life. It didn't last long. Within a few months, following a fatal brawl between members of the Comancheros and Hells Angels outlaw motorcycle gangs in the arrivals hall at Sydney's domestic airport, he was back in charge of another discrete unit at the State Crime Command, Strike Force Raptor; it was a proactive division of the Gangs Squad that in many ways was modelled on the work of MEOCS TAG and its predecessor at Task Force Gain.

Into Adney's place stepped Mick Ryan, the veteran investigator who gave the Squad's induction speech on the day it formed. He transferred into the role after a brief hiatus working at the Child Abuse and Sex Crimes Squad where he dealt with horrific and sadistic criminality, much worse than anything he'd encountered in the realm of organised crime. For that reason alone, he was glad to be back.

Ryan was a different style of detective to Adney. The way Ryan saw things, the TAG office needed to be a training ground for the CI teams on Level Three, an incubator where detectives could be cultivated for long-term investigations. In Ryan's mind, there had been too many short-term missions and not enough syndicate-busting strike forces. Over the subsequent months, Ryan steered his team in that direction.

*

On the afternoon of Abdul Darwiche's murder, Wallace received a phone call from David Hudson, the commander of the State Crime Command. He wanted to know what strategy was in place to prevent any further shootings. The murder itself, and locating Mohammed 'Blackie' Fahda, was a job for the Homicide Squad, but the job of preventing what was expected to be further bloodshed between the Darwiche and Fahda families fell squarely with MEOCS, he said.

In response to the call, Wallace ordered the formation of a rapid, proactive strike force that would essentially be a surveillance operation on the Darwiche family, a watch-and-see to intercept any potential attack of retribution. The MEOCS experience and incoming intelligence suggested the Darwiche family would have to stage a reprisal attack. Not to do so, some officers strongly believed, would result in a loss of face in the community.

As it stood, the Darwiche family's relationship with the police was already strained. Adnan's war with the Razzaks had brought them under intense scrutiny: their cars had been stopped and their homes had been raided on account of the feuding. Abdul Darwiche himself had his own potted history with the law. In 2005 he was charged alongside his brother Adnan with the attempted murder of Farouk 'Frank' Razzak at a house in Punchbowl. Farouk, the Razzak family's patriarch, had seen two men standing under a street light holding military-style rifles across the road from his house just before a volley of shots was fired towards him. In court, defence lawyers picked apart Farouk's evidence that he'd seen Adnan and Abdul holding the weapons, identifying inconsistencies that painted him as a liar. Abdul was acquitted by the jury in 2005 but Adnan was convicted in a separate trial a year later. The big difference between the two cases was the evidence of Khaled 'Crazy' Taleb, who by the time Adnan went on trial had been signed up as a star police witness – none of Taleb's evidence was heard during Abdul's trial and some police believe this is the reason he was acquitted. They continued their investigations into him in the years that followed.

He was placed under investigation for drug supply and in 2007 was refused a tow truck driver's certificate based on a MEOCS assessment of his character. The assessment, written by Mick Ryan, said that Abdul had assumed his brother Adnan's place in maintaining 'drug distribution networks in the south west of Sydney' and was seeking the tow truck driver's certificate to 'legitimise his activities'.

This all came to symbolise what the Darwiche family said was a systemic targeting and scapegoating of their family for crimes they did not commit. They pointed to Abdul's acquittal as proof that both he and Adnan were innocent of the crimes police had been accusing them of committing. The only reason Adnan had been found guilty was because of Khaled 'Crazy' Taleb, they said, calling him a liar who had framed Adnan in the witness box in exchange for an indemnity and financial reward.

But what angered them most in the aftermath of Abdul's murder was the police protection being offered to the Fahda family. They were moved into safety amid concerns for their welfare; meanwhile, the Darwiches had received no such support. If anyone needed protection, they argued, it was them; they were the ones at risk of further violence. Given that it was already their long-standing view that authorities had a vendetta against both Adnan and their broader family, this decision to protect the Fahdas seemed to aggravate their fragile relationship with police even further. When rumours later surfaced that Mohammed 'Blackie' Fahda had also somehow slipped out of the country, it cemented their loss of confidence in the police.

In the days following Abdul's murder, MEOCS detectives received word that reprisal attacks against the Fahdas were close to being carried out. Detective Senior Sergeant Paul O'Neill, the officer in charge of the proactive team trying to stop this retribution – Strike Force Lieutenant – noted in one report: 'Investigators are aware of volumes of source information indicating further shootings are imminent.'

If any reprisal were to happen then O'Neill figured it would take place after the three-day mourning period following Abdul's burial. In Islam, as O'Neill had learned through years of working in the realm of Middle Eastern organised crime, this is the period when normal life is put on hold, when visitors bearing food are received into the home, and decorative clothing or jewellery is generally shunned. On the third day, however, the formal grieving process ends and, in MEOC circles, generally, retribution follows.

On 19 March, on the third day of mourning, detectives mobilised in unmarked vehicles around the Darwiche family home on Petunia Avenue, Punchbowl, where dozens of people had converged.

O'Neill watched the house from his car with another detective, Belinda Dyson, sitting next to him. More detectives were parked around the corner waiting for a radio call to start following cars. The plan was to observe Abdul's younger brothers – Albert, Michael and Mohamed – and trail them as they left the property.

Around 9pm a car pulled away from the house and started moving in the direction of O'Neill and Dyson. There were two men inside; in the passenger seat was Michael Darwiche.

O'Neill radioed the backup team. 'Dark-coloured BMW,' he said, reading out the licence plate, putting them on notice to pull over the car once it rounded the corner.

The BMW slowed down alongside the unmarked police car and came to a stop right next to it, seemingly lining up alongside the driver's seat in the tell-tale way of letting a surveillance cop know they have been burned. O'Neill froze. Dyson didn't breathe. The windows of their car were tinted but not completely blacked out. Had Darwiche seen them? Had they been burned? O'Neill slowly pressed himself into his seat and stared straight ahead until he heard what sounded like a conversation taking place over the top of his car.

What O'Neill hadn't counted on was that his vantage point was directly outside the home of a 'friendly', a neighbour who had come outside to share a few words with Michael Darwiche, unwittingly it seemed, over the top of two detectives. O'Neill waited until the conversation ended, then watched as the BMW kept moving past him. He radioed Detective Jonathon Findlay and another officer, telling them the car was on its way. When they pulled the car over within a minute on Salvia Street, two streets over, they introduced themselves and asked both men to step out of the car.

The driver handed over his licence, identifying himself as Michael Darwick, a 36-year-old construction worker from Punchbowl. He and Michael Darwiche worked for the same company. Their names sounded similar but they weren't related. Asked where they were going, both men said they were heading to McDonald's for dinner.

Findlay searched the car as his fellow officer recorded the scene on a video camera. With gloved hands Findlay went through the centre console and glove compartment, finding nothing of any real value. The back seat looked normal except for a seat cushion that was out of place. Findlay lifted the cushion and found a Glock 23 handgun loaded with fifteen rounds of ammunition. By the time the search had ended Findlay had also found a street directory with a White Pages printout of four Fahda family addresses jammed inside as a bookmark. It looked like a hit-kit: a gun, a map and a list of addresses to Fahda family homes. At Bankstown Police Station both men invoked their right to silence and were charged with eight offences ranging from gun possession to the most serious: armed to commit an indictable offence.

When they applied for bail the next morning, a police prosecutor tendered documents written by Findlay stating both men were 'on their way to carry out a reprisal shooting when stopped by police'. Lawyers for both men called the police case weak, slamming it all as speculation; there was little evidence, the lawyers said, to prove either man knew there was a gun in the car. The gun, the bullets and the map had all been sent for trace evidence and DNA testing at the Division of Analytical Laboratories in Lidcombe, a twenty-minute drive away from the courthouse. Much later, as a result of these tests, it would emerge that Darwiche's DNA was found on the trigger of the Glock, which inextricably linked him to the weapon.

The magistrate agreed to give Darwick bail, but opposed it for Michael Darwiche despite a clean criminal record, an offer of an $800,000 surety, and an argument from his lawyer that he posed no threat to the community. His brothers, sitting in the court watching, left without saying a word to the waiting media.

Mohammed 'Blackie' Fahda, who police believed was responsible for the murder of Abdul Darwiche, went underground immediately after the Bass Hill shooting. And he stayed missing, unable to be located despite surveillance operations and surprise raids on homes belonging to his family members. His father, sister and cousins were spoken to several times and they always told police the same thing: we don't know where he has gone. In desperation, police released his mugshot to the media, but this, too, was unhelpful. As the weeks and months passed and interest in the case died down, so too did the manhunt to find him, though by then new rumours had surfaced suggesting his possible whereabouts.

By September, almost six months after the murder, police strongly suspected that Blackie had somehow made it out of the country despite warnings on his passport and his mugshot plastered through the media. For members of the Darwiche family, this was further proof that the police didn't care and were, in their minds, complicit in his escape. 'They knew it was Fahda who shot Abdul from the day it happened, so if they really wanted him, they could have had him,' Abdul's sister, Khadije, told the *Sunday Telegraph* newspaper on 5 September 2009.

Three weeks after those comments were printed, a phone rang in the office of the NSW Homicide Squad informing detectives attached to Strike Force Solomon that Mohammed 'Blackie' Fahda had been found in Tonga and placed under arrest by local security forces. Intelligence provided to the Tongan Police suggested Fahda had boarded a cargo ship as a stowaway, the MV *Captain Tasman*, and then jumped off the side into the ocean as the vessel approached Queen Salote Harbour. A local man was waiting for him in a boat and took him ashore.

Hiding in Tonga, Fahda slept on the floor of a drug dealer's house in Nuku'alofa and made attempts to buy a false passport to fly out to Saudi Arabia. In meetings with locals he identified himself as 'Mike' and, quite foolishly, told people he was wanted in Australia for the murders of two people, a boast that eventually made its way back to Tongan police officer Sosefo Tabueluelu, who set about trying to verify the information. Tabueluelu drove out to the drug dealer's villa on the side of a highway and set up a surveillance operation. He'd been told that the character known as Mike was hiding out there. Tabueluelu knew the dealer well enough to spot his wife and children inside the house and, sure enough, they were there with a man whom Tabueluelu had never seen before.

A Tactical Response Group team surrounded the villa the next afternoon, raiding the property and finding Fahda, or Mike, lying on the floor of a room watching television. Hauled back to the station, he blundered his way through an interview by telling officers that his name was 'Micky Bondo' and that he was on holiday from Fiji. He said he'd lost his passport, an answer that only became suspicious when he couldn't remember basic details that it might have contained, such as his birthday or address in Suva, where he had apparently boarded his flight. Finally, an officer decided to lay a trick question.

'What colour is the Fijian passport?' they asked.

'Dark maroon,' he answered, quickly and confidently, as if he'd known the answer for years. Except it wasn't correct. The Fijian passport, the officer said, is light blue in colour.

They kept Fahda in the Tongan station house for another week while his extradition was organised by Australian authorities. His fingerprints identified him by his real name and revealed he was wanted for one murder in Australia, not two as he had bragged to people. At one point, two men walked into the station offering a large bribe to break him out of his cell, prompting security to be beefed up on the order of the country's police chief.

Fahda arrived back in Sydney on 5 October handcuffed to Officer Tabueluelu after what had been a largely uneventful flight. At one point Fahda turned to the officer and said it was his dream to return to Tonga someday.

'When?' Tabueluelu asked.

Fahda thought about it for a moment. 'Twenty to thirty years,' he said.

He was met on the tarmac by detectives Joe Maree and Peter Hogan from the NSW Homicide Squad and taken back to the Sydney Police Centre in Surry Hills to be interviewed. There, he was given two phone calls. He used the first on his parents and the second on his lawyer. He agreed to be interviewed but mostly invoked his right to silence.

Detective Maree turned on the tape at 5:05pm and put the regulation questions to Fahda, asking him to spell out his name and confirm his date of birth before quickly settling into the point of the interview: the murder of Abdul Darwiche.

'Is there anything you'd like to tell us in relation to that here this afternoon?' Maree asked.

'No,' said Fahda, cutting off the interview. 'I don't want to go any further.'

Michael Darwiche and Michael Darwick went on trial over the apparent hit-kit found in their vehicle on 19 March 2009. Darwiche had already pleaded guilty to one of his offences by the time the hearings began – possession of an unauthorised pistol. Despite this, he and Darwick were contesting their charge of being armed to commit an indictable offence.

In the witness box, Darwiche was asked about the weapon and why he was armed with it in the first place. His explanation was simple.

He'd found the weapon behind a bag of baby clothes in a garden shed at Abdul's house, which he'd come to visit in the hours after the murder. It had been an accidental find, Darwiche told the court. Abdul had been carrying the gun around before his murder, but stopped doing so on Michael's advice, something that now left him with pangs of survivor's guilt because he might have been able to use it to protect himself at the service station. With the police apparently giving his family no support, Michael was hoping to use the gun in the event that his brother's attackers tried coming after him next.

'I was hoping if I was attacked … that if I held it out [the gun], it might buy me a few minutes to get away, to run,' he told the court.

The Crown's case aggressively pursued the alternate theory: that Darwiche and Darwick had only revenge on their minds that night – what other explanation could there be, the prosecutor asked, for having a Glock handgun, a street directory and a White Pages printout of Fahda family addresses all in the same car?

Darwiche's explanation seemed to put these circumstances back into some perspective. Taking the stand in front of the jury, he said that both he and Darwick had gone to Rookwood Cemetery that afternoon to visit Abdul's grave. As a mark of respect, he left the gun in the car, hiding it under the back seat's cushion when his friend wasn't looking. Darwick, he said, didn't know he was carrying a weapon.

'I have wrecked his life,' Darwiche told the court, turning to his friend in the dock. 'I made a mistake and he is paying for my mistake and I'm sorry.'

As for the White Pages printout of Fahda family addresses, Darwiche said that had been done to form part of a dossier the family was compiling for a private investigator. With the police being unable to find Fahda, his family had been hoping to contract a private investigator to help track down Fahda for arrest, he said.

The jury didn't take long to deliberate. They found both men not guilty of being armed to commit an indictable offence. Darwick walked free while Darwiche was ordered to serve a minimum sentence of fourteen months over his guilty plea to the gun possession charge. The sentence was backdated to the time of his arrest, which made him eligible for parole within a month of his trial finishing.

Having been extradited, Mohammed 'Blackie' Fahda pleaded not guilty to the murder of Abdul Darwiche and took his case to trial, arguing that he was acting in self-defence at the time of the shooting. He told the court that seeing Darwiche and talking to him at the petrol station had triggered a chain reaction of events that created a belief in his mind that he was going to be killed.

Fahda outlined how he had tried to leave the petrol station before the shooting but was unable to get out of the driveway because Darwiche had blocked it with his car. Minutes earlier when they had spoken, Darwiche had allegedly threatened him.

'He [Abdul] said he's going to kill us the way he killed my brother Ahmad,' Fahda told the court, though whether this was actually said or not is open to interpretation. Some witnesses heard Darwiche shouting out words that suggested he was the one under threat, including the line, 'What are you going to do? Shoot me in front of my fucking family?'

Some psychologists who gave evidence during the Fahda trial said the effect of seeing Abdul Darwiche at a service station not unlike the one where his brother Ahmad was killed, coupled with the blocked driveway and the alleged threat that had been made, would have created a paranoid delusion in Fahda's mind that he really was about to be murdered.

Fahda reiterated this in a letter sent to the judge from an isolated cell at Lithgow Correctional Centre where he was being housed for his own safety, a place where his only means of communicating with anyone was by shouting over a brick wall. 'It was not revenge that day,' he wrote to the judge. 'I panicked. I am still traumatised by my brother's death.'

He was found guilty of murdering Abdul Darwiche and sentenced to a minimum term of fourteen years in prison. An appeal against this sentence was dismissed in 2013. He will be eligible for release on 28 September 2023.

CHAPTER TEN

THE SHOOTING OF FADI IBRAHIM

CASTLE COVE, 11:35PM, 4 JUNE 2009

Fadi Ibrahim, the second youngest of the Ibrahim brothers, brought his Lamborghini to a stop outside his home in Castle Cove, a spit of land north of Sydney Harbour. It was Friday night and the nightclubs were just warming up. Friends were waiting to party with him in the city. In the passenger seat was his girlfriend, Shayda Bastani-Rad, a 23-year-old student upset about being dropped off at home. The plan was to have a boys' night out.

Dinner had been a lavish affair at Catalina, a restaurant on the water at Rose Bay, a place popular with visiting celebrities. Jay-Z and Beyonce had once dined there, as had Al Pacino and also Leonardo DiCaprio. By contrast, Fadi's dining companions that night were characters like Allan Sarkis, president of the street gang Notorious, and several other tattooed men in finely tailored clothes. At the end of the meal, Fadi threw down his credit card and picked up the $1200 bill before driving off with Shayda for the 25-minute journey back to Castle Cove, a route dotted with speed and traffic cameras.

It's also a world away from the western Sydney fibro where he had grown up with his five siblings. He lived in a designer pile with pruned hedges along its border and a wide driveway leading to a spacious garage. Everything about the property's design hinted at privacy: its windows were no larger than laptop screens. Evergreens guarded the main window view of the street.

As the Lamborghini idled, Fadi and Shayda continued their argument, oblivious to the gunman sneaking up alongside the driver's side door. Five shots slammed into Fadi's body through the open window – two in the chest, two in the arm, and another through his right shoulder. The assassin said nothing, and then disappeared.

Shayda dialled Triple 0 as Fadi lay dying, applying pressure on his chest wound as she spoke to the operator. 'My boyfriend's been shot,' she said, giving them the address.

At hospital, doctors wheeled Fadi into emergency surgery and placed him in an induced coma. The operation removed each bullet and most of his stomach as family and friends gathered in the waiting room. Menacing men with tattoos kept the press at bay; a photographer was kicked in the stomach as he tried snapping a picture of John, one of Fadi's older brothers and something of a revered figure within the family. As Fadi remained in a coma, John updated his other two brothers, Sam and Michael, on his condition.

'A bullet went through his liver but it didn't hit the main artery,' he said to Michael, the youngest brother, a 31-year-old prison inmate serving a manslaughter sentence in Broken Hill Correctional Centre.

'So he'll be fine,' John said, trying to keep the conversation light-hearted. 'He's not going to be able to eat as much as he did, which will probably do him good anyway.'

Michael Ibrahim didn't share his John's optimism. He was fuming that someone had taken a shot at their family. That's the way he saw it; there had been threats and fights in the past, but nothing like this – this was a targeted, calculated assassination attempt that appeared to send a message to the entire family. Michael wanted action, but John urged patience; the attack seemed too personal to be targeting the rest of the family, he said.

John never played the hothead. He never had to; Sam, his older brother, and Michael, the youngest, took care of all that. John was always the coolheaded hustler, the street-smart businessman. At the time of Fadi's shooting, he reportedly owned more than twenty nightclubs in Kings Cross – the neighbourhood that had taken him under its wing when he first showed up as a teenager, still living in his mother's fibro and wagging class at Merrylands High School. It was Sam the tough guy and John the wise guy in those days when they went to work for the Bayeh brothers, Bill and Louis, the Bigs of the Cross. This was the late 1980s in the area's heyday of smokey nightclubs, burlesque and vice.

Working with the Bayehs created immense opportunity. Sam handled security while John played the gofer, driving the cars and running errands. He watched. He listened. Legend has it that he'd stepped into a fight on the Bayehs' behalf and got knifed in the process. The scars tell the story; they start at his waistline and stop at his sternum. If not for that, who knows what might have happened? But from then on, his future had been redefined, his loyalty affirmed. If he'd been shown the ropes before, then after the stabbing he was thrust into the action, buying into the local nightclub trade at the age of nineteen with his first venture, The Tunnel, a venue nestled on a quiet alley between Darlinghurst Road and Victoria Street, the main drag. From there he expanded: plans for a gaming licence, strip clubs and more real estate. Police attention followed – they suspected drugs. How else was he making his money? It was a question that would trail him for years. During the Wood Royal Commission in the mid 1990s it was put to him that he'd become the lifeblood of the Kings Cross drug trade. His response? 'It would seem that way,' he told the commission, 'but no.'

Drug dealing in the Cross tended to follow a formula back then. There were two main factions driving the trade – the Bayehs were on one side and Danny Karam, the gangster, was on the other. A handful of syndicates operated beneath them, paying tax or protection money to have their street dealers work the area.

Things got faster around 1996. This was when John and Sam had fallen out with the Bayehs. The Royal Commission had turned people against each other. Rumours of police assistance had spread throughout the Cross. Everyone was co-operating. Then, no one was co-operating. When Bill was hauled off to prison for drug supply, his strip club The Love Machine, a key piece of real estate, went up for grabs. Sam and John moved in fast, seizing the club with both hands in what was to be the beginning of an aggressive expansion.

Police were circling, but they were flush with other priorities. Strike forces looking into the Ibrahim brothers were shelved as their focus shifted. An emerging problem known as Middle Eastern organised crime was starting to rear its head. Danny Karam was still alive and causing havoc with his group, DK's Boys. An open-air drug market had appeared on Telopea Street, Punchbowl. With those guys hogging the limelight, John kept his head down. He quietly built an empire, accrued wealth and took on police suspicions with a come-at-me-with-everything-you-got type of attitude. Sam was less discreet. He joined the Nomads and climbed the ranks – chapter vice-president, then president – his arrival in the gang signalling a new era for the bikie culture. Once, they had been notoriously racist, an exclusive realm of white Australian men of Anglo-Saxon heritage. But now, with Sam's arrival, a new era had come to pass, opening them up to Middle Eastern and Islander recruits.

The death of Karam and the dismantling of his crew created a power vacuum in the Cross and the Ibrahims walked into it. More nightclubs and expansion followed. Their control of Kings Cross moved into Darlinghurst. Then Double Bay followed. They bought into venues like UN Nightclub, Dragonfly, Embassy, The White Blue Room, Mylk and China White. There was The Love Machine, of course, and also Porky's, another Kings Cross institution. In conversation, John was easygoing, but in business he was ruthless, a savage character who demanded it all. During one telling conversation at the Mr Goodbar nightclub, noted in police files, John revealed this side of his character, telling someone: 'I don't care if I own ten per cent or one per cent,' he said. 'I own the club.'

By the mid 2000s police tried their hand again at the Ibrahims. At least two separate drug strike forces had looked into John and members of his family – Strike Force Sombre and Strike Force Lancer – but the police could never prove anything. No one ever went on paper with any complaints against John. On 21 June 2009, the *Sunday Telegraph* reported that John observed this himself during a conversation secretly recorded by police in 2003: 'I've been on charges for murder, f****** attempted … it doesn't mean they get me. Because they come up with all this bull**** to get you charged, and then; but the time you get to court, everyone's gone, you know what I mean?

By the time Fadi was shot, John had virtually left that world behind. He was done with the headaches of the underworld and cringed at the unflattering news articles that appeared in print anytime one of his brothers got arrested. For John, life had evolved.

His family had been looked after, everyone had a house, and life was pretty good. Even the police seemed to have given up on caring; it's the other brothers, they said. John's gone clean.

And that was that: John had gone from the police pages to the social pages, turning up at beachside parties and rubbing shoulders with celebrities. In photographs there'd be one hand around a stunning bombshell and the other holding a drink. Meanwhile, Sam was in prison on a kidnapping charge, Michael was serving out a manslaughter sentence, and Fadi, who was described in the media as a loan shark but who called himself a builder, was driving a new prestige car every few weeks.

Detective Sergeant Brad Abdy was a new addition to MEOCS CI, Team 1. He'd moved over from a detectives' office in the suburb of Liverpool where a corruption scandal had poisoned morale and motivated some police to seek a transfer. He caught the Fadi Ibrahim case the morning after the shooting, showing up at the crime scene at about 7am dressed in a suit and carrying a notebook. Forensic crews had been working all night, photographing the car and swabbing it for fingerprints and DNA. There had been few witnesses located during the initial canvass of the street and those who had been found said they saw nothing of substance. For Abdy the scene itself gave away no secrets: the gunman had left no calling card, there was no scent for the Dog Squad to follow. Everything about the shooting had been perfectly executed. Its only failure had been that Fadi, now in a coma, had survived. He was Abdy's prime witness, or would become one once he was brought out of his coma. That would be weeks away. As Abdy moved through the crime scene outside the house he looked for links, a stray footprint in the grass, a cigarette butt. He studied the golf course facing the house and examined each tree for its adequacy as a hiding spot.

Central to the case were a handful of questions: How did the assassin get to the scene? Was there an accomplice? Did the gunman wait for Fadi to arrive? Or was he followed from the restaurant?

Every investigation, no matter how dismal it may first appear, gets a small leg up – it's a witness sipping tea as the gunshots go off, or a jogger who hears the screeching tyres and glances at the licence plate. In Abdy's case it's a CCTV camera located just above the garage of Fadi Ibrahim's home. It captured the entire shooting on video, recording it onto a tape that Abdy watched again and again, somewhere in the vicinity of 400 times in his search for answers. This was 2009, a time when camera technology was in its infancy. The tape was poor quality, infrared and too far away to capture facial features, but it was still full of subtle hints. Each replay gave Abdy a little more insight into the weight and stature of the grainy assassin in the images. It was clearly a man, he thought. Shadows on the road hinted at the height and the gunman seemed relaxed as he walked, striding casually like this had all been practiced, or done before. Abdy paused the tape and enhanced segments, dialling up the light sources where he could, mulling over questions between each replay. He could only hope ballistics would match the bullets pulled out of Fadi with another same-calibre shooting, one where the suspects were already known. If not, this would turn into another gangland hit – one where the walls go up, the victim says nothing, and no one goes down.

The footage was poor quality but almost redeemed itself by revealing a potential witness – a passing motorist who'd driven past the Lamborghini just as the gunman crept up to the car. Maybe they saw something? Abdy later learned the motorist had been picked up during the intial canvass, a young man on his way to a party. He hadn't seen anything; he couldn't even remember seeing a Lamborghini that night. Just my luck, Abdy thought – had it been a less affluent suburb, where Lamborghinis aren't as common, it's possible the kid might have paid more attention.

His team reviewed every traffic camera from Catalina to Castle Cove, watching the Lamborghini in real time to follow its route and painstakingly track every car around it. This was gruelling work and hours upon hours of camera footage had to be trawled through and scrutinised to try to spot a tail, a pattern, someone stalking Fadi Ibrahim through the Cross City Tunnel or over the Sydney Harbour Bridge. It took days and gave him nothing in the end; the gunman was starting to become a wraith-like apparition that appeared on Neerim Road just as Fadi's Lamborghini slowed down.

The only other witness to the shooting was Shayda, Fadi's girlfriend, who had little to offer in her statement; all she could remember was the gunshots. She didn't see a face. Her previous boyfriend, Faouxi Abou-Jibal, a friend of Fadi's and accomplice in Michael Ibrahim's manslaughter case, had been murdered three years earlier.

Within the first twenty-four hours partner agencies like the NSW Crime Commission began sending Abdy reams of intelligence from their sources in the field, their existing holdings, and tip-offs they'd received that were, at times, years old. These ranged from rumoured gripes to known conflicts that stretched as far back as the early 2000s. Informants loyal to MEOCS were reporting in with gossip picked up around the café tables of Bankstown where groups of excited men were hashing out their own theories. Abdy was deluged with possible motives, too many, most of them speculative: the shooting was a message to John Ibrahim; the shooting was a warning over the nightclub trade; the shooting was a show of force that the family members weren't invincible. Others suggested old scores being finally settled. A man who'd fallen foul of the Ibrahims and had his leg broken with a claw hammer was mentioned several times. Abdy took note but, as this speculation continued to pour in, he was working on one of his own theories that no one else knew about.

Abdy had started at MEOCS in April, two months earlier, walking into a new assignment that was already running into the Ibrahim family, a secretive investigation known as Strike Force Bellwood. It was an intelligence probe much like the cold start that Memmolo's team had tried on the Kalache family a year earlier – the idea was to gather information and then look for angles into the targets.

Bellwood had already been running for two months and had made inroads into Fadi's older sister, Maha Sayour. She lived in a two-level property on Pearson Street in the Sydney suburb of South Wentworthville, a house that had been midway through renovations for too long; it was perpetually unfinished. Barely days into Abdy's tenure at MEOCS, Sayour's house was raided by a team of detectives, including Abdy, who found himself standing in the middle of her living room as ninety-five heat-sealed bags of cash were pulled out from a roof cavity in the kitchen, a hole that seemed to have been purpose-made for the property. When the money was counted back at the station the cash totalled $2.86 million. Sayour insisted she had no idea how the money got there and said she had never seen it, telling the detectives cheekily, 'If I had big sums of money I would have finished the bloody house, trust me.' Unable to prove that Sayour knew the money was hidden in her kitchen, the police case struggled at trial and Sayour walked on all charges. Abdy, however, could see a bigger picture.

He knew all along the money most likely didn't belong to her; whether she knew it was hidden in her house or not was beside the point. Abdy believed the money most likely belonged to her youngest brother Michael. Even though he was in prison, Michael needed the money more than she did, Abdy thought.

It had been widely confirmed that Michael Ibrahim was the architect behind the street gang known as Notorious, a group that was using Kings Cross as its base of operations. Various theories were tossed around about why Notorious was formed but the prevailing one was that it had been set up to protect the Ibrahim family's interests in the red-light district; with Michael in jail and Sam in and out of prison, there were few safeguards to insulate the family from a war in Kings Cross. In the eighteen months leading up to Fadi's shooting, tensions had been brewing through the area. The Comanchero outlaw motorcycle gang had already made their interests well known by showing up unannounced in great numbers at Ibrahim-controlled clubs and attempting to buy up real estate in the area. Rumours of contract killings began circulating.

To be sure, Notorious appeared to have been formed in response to this posturing. The group's membership base was growing and was largely a mix of Islander and Middle Eastern men, most of them young and trigger-happy types who were reckless and willing to carry out crimes to make a name for themselves. The perks waved under the noses of these men to recruit them into the club included payment of legal costs and other bills should they ever be arrested or charged. Along with these costs were other tangential expenses, including clubhouse leases, vehicles and weapons. In other words, a gang like Notorious needed a big sum of cash behind it; and that's where Abdy believed the money in Sayour's house came into the picture.

In his mind, the $2.86 million was Michael's war chest, a fighting fund to pay for his gang's expenses. Without that money, pressure would build on its hierarchy to come up with a new source of income, and Abdy could already see the tension building between Michael Ibrahim, the gang's notional founder, and Notorious's notional president, Allan Sarkis, who'd been having dinner with Fadi on the night he was shot. Michael regularly used the prison phone at Broken Hill Correctional Centre to call Allan Sarkis. These were monitored and recorded calls. In the immediate aftermath of Fadi's shooting, Michael had joked with Sarkis that he might have set up his brother for the shooting, tipping off the gunman when he left the Catalina restaurant. Sarkis didn't see the funny side to the joke, but Michael reassured him.

'If I thought it was true,' he said, 'mate, you'd be dead already.'

A new lead walked into the frame on day three of Abdy's investigation. His name was 'Jack', a police informant, his true identity suppressed by a court. He was a drug dealer, a stylish one, a playboy who wore designer clothes and jumped the queues outside nightclubs, slapping hands with the bouncers as he walked inside. He wasn't a gangster – he had a degree in property economics – but he liked to be around them, loved the notoriety and all the spoils that came with it. And they liked him – he knew how to find houses that were perfect for cooking speed and, if things got desperate, knew the kind of people who could cook up a batch.

Becoming an informant hadn't been part of Jack's plan, but that's just the way things worked out. It was all thanks to his brother-in-law, 'Tommy' (a pseudonym). He'd been running a speed lab that caught fire and aroused the attention of police, landing him in Long Bay Correctional Centre where, in late 2008, Michael Ibrahim was serving out part of his manslaughter sentence. Michael still had another five years until he could make parole.

He and Tommy became friends in prison and whenever Jack would visit, which was most weeks, they would all get together in the visiting yard and trade gossip about people up in Kings Cross – who's been arrested, who's out of prison, what's going on up at the strip. Michael hung onto this stuff and Jack was happy to oblige with offers to smuggle contraband into the prison – DVDs, drugs, anything that could feasibly be snuck past the guards in the minimum-security centre.

When Michael was moved to Broken Hill, Jack stayed in touch with him, agreeing to fly the two-and-a-half-hour journey to visit and keep up the relationship. Sure, they didn't really know each other that well, but that was Jack's personality – he admired Michael in some ways and wanted to be friends with him. Call it awe; a mix of fear and respect. But there was another side to this relationship as well.

What Michael Ibrahim didn't know was that Jack was a Gangs Squad informant with a set of handlers who he reported to regularly: Mark Gorton and Sharon Smithers. They were collecting intelligence on Notorious, the street gang that Michael Ibrahim had founded. What better way to get information about Notorious than for Jack to mine his new friend for tidbits of information. Gorton and Smithers told him that if he could provide useful intelligence about the street crew, it could assist his brother-in-law, Tommy, with his case when it came up for sentencing. It was a fair deal, Jack thought. Besides, he could pick and choose what he gave them.

About three days after Fadi got shot, Jack called Smithers from a payphone and told her he had information about the shooting, if she wanted it. He said it was too early to say who was behind the attack – no one knew for sure – but suspicions were rife within the Ibrahim family. He read out some names of potential suspects and said he would contact her again later.

Smithers called Brad Abdy, the head of the investigation, when she got off the call. She told him she couldn't identify her source, but had names of suspects she could provide. Abdy wrote them down in his police notepad.

One name was Mark Buddle, the head of the Comanchero outlaw motorcycle gang. Daniel Callahan, a bikie associate, was another one, along with Hugo Jacobs, a man who owed money to Fadi Ibrahim. The last was John Macris, a name which Abdy hadn't heard before. He already knew about the others, but discounted them as suspects; Abdy just didn't believe those men had the kind of tensions with the Ibrahim family that would lead them to attempt murder. It was known that the Comancheros had taken out contracts on John Ibrahim in the past, but Fadi? It seemed too unlikely. Abdy wrote all four names down anyway and hung up the phone. He tapped his pen against the name Macris and then drew an asterisk next to it.

On a Friday afternoon, the week after Fadi was shot, Jack flew to Broken Hill Correctional Centre for another one of his usual meetings with Michael Ibrahim. Joining him was 'Ayman', whose real name has also been suppressed by a court order. Ayman was a shonk, another middleman in the drug trade who was on bail for a trafficking offence in Victoria.

Michael sat in front of them at a table in the visiting area, and was angry and agitated about the shooting. He was certain that whoever had gone after Fadi had done so to intimidate the entire family. He leaned in close when he spoke, whispering his sentences and switching between English and Arabic, which Jack couldn't understand.

At one point, after an extended conversation with Ayman in Arabic, Michael turned to Jack and said that he knew who shot Fadi, mouthing the word 'Macris' to him across the table.

Jack was skeptical. He knew John Macris and his history of conflict with the Ibrahims but the notion still seemed unlikely. 'He doesn't have the balls,' Jack said. Michael assured him it was true. He'd worked out the logic in his head using his deductive leaps that couldn't be questioned; they were foolproof and brutally simple.

'He hates us and we hate him,' Michael said, a fact that, in his mind, seemed to seal his argument. He asked Jack if he knew where Macris could be found, the implication being that a reprisal would follow.

Jack said the cops were all over the case and looking at everyone; it was a bad idea.

At this, Michael snapped. 'Do you think I wanna do this? I'm forced into a position now here, I have to do something about it. I'm dirty on my brother Fadi for bringing this drama to us, buying his Lamborghini, buying his Bentley, showing off all his money, bringing heat on the family and terrorising Macris. Fadi thinks he's a gangster but he's not, he's a wimp. Even with all his money he's too much of a tightarse to pay a couple of coconuts to walk around with him and protect him and now I'm left with the problem and I've gotta do something about it or people are gunna think that they can take the Cross.'

Jack reeled from the shouting. He figured it was pointless arguing and he placated Michael, telling him he'd once seen Macris in a chicken shop around Woollahra, a leafy, affluent suburb of Sydney's east known for its high concentration of wealthy retirees.

'If I bump into him I'll call Ayman and tell him where he is, but I can't guarantee that I'll even see him again,' Jack said.

Later, when he got back to Sydney, Jack called Smithers and told her about his conversation at the prison. He omitted most of the important details, specifically the parts of the conversation where Macris's name had been mentioned and the part where he'd been asked to track him down. Instead, he told Smithers there was still uncertainty about who shot Fadi, which wasn't true, and he volunteered Ayman's name as the likely triggerman for any future revenge plot to be carried out. What neither Jack nor Smithers knew, however, was that Ayman himself was also a police informant.

His handlers worked at MEOCS and had reached out to him within days of Fadi Ibrahim's shooting. As far as sources went, he was a godsend, a grass who sat within the Ibrahims' inner circle of family and someone who was far more forthcoming with information than Jack had been with Smithers. Through Ayman and his handlers, Abdy was given a full rundown of the history between the Macris and Ibrahim families, including the catalyst for their acrimony, recent developments in this feuding and, of course, the tentative plotting to seek retribution against them, which at that stage Abdy wasn't too concerned with. And why would he be? From what Ayman was telling his handler, no one even knew where to find John Macris.

From what Abdy could gather, the conflict had started over a nightclub refurbishment, but the story went back much further, back to the mid 1990s when John Ibrahim was running the EP1 nightclub and John Macris was a club guy who hung around the Cross on the weekends. The two Johns met through the club scene and saw each other on most weekends, eventually becoming friends and drinking together whenever they bumped into each other. A stint in prison took Macris out of this circuit for a while; it was a drugs charge that saw him arrested in 2000 and dragged through the courts – he was sentenced, then appealed, then retried, then finally released in 2006.

Once out of prison, he got back into the building trade, which is what he'd been doing before his arrest. He hadn't seen or heard from John Ibrahim in years until suddenly, just months after his release, Ibrahim reached out with a proposition. He needed someone to remodel his nightclub on Oxford Street, Mr Goodbar, and he figured Macris, fresh out of jail, would be interested in the work.

Macris hesitated. He didn't want to be involved with the Ibrahim family or John's hot new club. It wasn't personal, but there had been stories.

Ibrahim twisted his arm, gently.

By Christmas 2006 Macris had dropped nearly $300,000 on the Mr Goodbar fitout and still hadn't received a single payment in return. He approached Ibrahim to talk, telling him the club needed another $100,000 before it would be finished.

According to evidence later given by Macris, Ibrahim shrugged and said he didn't have the cash to pay him for the work he'd done. That would only happen, he said, once the club had opened and they could spin a profit from the drink sales. But, Ibrahim continued, if Macris was prepared to finish the job using his own money, then he could become a partner in the venture and take a share of the profits indefinitely.

Macris figured that Ibrahim was a showman of sorts and his clubs generally appeared to be extremely successful. He took the deal and kept his mouth shut, funnelling more cash into the business and holding out for the big payday when the club finally opened. When that day came, however, all that arrived was bitter disappointment. Whenever Macris asked about his share of the weekly takings, Ibrahim told him there was nothing to hand over. The club was barely breaking even each week – no one knew why it wasn't taking off.

Things got more complicated when Macris's younger brother Alex entered the picture. He was nine years younger than his brother and had become close to the Ibrahims while John Macris was in prison, at one point even working for Michael Ibrahim as a driver, or so Michael had told people, and had done some work as a money collector for the family.

Alex had his own business ventures running independently of his brother, including one with Michael Ibrahim. When the deal went sour, resulting in a debt of $1.2 million, the Ibrahims turned to John Macris to step in for Alex and pick up the debt.

This was hammered home to John Macris one day when he sought out another meeting with the Ibrahims about the $400,000 he was owed over the Mr Goodbar nightclub refurbishments. Instead of being given back his money, he was told that his equity was being taken away to pay off the debt Alex had incurred – the precise nature of this debt cannot be printed; suffice to say it was a business deal of sorts.

Macris didn't understand the logic. It wasn't his debt to pay, he said, but he was told it didn't matter. Alex wasn't capable of paying back the money, so John Macris was told he would have to cover him. Once the $400,000 share was factored in, John and his brother were told they now owed the Ibrahim family a balance payment of $800,000.

From then on, both the Macris brothers avoided Kings Cross, staying away from the Ibrahims and their clubs across the city. It didn't stop the Ibrahims finding them, however. One afternoon John Macris was sitting in traffic when someone leaned through his open window and tried to punch him in the face. When he looked up he saw Fadi Ibrahim standing by the car with a group of burly Islander men behind him. They ran off a moment later, possibly due to the moving traffic; the fight was over before Macris had any time to react. There were other incidents, a drive-by shooting, a kidnapping, which law enforcement had discovered.

But the most critical incident happened a few weeks prior to Fadi's shooting when a fight broke out at the Ivy nightclub in Sydney's CBD. Fadi had spotted his girlfriend, Shayda, speaking to Alex Macris on the dancefloor. They were old friends, so this wasn't unusual. In fact, Alex had introduced Shayda to her ex-boyfriend, Faouxi Abou-Jibal, not long before his untimely murder in March 2006.

As Alex and Shayda continued talking, Fadi emerged from the darkness and threw a punch, hitting Alex in the face and putting him on the floor. As far as motives went, at least for Detective Abdy, the fight seemed like one of the strongest lines of enquiry yet for the shooting that followed a few weeks later, far greater than any of the other historic feuds or theories touted so far. From that moment on, Abdy began looking far more closely at the Macris brothers as his chief line of enquiry.

*

The investigation into Fadi Ibrahim's attempted murder was given the codename of Strike Force Proudfoot. It was split into two competing tranches of enquiry on the basis of Ayman's incoming intelligence. On one side was the need to solve the shooting, which had a field of suspects and a couple of good leads. On the other side was the payback hit against the Macris brothers, particularly John

Macris, that was gathering steam from behind the bars of Broken Hill Correctional Centre.

Ayman couldn't say exactly how, but Michael Ibrahim had managed to get his hands on a smuggled phone in the prison, which allowed him to call out at all hours and check on the progress of the Macris plot. It also gave him more control.

The original plan had been to use Ayman as the triggerman, but this had now changed, Ayman told his handler, explaining that Michael thought of him as an unreliable character, someone who didn't always answer the phone and disappeared for days on end. And he was right: Ayman had no intention of shooting anyone and, being a police informant, he planned to stifle the plot at every turn. Frustrated by Ayman, Michael had contracted a new hitman to go get Macris once he'd been located, someone he considered to be a professional in this field: his name was Rodney 'Goldie' Atkinson.

Michael spoke about Atkinson in glowing terms. During one call to Allan Sarkis, the president of Notorious, he described the debt collector as a 'good kid', someone who could get any job done like a soldier. 'You tell him go, he'll go,' Ibrahim said in the recorded conversation. 'He won't come back till it's done.'

It had only been a few weeks since Fadi had been shot and Abdy still regarded any talk of reprisal as premature. For one thing, none of Ibrahim's cohorts had been able to locate Macris or where he lived and, secondly, immigration records suggested he was out of the country on holiday for at least another month, or so Abdy had gathered from the departure card Macris had filled out at the airport.

Still, he had concerns, particularly with the entry of Atkinson to the frame. His involvement raised the stakes and showed a much stronger level of commitment to carrying out some kind of retributive plot. Until then, it had all been just talk. Abdy had seen it a hundred times before: a big-noting crook swears revenge on an enemy only to sleep on it and move on within a week when it becomes apparent that a gun and triggerman aren't so easy to find.

Of course Abdy had heard of Rodney Atkinson, the famed underworld enforcer. He had been one of the key targets from the Strike Force Skelton investigation into Bassam Hamzy during 2008. He was also under investigation by the NSW Crime Commission over the unsolved murder of Todd O'Connor, a manager of the Mr Goodbar nightclub in Paddington. O'Connor, aged forty-one, had been mysteriously gunned down at a park in Tempe on 5 October 2008 while picking up a debt, which police claimed was being collected on behalf of Fadi Ibrahim. The autopsy pulled three bullets from his head and seven of a different calibre from his body, indicating two gunmen, neither of whom have ever been caught.

Atkinson hadn't been arrested or charged by Memmolo's team over his dealings with Bassam Hamzy. Not yet, anyway. At the time of Fadi's shooting in June 2009, he was still a free man, still out on the streets and meeting with Michael Ibrahim at Broken Hill Correctional Centre, or so the jail's visitor logs revealed. Records would show that Atkinson turned up at the jail twice – on 1 July and 5 July. On both occasions he'd arrived under the name Castro Gard'e, an alias police had on file.

Meanwhile, Abdy turned his attention back to Fadi, who doctors had brought out of his induced coma. A 24-hour police guard had been posted outside his room for protection. Listening devices had been hidden inside to record conversations, but they had picked up nothing of value to the investigation.

Fadi's recollection of his shooting, which he agreed to recount to Abdy, was vague. He hadn't recognised the attacker and couldn't remember much at all, save for the gunshots. Abdy wasn't surprised.

He didn't expect that Fadi would be much help to the investigation – the code of the street and all that – but he also believed that, as a victim, Fadi was probably telling the truth about having a memory lapse. Most shooting victims suffer the same thing from the trauma of being shot; Abdy had seen it before.

The detective dropped the names of certain people to try to stimulate Fadi's memory and gauge his reactions. John Macris and Alex Macris were mentioned in passing.

'I don't think it was them,' Fadi said. 'I've got no clue who it was.'

Was he being truthful? Abdy couldn't tell. Did Fadi know a reprisal attack was being planned? Had he been told in advance to play down his suspicion of the Macris family? Anything was possible, Abdy thought. The rest of the hospital visit was spent listening to Fadi justify every dollar he'd ever earned as he implored Abdy to stop viewing him as a gangster. 'I'm a builder,' he said. Abdy laughed. 'You've never built anything in your life.'

Later he would hear Fadi talk candidly about the shooting in subsequent phone calls to his brothers, always sticking to the same line about doubting Macris. Abdy remained skeptical, but Fadi's tone suggested he was genuinely clueless about why he'd been shot. Then again, Abdy thought, Fadi probably knew his calls were being monitored.

*

The next time Jack called Smithers, his handler at the Gangs Squad, he'd just come back from another visit to Broken Hill Correctional Centre. It was 17 July and his role by then had been dialled up significantly. Previously Michael Ibrahim had asked Jack to find Macris's address. Now he wanted him to get a photograph of his face as well. Jack mentioned none of this to Smithers. All he told her was what Abdy's team already knew: that Macris was a target for retribution and plans were being made for a get-square.

In doing this, Jack was playing both sides. He was pretending to help Michael Ibrahim plan his conspiracy plot, and he was also pretending to help police by feeding them inconsequential details. What he didn't realise was that Ayman had been steadily feeding back the real story to Abdy's team, which put Jack squarely in the frame as a middleman in the plot, even though he was, technically, assisting police.

Not that Abdy was aware of this assistance. He didn't know that Jack was an informant working for the Gangs Squad; all he knew was that Smithers had a source somewhere in the Ibrahim camp providing intelligence. Conversely, and somewhat ironically, Smithers didn't know that Jack had become a central target of Abdy's investigation, or that his mobile phone calls were being intercepted – she was just taking down the information and passing it to Abdy, whose days were being spent listening to incoming and outgoing telephone calls from several numbers; it was one of the few ways he could monitor the conspiracy plot against Macris and how it was developing. Weeks passed in this way. In addition to Jack's phone, he had intercepts running on Michael Ibrahim's smuggled jail phone, Rodney Atkinson's phone and Fadi Ibrahim's phone. Whenever they changed numbers, Ayman would come to the rescue.

Fadi's calls seemed to indicate a growing frustration at the progress of Abdy's investigation. The field was wide open with persons of interest, including the Macris brothers, but there were no firm suspects in the mix. Abdy had even shown Fadi the CCTV footage of the attack in the hope it might jog his memory, which it didn't.

But Fadi's main gripe was being stuck at home; here was a guy who drove fast cars and ate out in fancy restaurants and now, because he'd been shot, even simple tasks had become a burden.

'I'm like a fuckin' disabled person,' he said to his brother Michael during one call in early August. 'I don't want to leave the house, I can't defend myself. It stresses the fuck out of me. Before ... I could defend myself. It's shit.'

Abdy was paying close attention to these conversations. He wanted to know if Michael would make admissions about the plot against Macris. He also wondered if Fadi was already aware of it. At that stage, it wasn't clear. Abdy waited for Macris's name to be mentioned, but there was a conspicuous lack of dialogue about him, which in itself was suspicious. Why weren't they mentioning him? Michael was actively trying to find him and yet he was saying nothing over the phone. Two reasons for this sprang to mind: either Michael was taking care of the matter quietly and keeping Fadi out of it, or the conversations were staged. Abdy kept listening as the men vented their frustration and confusion about the identity of the assassin.

'When your little brother Mick gets out he's going to find him,' Michael said of the gunman. 'I'm going to cut off his head, I'm going to stick it on the front post of his house.'

'But that's the thing, Mick,' Fadi said. 'None of us know who he is.'

Michael moved to reassure him. 'In time, brother. In time it will come out.'

Two weeks later Jack was summoned back to Broken Hill Correctional Centre for a progress update on finding Macris. He still hadn't found an address or photograph. At the airport he spotted Fadi Ibrahim at the boarding gate with an entourage around him – guys from Kings Cross like Semi 'Tongan Sam' Ngata, the Ibrahim family's long-standing security guard, and Jim 'Sid' Habkouk, another close friend who acted as a driver and gofer for the family. With Jack included they were a group of six heading to the prison. For Fadi, it was the first time he was seeing his brother since the shooting.

They walked through the gates of Broken Hill Correctional Centre and took seats in the visiting area, a few minutes before Michael walked out. Fadi showed a more playful side to his character, hiding between two vending machines and surprising his brother by jumping out when he arrived. Afterwards Fadi lifted his shirt and showed off his scars, telling Michael about how awful it had been to be cooped up at home. He'd been recuperating at their mother's house.

Jack couldn't hear what was said, but he saw Michael lean in and whisper something in Fadi's ear. Whatever it was, Fadi seemed to reel at what he heard. Jack figured it must have been about Macris.

'Are you sure?' Fadi asked. He seemed genuinely surprised by what he'd just heard. 'I thought it was someone else,' he said.

A few hours later, as the group of six walked through the streets of Broken Hill looking for a place to grab lunch, Fadi motioned to Jack to fall behind a few steps to speak in private. Their conversation gravitated quickly towards Macris.

'So, is this thing going to happen quickly?' he asked.

Jack said locating John Macris was still a problem. 'Nobody knows where he is,' he said.

'I can help you with that,' Fadi replied. As it turned out, his girlfriend, Shayda, had gone to university with John Macris's girlfriend, Aimee Fischer-Gray, and had been to their house in Chippendale for study group assignments. Macris had been uncomfortable about it too. He'd even asked Shayda to keep the location a secret.

A few days later Fadi called Jack to a meeting in the car park of Royal North Shore Hospital where he was having a check-up for his injuries. As Jack approached, Fadi pulled out a real estate brochure from his pocket and passed it when they shook hands. The brochure went straight into Jack's pocket. He didn't even look at it.

'Please … don't fuck around. Get it done ASAP,' Fadi said. 'I need it.'

Jack nodded and reached back into the pocket, placing a protective hand around the folded brochure.

On the drive home he took it out and looked at the address: it was a house in Chippendale in the inner-city of Sydney.

Jack's instructions were to pass the address to Rodney Atkinson, the triggerman. Michael had been telling him this during their conversations. But Jack barely knew Atkinson. He didn't feel like he could trust him. Instead, he called Ayman, still none the wiser to his suspicious behaviour. Somehow, every time Ayman had been asked to do something, it never got done and his phone was always off whenever he was needed most.

They met at a car wash in Parramatta and then walked to a nearby café where they ordered coffee and split a banana bread. Jack had a backpack with him and pulled out an envelope with a slip of paper inside. He'd already thrown out the brochure Fadi had given him, ripping it up and flushing it down the toilet. It was evidence, he thought; if for some reason the brochure ever got seized by the police, his fingerprints would be found all over it. To cover himself, he'd slipped on a pair of latex gloves and transcribed the address with his left hand, to mask his handwriting.

Ayman took the envelope and assured Jack he would deliver it straight to Atkinson. Then they walked back to the car wash where Ayman's Mercedes-Benz was waiting, driving off in separate directions – Jack heading back east to the city and Ayman heading to a park where he'd arranged to meet his handler from MEOCS, Jeffrey Hohnen. At the park, Hohnen took the envelope and studied the address on the slip of paper, immediately noticing a problem: it was the wrong house. John Macris didn't live at the address but at the property next door.

With the efforts to get Macris suddenly accelerating, Abdy drove out to his house and decided to inform him his life might be in danger. Abdy hadn't seen any great need to tell him up until this point – Macris had only just returned from his overseas holiday and, until the developments of that afternoon, the plot to assassinate him had been stifled at every turn. Even now, Ayman had delivered the address to police instead of Atkinson like he'd promised, buying the investigation a bit more time. That said, even if Ayman had kept his word, Atkinson still needed a photo of Macris and a gun to get moving.

Security cameras were installed around Macris's property and he was told to remove all his pictures from Facebook. Abdy suggested he move into a hotel room temporarily and gave the same direction to his neighbours in the townhouse next door. It was their address that was mistakenly provided to Jack on the real estate brochure. Having been told the NSW Police Force would pay for their accommodation, the middle-aged couple promptly booked a room at the five-star Sheraton on the Park Hotel in the CBD, leaving the Force to pick up the astounding tab.

*

Michael Ibrahim fumed at Jack when he found out he had delivered the address to Ayman rather than Atkinson. Threats were made and Jack was accused of bringing the whole plot to another grinding halt. When asked, Jack lied about Atkinson and said he'd lost his phone number. Michael didn't buy it. He raged at Jack, shouting down the line that he'd been useless at every turn, almost traitorous, whether it was finding an address for Macris, a photograph of him, or making a simple delivery like he'd been instructed.

Jack's problem had been his conscience. He didn't want to be part of any plot to have Macris killed, but at the same time he wanted to stay ingratiated with the Ibrahims and work his way into their inner circle.

Fearing his life may depend on it, he drove to Fadi Ibrahim's house to ask for his help. Jack thought that if he could get a photograph and deliver it with the address then he might redeem himself to Michael. The house was immaculate; it looked like the interior of a designer showroom, filled with modern furniture and reflective ornaments. Jack pulled up a chair next to Fadi at a long table in the dining room where a laptop was set up. Using Shayda's Facebook profile, they accessed Macris's girlfriend's page and printed off a picture of Macris in a grey t-shirt at a party. It was cut down to a reasonable size, printed and placed into an A4 envelope, which was delivered that night to Atkinson with another copy of Macris's address, written down with the same precautions as last time. It was all for nothing, though. By then Atkinson had already been given a photograph of Macris, receiving it from Jim 'Sid' Habkouk, the Ibrahim family's driver and confidante. Tired of Jack's bullshit, Michael just called Habkouk and asked him to make the delivery and get things moving.

With the photograph and address in place, the only thing missing was a gun. For Brad Abdy, this meant it was time to make a few decisions. He had a solid 'telephone brief', as it's known in the police force, a circumstantial case made up of tapped phone calls and coded conversations. With Ayman's evidence to corroborate the phone calls, he felt the investigation was in a good position to make arrests. But even Abdy knew a jury would need more proof of what kind of conspiracy was being planned. Was Michael Ibrahim trying to kill Macris or simply rob him for money? For the case to succeed Abdy needed to prove definitively that the goal was murder. Without a gun or something more substantial to suggest that a slaying was on the cards, there was ample room for a good defence lawyer to throw enough doubt at a jury and tell them that, sure, a conspiracy was afoot to steal, or bash, or harm; but not to kill anyone.

A decision was made to keep the investigation running a bit longer – a gun would be a compelling piece of evidence to put before a jury and Abdy knew that Atkinson was in the process of trying to find one.

This had been another sticking point in the conspiracy plot. A new gun was expensive, costing anywhere between $5000 and $10,000, depending on the type of weapon. Abdy read the intercepted text messages between Atkinson and Michael and could see the frustration building. All sorts of factors had to be nailed down: the cash, the transfer, finding the gun itself from a willing buyer.

Finally, on 12 September, Atkinson wrote a text message to Michael Ibrahim: 'Got a girl, she's hot, need 7, get them to put it in my TAB account.' Abdy knew this was code. Atkinson was asking for $7000 to buy a handgun.

Abdy's plan was to wait until Atkinson had picked up the gun and, only then, move in for an arrest. Atkinson was placed under close surveillance and scrutinised to make sure the weapon didn't sneak into his hands without their knowledge; they couldn't afford to wait – once he had the gun, it was time to move.

As these preparations were made, Abdy reached out to Smithers and asked her to set up a meeting with her source. By then, Abdy had become aware that Jack was her informant – the penny had dropped during one of their phone conversations. Something twigged as the two detectives compared notes – Abdy had a realisation and he asked Smithers directly.

They all met at Burnside Gardens, a park area in Oatlands northwest of the CBD, right next to Parramatta. Jack was there with his lawyer. Abdy arrived a few minutes later, walking over with Smithers standing next to him.

Abdy told Jack that there was evidence implicating him in the plot to have John Macris killed. Discussions had been overheard which suggested he'd been complicit in the search for Macris's address and photograph. Jack nodded, saying nothing. He kept listening as Abdy outlined arrangements that could help him evade the charges. Abdy wanted Jack to roll and suggested he wear a body wire to record some conversations with Michael Ibrahim. Jack said no. It was too dangerous. The other option, Abdy said, was to make a formal statement to police, co-operate fully, and give evidence in court. Jack nodded and said he would consider his options. He wasn't a fan of any of those proposals.

Before they parted Abdy asked Jack if he knew the name of the triggerman hired to shoot Macris. It was a throwaway question, a test to see if he would tell the truth. Abdy, of course, already knew that Rodney 'Goldie' Atkinson was being paid to do the job.

Jack said he didn't know. Another lie.

Two days later, the arrests began.

Abdy knocked hard on the front door of Atkinson's townhouse, calling out for him to open up.

'Rodney,' Abdy shouted into the door. 'We have a search warrant!'

It was about 8:30am, Wednesday, 24 September. The townhouse was located on Penelope Lucas Lane, just across the road from Rose Hill racecourse. Standing behind Abdy were half a dozen detectives, including one with a camera to film the search.

Surveillance officers had watched Atkinson meet a gun supplier the previous night at Parramatta railway station, a man who had brought the weapon, a German made Ruger pistol, all the way from Newcastle. With the gun in play, the decision had been made to move on Atkinson first thing in the morning.

He opened the door wide and greeted the detectives cordially, signalling his intention to co-operate. He inspected the warrant and its mechanical, itemised contents: 'firearm parts', 'ammunition'. Abdy asked whether any of the items listed were inside his house.

'Oh, fuckin' heaps,' Atkinson said.

As Atkinson was read his rights, search officers moved through the doorway and spread out across each room unzipping bags and opening drawers. One of the search officers, looked in a cupboard above the fridge and found a Ruger pistol in plain sight with a silencer jammed onto it. Next came a hit-kit a few minutes later. Inside it was a police badge and business cards belonging to a serving officer, two latex gloves, a .45-calibre pistol, a photograph of John Macris, and a torn piece of envelope with the address in Chippendale written on it.

Across town, Fadi Ibrahim, still recuperating and requiring ongoing medical treatment, presented himself to Waverley Police Station with his solicitor and was placed under arrest. He'd been summoned by phone to appear while the search of Atkinson's home was continuing. This happened often during arrests considered low risk. Ibrahim declined to be interviewed at the station and was taken into custody. It was front-page news the next morning: three months since he'd been shot, Fadi Ibrahim was being accused of orchestrating the payback. Both he and Atkinson were charged with conspiracy to murder. Charges against Michael Ibrahim and Jim 'Sid' Habkouk followed soon after.

Abdy watched Jack to see how he would react to the arrests. The hope was that he would read about the charges in the paper and contact detectives to make a deal. Abdy waited but never heard from him. Three days later he was arrested outside his solicitor's office and charged with the same offence as the others: conspiracy to murder.

Jack turned down several offers to make a statement while in custody. Each time detectives would visit, he sent them away empty handed, telling them he would think about his options. 'I still haven't made up my mind,' he said on 2 November to some detectives who came to visit.

Abdy already had Ayman on his side, ready to assist and give evidence in court, a brave move, but Ayman had his motives, namely the drug charges he was facing in Victoria. Abdy felt that a statement from Jack would make his case irrefutable. With Jack, the prosecution case would have not one but two people directly involved in the conspiracy giving evidence against the Ibrahim brothers and their alleged co-offenders.

On 29 January, Jack finally agreed to make one of two statements to police in exchange for an indemnity against prosecution. After three months of telling Abdy he was still weighing his options, Jack was moved to the protection wing of Long Bay Correctional Centre where he gave a 45-page recap of everything that had taken place during the conspiracy plot – from his first meeting with Michael Ibrahim in prison to the day he delivered Macris's photograph to Rodney Atkinson.

The case went to trial in good shape. Abdy had Atkinson with a hit-kit in his house, recordings of Michael Ibrahim, and two pivotal players attesting to the fact that every recorded phone conversation, analysed by the Strike Force Bellwood detectives, had been geared towards shooting John Macris.

But as the case proceeded in court it took several knocks. First, Fadi Ibrahim was ruled unfit to stand trial due to his injuries, a bitter blow for the detectives. They'd worked hard to bring him to the dock, but his lawyers successfully argued he was too ill to attend the proceedings and so the charges were withdrawn.

Then the charge against Jim 'Sid' Habkouk, which arose out of an allegation that he had delivered a photograph of Macris to Atkinson, was thrown out of court. His defence lawyer had successfully argued that Habkouk had delivered an envelope to Atkinson but no evidence had been produced to show that he knew what was inside of it.

That left Michael Ibrahim and Rodney Atkinson in the stand. Both defendants pleaded not guilty to their charges of conspiracy to murder, which, on the strength of the police case, seemed unwinnable.

Defence lawyers for both Ibrahim and Atkinson mounted the argument that their clients had intended to collect money from Macris rather than kill him.

Their joint trial had proceeded smoothly until a television news report, revolving around an unrelated shooting that mentioned members of the Ibrahim family, derailed everything. Fearing the jury might be prejudiced by the coverage, the judge ordered a new trial and empanelled a new jury for hearings starting in April 2012. From here, everything went downhill.

For reasons that weren't clear – though rumours of a cash incentive did make their way back to Abdy – Ayman fled the country before the second trial commenced, sending a text message to Abdy in advance to apologise for his absence.

Without Ayman, the trial drew more heavily on Jack's evidence to prove the conspiracy – Jack, after all, had intimate knowledge of the plot and remembered Michael Ibrahim's conversations, his statement laying out their many discussions in exquisite detail. In court, however, his chequered past was laid bare as Ibrahim's and Atkinson's lawyers went to work on him, their attacks designed to prove he was a self-serving drug dealer who was only giving evidence under indemnity to save himself. He was painted to the jury as a liar and pretender, a man who admitted to supplying drugs, procuring chemicals and taking acting classes, revelations that all caught the prosecution off guard.

The killer blow came when Jack was asked about lengthy interviews he had given to officers with the NSW Crime Commission while he was still in prison. These had occurred before he'd agreed to co-operate with the NSW Police Force.

Damning comments were made during these interviews with the commission. Jack was asked about allegations he'd made against the Bellwood detectives, including Brad Abdy, suggesting they had threatened and coerced him into making a statement. Abdy and his colleagues flatly denied the allegations, but, in front of the jury, this dirty laundry was untidy and difficult to explain. Consider: if

Jack's statement had been forced by coercion, then his credibility was ruined. If he was lying about being threatened then, well, he was a liar and his evidence would still lose all credibility. Either way, the revelations shattered the evidence of their only witness and snookered the prosecution case.

On 10 December 2012, the jury acquitted both Michael Ibrahim and Rodney Atkinson of conspiring to murder John Macris, finding that it couldn't be proved beyond a reasonable doubt that they had intended to kill him, rather than rob him.

Atkinson pleaded guilty to possession of the firearms found during the search warrant on his home, which saw him handed a minimum seven years in prison. He successfully appealed this sentence in November 2014 and it was dropped to a term of five years and three months.

It was while serving out his sentence for possession of firearms that Atkinson received a visit from Strike Force Skelton detectives. Having finally collated all their evidence and tied up each loose end, they were ready to charge Atkinson over the alleged kidnapping of South Australian drug dealer John Baroutas back in June 2008. The case proceeded to court but was eventually thrown out on a legal technicality – the charge had been set out based on NSW legislation and, therefore, wasn't applicable to a crime committed in South Australia.

He has since been released on parole and gone on to reinvent himself as a cage fighter, telling a newspaper in 2016 of his struggle to find contenders, based on his reputation: 'I have had heaps of fights lined up, but they all pulled out after Googling me.'

CHAPTER ELEVEN

GANGS OF AUBURN

Late one night in the spring of 2009 the glass entry to Auburn Base Hospital slid open to reveal Manih Zaoud at the entrance. A nurse took one look at him and rushed over with a stretcher. His arms were draped around two friends and he was staggering inside with a gunshot wound to his chest.

Within minutes, two local officers had arrived at the hospital – standard protocol states that police get called for anyone presenting with gunshot wounds. They stood at Zaoud's bedside once he was out of surgery, under no false illusions that he would actually speak to them. Barely into his twenties, Zaoud was a member of one of Auburn's most prominent families and was, along with his brothers, a senior figure of the Muslim Brotherhood Movement. They were a street crew dominating in the area, one that acted as a feeder group to the Bandidos outlaw motorcycle gang, providing fresh blood to its ranks. When the officers asked Zaoud what had happened, he just shook his head; another unco-operative victim.

This had become a common theme in Auburn. Gunshots rang out, people got hurt, and no one saw anything. Problems were sorted in-house, handled between families. Officers would turn up to the hospital and hear the same excuse each time: 'I was jogging in a park and I just felt something sting my leg. Didn't see anything.'

By 2009, Auburn had become a classic MEOC enclave swarming with gang activity, much like the no-go zone of Telopea Street, Punchbowl, had been before it. Union Road was notorious, a street where police had to abide by a separate set of operating procedures. Police cars had been smashed with rocks. House bricks and full cans of soft drink were thrown from behind the walls of houses. Officers were told not to drive along the street without heavy backup.

Two streets over was Pine Road, home of the Dib family. Their house had been shot up almost as many times as it had been raided. An ugly brick wall had been built around it to keep the bullets out. They had two sons, both influential characters in the area. One of them, Mahmoud Dib, was a senior member of the Bandidos Parramatta Chapter, its sergeant-at-arms no less.

Over the years, several gangs had planted their flag over the area, but in 2009 it was the Bandidos who carried the numbers. The suburb was a cauldron of hostility and mixed allegiances: there were members of the gang living alongside freshly recruited members of Notorious, the street crew founded by Michael Ibrahim. There were Hells Angels living on Norval Street and Comancheros on Albert Street. Added to this powderkeg were several prominent crime families: the Hamzys lived in Auburn, as did the Kalaches.

The result was an area that led an evolutionary trend sweeping through Sydney's underworld: the union of Middle Eastern criminals and outlaw motorcycle gangs. Jacked up on steroids and unfazed about squeezing a trigger, Middle Eastern criminals were the perfect recruits for gangs trying to bolster their numbers. They were reckless hotheads who taunted rivals and didn't suffer the consequences. A gang stacked with Middle Eastern crime figures was a gang at war with something. They picked fights and wrested back drug turf. But they came with perks, acting like ambassadors to local crime families that controlled territory and wielded power. Eventually, someone put two and two together: the gangs had the drugs and the families had the turf. Combining both was a marriage of convenience, much like what the institution was first created for, a merger designed to set down roots, increase business opportunities, grab land and maximise wealth. And that's what happened: the gangs got their territory and, in return, the families got an army.

The Muslim Brotherhood Movement (MBM) worked within this environment, recruiting from a pool of impressionable young people who worked out in the gyms and hung out in cafés. The four Zaoud brothers were the shotcallers of this crew, their central meeting place a converted pool hall on Auburn's Cumberland Road, the Rolling 8-Ball café. MEOCS detectives and local police had kept this café under close surveillance since it opened, about a month before Manih Zaoud was shot on 7 September. The site had previously been known as the House of Pain gym and owned by the Kalache family. Police intelligence suggested the café was a front, its name a not-so-subtle hint at the trade taking place inside – an eight-ball being the street reference to one-eighth of an ounce of cocaine, or 3.5 grams. When the café was raided in the same year it opened, a bag of ecstasy pills was discovered behind the counter. The owner of the pills, however, was not identified.

To Deb Wallace, the Commander of MEOCS, the MBM were a ragtag bunch, a disorganised rabble, poorly led and lacking a hierarchy or any sense of discipline. They stood for nothing. Even the gang's name was a rip-off, stolen from a political movement based in the Middle East. But even though it lacked a direction, the shooting of Manih Zaoud presented a challenge for law enforcement. As a figurehead of the street gang, the expectation was that Zaoud would recover from his injuries and then mount a reprisal attack on the man who had shot him. It's an old adage at MEOCS, one of many: today's victim is tomorrow's shooter. The priority was to prevent more violence.

The case fell to Detective Senior Sergeant Paul O'Neill, a team leader in the TAG office. O'Neill was a natural at procuring informants, one of the best. He studied Arabic in his spare time and was someone who could keep criminals talking for hours until they were admitting things even he was surprised to hear: how powerless they felt on the streets; the arrogance of young gang members; the lack of respect for the older generation.

O'Neill had street assets all over Auburn – 'the hood mail' as it was known around the office – and within a few phone calls he knew everything he needed to know about the Zaoud shooting. It was over a car, a deal that went sour. Zaoud had been the buyer. Negotiations broke down and, for reasons best known to the seller – another MEOC identity in the area – a gun was pulled and pointed at Zaoud. He took one in the chest while the man standing next to him came under fire, emerging uninjured. That man was Rabii Kalache, one of the strongmen of Auburn, barely a year out of prison after fifteen years in maximum security. O'Neill could see this was still going to be a big problem. Shooting Manih Zaoud was one thing, but taking on a Kalache was probably worse.

The gunman went underground almost immediately; even he knew he was in trouble. He was a marked man and everyone in Auburn knew it. O'Neill went into damage control to try to find him, visiting his friends and relatives. O'Neill didn't want to arrest him, he wanted to warn him – there was a duty of care at play. Sure, the gunman had shot a man but the need to prevent a homicide took precedence.

Most of the man's relatives slammed the door in O'Neill's face. They didn't trust the police at the best of times. Behind the scenes he worked the phones trying to get in contact with the gunman, calling around, looking for phone numbers, trying to reach people who could get a message to him in hiding. Squad cars were stationed outside his family's home to ensure the people inside didn't become collateral damage. Within a day more intelligence had come through about the retribution: the gun that would be used in the attack was being hidden in a house on Cumberland Road, across the road from the Rolling 8-Ball café. An emergency search warrant followed to search the house in the late afternoon of 9 September, a move that risked raising the ire of the local community – it was the middle of Ramadan and the execution was slated for 6pm, right smack in the middle of the time families would be breaking their fast.

For O'Neill and his superiors, the imperative to move was strong: wait until the morning and the gun could be gone. Informants were suggesting it could even be used that night. By 6pm he was standing outside a home owned by the Hadife family, a premises rated low risk on intelligence databases for any kind of assault. There were only a few reports on file for the people living inside. They were clean. A young man living there had once put his feet up on a train carriage seat – that was the extent of their criminality. Across the road, more officers were preparing to raid the Rolling 8-Ball café. Above them was a PolAir chopper with a camera rolling in case the scenes got wild, which they soon did.

The café, rated as a medium risk of violence, was an easy search carried out with no issues. It was the Hadife family property which became an unlikely scene of violence. Members of the household raged against officers at their door for executing their warrant during Ramadan. A punch was thrown, cutting a senior constable's forehead open. A woman jumped on another officer's back. In the chaos a pulse of capsicum spray ricocheted and hit O'Neill near the eyes, turning his face a deep shade of orange.

A post on social media called for residents to gather at the scene. 'Kefeirs raiding brother's house, everyone get down hier!!' the message said, using the slang word to refer to non-Muslims. About 200 people appeared, threatening to push through the perimeter created by police officers. Bottles were thrown, but no injuries were noted. Eventually, after a few hours, the crowd dispersed with the help of local leaders who called for calm.

The next day O'Neill received a phone call directly from Ken McKay asking for a report into the incident. McKay had approved the warrant, but wanted to know the reasons for the flare up. The media had taken an interest in the story and some community representatives were suggesting heavy-handedness by police. It was the Ramadan aspect that everyone was interested in, creating a hot button question for debate: should the police have raided a house while families were breaking their fast? Most commentators said yes and applauded the police for their actions.

Some said no, arguing that the move was disrespectful. It was the kind of scenario that might have been canvassed back in 2006 when MEOCS officers attended the North Cronulla Surf Club for lectures on cultural sensitivities. What most critics overlooked was the fact that inside the backroom of the Hadife property was a stolen firearm, a dirty gun that had been doing the rounds of the underworld since it had gone missing in 2003.

McKay, the newly appointed Director of Organised Crime and former MEOCS commander, was happy to speak about this thorny issue on camera. To him, it was an open-and-shut case. At a press conference, he responded stridently to the claims that police had acted insensitively. 'A lot of people like to use excuses for their behaviour,' he told reporters. 'There's a way to solve that: don't commit crime. This is New South Wales. We have laws in this state we must all abide by and these people have to abide by the same laws.'

With the gun out of play and the risk of retribution cooling, O'Neill's team shifted away from the reprisal attack and refocused their efforts on Rabii Kalache. This was MEOCS methodology in action: you pick up a case, you mine it for new targets and then you plough forward into the next job. Over the course of the Zaoud investigation a wealth of information had come to light suggesting Rabii Kalache had been involved in significant movements of cocaine since his release from prison, buying ounces at a time in deals worth thousands of dollars.

The Kalaches were still considered high-profile, influential and sought-after players on the MEOCS radar. While Strike Force Skelton hadn't been successful in building a brief on any of the brothers, some of them had still been put in jail as a result of peripheral operations. Nasser Kalache, for example, had been given a four-year prison term in 2009 over a series of mortgage frauds dating back to 2003. Another brother, Bilal, was arrested at the family's Chester Hill pizza shop, Nasr's Gourmet Kitchen. He was wanted on outstanding warrants at the time, minor traffic matters, his arrest planned as a mini-sting.

It began with the arrival of Detective Vlad Mijok, in plain clothes, coming through the front door of the pizza shop. He approached the counter looking like any ordinary customer, but his true motive was to try to sight Bilal inside. The officers didn't know if he would be inside or not, so the effort was something of a gamble.

Standing near the back door, in case Bilal did a runner, were Detectives Dave Roberts and Tom Howes. They had planned everything with Mijok in advance. After a few minutes, Roberts called Mijok on his mobile.

'Did you get the special?' he asked, a coded question. It had been agreed between the officers that if Mijok said yes then it would signal that Bilal was in the shop. Mijok kept Roberts on the line until he saw Bilal moving around the back of the pizzeria and then said yes, he'd ordered the special, which prompted all three detectives to swarm at the same time.

Bilal was a professional boxer who had fought on the undercard of an Anthony Mundine fight. His arrest turned into a struggle and ended up on the footpath outside the shop, requiring all three officers to manhandle him to the ground. A search of his pockets turned up $5000 in cash. In his underwear were nine foil packets of heroin. Later, he would plead guilty to supply charges. As he was being led to the police car, an old man working in the pizza shop's kitchen ran outside. He was holding the pizza that Mijok had ordered; he wanted to know if any of the officers still wanted it.

With Nasser and Bilal locked up, and with Hassan Kalache still completing a 22-year sentence for murder, the opportunity to pursue a fourth Kalache brother on drug supply charges was something O'Neill found irresistible. Rabii's methodology was similar to many drug suppliers': he threw away his phone every two weeks and subscribed his new numbers with fake identities. A separate police squad had already been listening to Rabii's phone calls and passed their intelligence to O'Neill, propelling his case forward and expediting the arrest. When that day came six months later, in February 2010, Rabii was relaxed and easy about the vehicle stop that saw him pulled over in a Nissan X-Trail along

Cumberland road, Auburn. Cops pulled two mobile phones from his pockets along with six keys to a South Granville townhouse that had been under surveillance for months. Rabii insisted he didn't live there, but O'Neill didn't buy it; the Foxtel account was registered in the name of his wife. A surveillance detail had also captured him coming and going from the premises.

At the townhouse, O'Neill and his team moved through each room until they reached the bedroom upstairs. In a TV cabinet was a handgun and eighty-two rounds of ammunition. There were Medicare and student cards in Rabii's name along with tidy bundles of cash, which were counted back at the station and totalled $135,555. The gun alone would have been enough to send Rabii back to prison, but O'Neill got his big break in the wardrobe, finding just under 150 grams of cocaine packed into resealable freezer bags. Sent for lab testing, the purity was revealed to be as high as sixty-seven per cent. Good gear, O'Neill thought, barely any jump, which meant Rabii's supplier was probably close to the importer. Tests on one of the freezer bags gave the detective his next lead, a latent fingerprint belonging to a man living in Villawood. His name was Gehad Arja – barely any intelligence, few prior convictions. On paper, a nobody. His only brush with the law had been a drug supply charge he'd been acquitted of nearly a decade earlier after selling something to an undercover officer in Queensland. Apart from that, he was clean. O'Neill hadn't heard of him.

Informants told a different story about Arja, talking him up as one of the biggest movers of cocaine in southwestern Sydney, an upline guy with a strictly business approach and a very low profile – he dealt to a small, trusted circle of people, drove an average-looking car, lived in an ordinary-looking house, avoided conflict, and spoke very politely to people over the phone.

If anyone had a complaint, they could contact him directly. It was said he was moving up to a kilogram of cocaine a week, an astronomical amount – something in the vicinity of $250,000 worth of product. With a fingerprint on a bag, O'Neill had found his next case – he had gone from a shooting to a drug arrest and now he was on the precipice of the rarefied atmosphere of the upline supplier.

The investigation into Arja started from scratch, a cold start. There were no sources in his group, no one who could introduce an undercover agent, and no one who could wear a body wire to record a conversation. That meant months of work, minimum, but the rewards of success stood to be great. An informant put the challenge to O'Neill in these terms: 'You will never get him. He's too good.'

The investigation – Strike Force Gradwell – was launched in June 2010, sending O'Neill and his team deep into the backstreets of Villawood, the suburb where Arja's operation appeared to be based. Aside from a fingerprint on a drug package, they had his address – a house on Alcoomie Street – and a phone number, both of which had been pulled from standard government databases. From what it looked like, he wasn't trying to hide from anyone. Soon O'Neill was tapping into Arja's phone calls, getting bombarded with hours of useless chatter about family affairs and events for the kids. Everything about these conversations suggested he was nothing more than an ordinary father as opposed to the cocaine king of the southwestern suburbs. It was only when O'Neill and his team started looking closer at the house on Alcoomie Street that a few anomalies emerged.

For a start, it belonged to Arja's parents; he didn't live there, even though he'd listed it as his residence. Surveillance was a tricky task. The house was located on a street of eyeballs, a part of Villawood known as the Bronx, which had deteriorated into back blocks of long-term unemployment and generational welfare. The street itself felt like an old village: residents were distantly related and nosey about each other's affairs. Anything unfamiliar – a new face, a new car – came under close examination. That might sound like good old-fashioned community vigilance, but for police on observation it was a nightmare; you couldn't put a plainclothes cop anywhere near Alcoomie Street without someone walking over to ask a few questions.

In 1996 the television program A Current Affair took a film crew to Villawood to spend time at the local housing estate. A local gang known as the Villawood Bronx Boys had apparently hijacked the premises and turned it into a hive of drug activity. Among their key members was Gehad Arja, who was interviewed at length by journalist Mike Munro and made a point of showing Munro how the housing estate was rotting with neglect. That's why the local kids were taking up crime, he said. There were football fields with no goalposts, basketball courts with no hoops. The kids were bored, he said. 'They put up basketball courts for us, they take them down. They put up a football field, they take it away. They put up the swings, they take them away,' he told Munro. 'What do you expect little kids to do? What do you expect *us* to do?'

Villawood and Fairfield were Assyrian territory, areas with their own brand of extremely violent disputes and turf wars. On one side were the Bronx Boys, based in Villawood. Their rivals were the Fairfield-based Assyrian Kings, a gang whose members had been linked to the murder of a police officer in 1995 and then, much later, Dimitri Debaz, the Bronx Boys' leader. Debaz's killers, Raymond Youmaran and Raphael Joseph, had fled into hiding as an intense campaign of retribution played out to try to find them. People were kidnapped and tortured in a bid to pry information on the killers' whereabouts: a man was left in a burning car with his kneecaps shot out; another was found with his face sliced open and a caustic liquid poured onto his neck. A homemade bomb filled with nails was detonated outside the Youmaran family home and police who examined the device said that if someone had been standing nearby they would have been shredded to pieces.

Three months after starting his investigation into Gehad Arja, O'Neill had the necessary paperwork to put a covert camera somewhere near the Alcoomie Street property. This would solve his problem of how to run surveillance on the premises without getting burned by neighbours. His goal was to try to watch some of the people who he had overheard calling Arja and arranging to meet with him at his parents' property. These meetings had all the makings of drug transactions: a car would turn up, stay a few minutes, then disappear.

There was something about the house that had made O'Neill sit up and take notice. But as he felt his instincts gathering pace, he was coming up against an alternative force from Mick Ryan, the TAG commander. Ryan was growing impatient with the Gradwell investigation. Now into its third month, there had still been no firm evidence of any cocaine supply and while O'Neill had his suspicions, good ones, he had little else. In the meantime, the case was swallowing up staff and costing too much money in overtime. Installing cameras and listening to telephone intercepts were straining the TAG's budget and Ryan knew that to persist would mean months of investment. He gave O'Neill a couple more weeks and said that if he didn't get a result soon, or some type of stronger indication of supply to work with, the case would be shut down.

Within a few months of his conversation with Mick Ryan, O'Neill had added two new people to his target list in addition to

Gehad Arja. They were his older brother, Jamel Arja, and his cousin, Toufic Arja, both of whom he suspected either brought the cocaine to the Alcoomie Street property to sell to customers, or cut up the product and packaged it in the shed at the back of the house.

Mick Ryan still grew tired of the case and came to a compromise with O'Neill. In his view, an investigation like Strike Force Gradwell needed a full-time contingent of detectives, and a lot more of them to get the job done.

In late 2011, under an agreement between Ryan, the Squad's commander Deb Wallace, and Detective Inspector Mark Jones, a deal was reached to have Strike Force Gradwell moved from the TAG office up to the CI floor. Mark Jones was happy to absorb the project. His team was just coming off the final stage of another matter, Strike Force Caramana, which had made phenomenal seizures – ten kilograms of methamphetamine, four kilograms of pseudoephedrine and nine million black market cigarettes – and were interested in adopting an investigation that was already up and running.

The decision boosted O'Neill's team, taking it from four detectives to a team of sixteen. A year later, Strike Force Gradwell was still going and had ballooned into a long-term investigation that required extensive electronic surveillance and a beefed-up staff to manage it. Detectives jokingly renamed the case 'Strike Force Gradual' because it had taken so long to hit its stride. Over twelve months O'Neill had placed listening devices outside the Alcoomie Street property and into a shed at the back of the house where he suspected Arja had been packaging the cocaine. He had mounted operations to put tracking devices on cars, upgraded the camera equipment that had already been installed, and eventually identified the core members of Arja's syndicate and their modus operandi.

Several strokes of good luck followed. On one day, detectives were listening to one of Gehad Arja's phone calls when they heard what appeared to be a ringing sound coming from his pocket, revealing for the first time that he had a second number – a covert phone, as it's known – that he used strictly for his cocaine supply business. The discovery, while small and a bit late to the case, led to the unravelling of Arja's modus operandi. On his second phone, he spoke freely about his transactions.

Arja had his own style of dealing cocaine, one that was different to most of the other suppliers that the detectives had encountered. Every four to six weeks he would pull up outside his customers' homes and hand over a box with a brand-new mobile phone inside, a phone they could use to call him. It would only have one number programmed in its memory – Arja's number – which similarly changed every four to six weeks. He worked with a small group of clients, no more than ten people at a time, all of whom were buying several ounces of cocaine, big amounts that cost tens of thousands of dollars. Arja used a code when they spoke, a cipher he'd invented to throw off anyone listening – 'ounces' were referred to as 'sticks', the street name used to describe a $20 deal of cannabis. For a while, as a result of this code, there were some on O'Neill's team who became convinced the Arjas were supplying sticks of cannabis, rather than cocaine. With Arja's covert phone being intercepted and the listening devices in place, the case began to gather the kind of momentum that started making arrests seem possible in the near future. The audio had given them vital intelligence about where the cocaine was being stored, the names of Arja's biggest customers, the cutting agents he was using to dilute his cocaine, and other useful pieces of intelligence, like his plans to buy a pill press and potentially expand their operations.

But there were setbacks as well – technical problems that stood to jeopardise the entire investigation. In early 2011 the covert camera filming the drug deals outside the house on Alcoomie Street lost its feed, so a support team was dispatched to try to fix the problem. As they worked on the camera as discreetly as possible, Jamel Arja, Gehad's older brother, watched them from across the street, leaning against a car and casually smoking a cigarette.

Something must have twigged in his mind that the work was unusual. A few minutes after the feed was restored, O'Neill watched as an unfamiliar car drove past with a ladder attached to its roof. It appeared to slow down just past the camera, which then wobbled about a minute later and abruptly stopped working again. Pieces of the camera were later found in a park nearby.

A sardonic Gehad Arja turned up to Surry Hills Police Station a month later with a barrister in tow and a tracking device in his hand that had been found on his car. This was his way of letting the police know that he was aware of their investigation. Two uniformed officers met him in the station foyer, took the tracking device, said thank you, and then walked away without saying much more – O'Neill was watching Arja with a surveillance team nearby.

With both the camera and the tracking device uncovered it appeared the case was finished. Arja was well and truly aware that he was being watched by detectives; why else would he turn up at a police station to personally hand back a tracking device?

But one thing working in O'Neill's favour was Arja's sense of arrogance. The warning signs were there for him to take, but he refused to believe the cops had his syndicate worked out. The camera had been found outside the Alcoomie Street property and, in Arja's mind, that meant the police didn't know about his safe house, his covert phone, his routine drop-offs and his secret codes.

Let them raid the property, he must have thought. It's a front! What are they going to find? Spoons? Bowls? Trace elements of cocaine?

O'Neill knew that raiding the house on Alcoomie Street would amount to a waste of time, but he also knew that Arja was expecting the house to be searched; if it didn't happen, he would query why.

When officers arrived on 10 August 2011 they were welcomed inside and shown around, getting a tour of each room, the kitchen and even the shed at the back of the property where the Arjas routinely diluted their product. Both Gehad and Jamel co-operated fully during the search, addressing the officers as 'sir' and 'gentlemen' and answering all their questions. Gehad still claimed he was living at the property and showed officers his bedroom, which had no clothes in the cupboard.

The raid was mostly for show. No charges were laid, but some evidence was seized – bowls, cups, spoons, digital scales, fingerprints and DNA swabs. As the police cars pulled out of the driveway the Arjas waved to the officers and told them to come back any time. A month later, the detectives came back for real. They started at Gehad's house, arresting him and then using his phone to send a text message to his cousin Toufic. He was at his workshop in Condell Park when the message came through: 'Someone wants to see you, how long?' He responded, indicating he would pick up some cocaine and meet the buyer at his workshop. Officers followed him to the safe house, a two-storey home in Bass Hill, and then arrested him when he returned to the workshop. He was carrying two bags of cocaine at the time.

When O'Neill and a team of officers raided the safe house that day it was mostly empty; he suspected that the bulk of the product had just been sold. Had the investigation moved a bit earlier, it's likely that more cocaine would have been seized, resulting in greater sentences. All three men pleaded guilty to their charges and were out of prison within four years, which was less time than what was given to Rabii Kalache, who had been caught with a fraction of what the Arjas had supplied. O'Neill calculated that over the nine months they were under investigation, the Arjas trafficked 5.89 kilograms of cocaine.

One reason for the low sentence was their lack of any criminal record. While the trio had been moving kilos of cocaine, which should have attracted a much longer prison term, on paper they looked like cleanskins, first-time offenders when they went before the judge. Today, all three men are no longer in prison.

CHAPTER TWELVE

SIGNAL ONE

It takes a tragedy to make a change. After the death of Roni Levi on Bondi Beach in 1997, the cops introduced capsicum spray to their toolkit. The fatal shootings of two policeman at Crescent Head in 1995 saw them replace their revolvers with Glocks. The Lawford Street murders brought in Task Force Gain, a reaction to an out-of-control problem with Middle Eastern organised crime in southwestern Sydney. And Cairds Avenue, Bankstown, a low-risk raid to interrupt a drug deal, would change the face of modern-day search warrants across the NSW Police Force.

And yet it began like so many other search warrants that had come before it at MEOCS: a routine tip-off from a cultivated informant. Dave Roberts had arrested the source years earlier, and on the morning of 8 September 2010 Roberts reached out to try to glean some intelligence. About anything – that's how the TAG detectives worked. By midday Roberts was at the wheel of an unmarked police car and the informant was sitting in the back seat next to Detective Richard McNally who was taking down notes of what the source was saying. A deal would be going down that night: six ounces (170 grams) of cocaine, a Bankstown unit block, the whole thing worth $45,600.

Roberts turned into Cairds Avenue, Bankstown, and slowed down near a cream-brick building on the corner with Carmen

Street. 'That's it,' the informant said, pointing at the building. It was about four storeys high and full of apartments. Roberts studied its facade. It didn't have the bleak look of a drug complex, like the towers of Redfern or Waterloo. There were no broken windows or shattered intercoms. Instead there were street-facing balconies, a neat lawn and a landscaped garden. It seemed like an unlikely spot to be moving such a large amount of cocaine – Bankstown Police Station was only a short walk around the corner.

In his notebook, Detective McNally wrote down details about the dealer, an Asian-looking man, aged in his mid-fifties. His nickname was 'Miagi' and his deals worked like so: buyers and sellers were invited to his basement car park and placed in separate garages. Miagi played the middleman, working out prices, providing the location, and taking a cut from each sale.

What kind of buyers are we talking about? Roberts asked.

Serious criminals, the source said. A member of the Kalache family had been to the garage. So had members of the Hamze family.

The source had been the upline, selling to Miagi. Two nights earlier, he had bought two ounces of cocaine, low-grade junk, barely worth the asking price of $4500. To the source's surprise, not only did Miagi pay for it, he wanted more – another six ounces as soon as possible, which was very suspicious.

Roberts asked why.

The source explained that it meant Miagi was either working with the cops or about to rip off the drugs. Why else was he prepared to pay so much money for such a large amount of terrible cocaine?

Roberts saw his point. What about guns? he asked. Have you seen any guns? Does Miagi carry?

No, the source said, nothing like that. The question came up a few more times and the answer was always the same. McNally wrote down the word 'Gun' in his notepad and struck a line underneath it to emphasise that the question had been asked.

By now it was nearly 1:30pm. Roberts dropped the source off on a street corner not far from Cairds Avenue and started driving with McNally back to MEOCS HQ. He called Mick Ryan, the TAG commander, on the way and walked him through the source's information: a drug deal that night, six ounces of coke, $45,600 in play.

'It can probably be done today,' Roberts said to Ryan, referring to a raid. 'Strike while the iron's hot.' He wanted to move that night and catch Miagi with the drugs and cash. Move too late and you run the risk of losing both, he said.

Ryan agreed, but he generally didn't like night raids and tried to avoid them; better they be done in the daytime, he thought. But in this case he agreed with Roberts; it was better to move sooner rather than later. Besides, he thought, Miagi wasn't a raging Middle Eastern criminal with a gun strapped to his ankle. He was a middle-aged Asian male who, according to the informant, didn't carry a firearm. Having a source in play was also reassuring – it meant the team would get live updates on the movements of people, the arrival of drugs, and any surprise appearance of weapons. With that in mind, Ryan gave his approval to move ahead.

When they got back to the office, McNally pulled up a chair at his computer and started searching the COPS intelligence database for reports about the unit block at 41–43 Cairds Avenue. He wanted something to corroborate the source's information – if drug dealing was a regular occurrence in the building's basement car park then hopefully someone would have already made a complaint about it. And he was in luck. A week earlier a report had been filed by a Bankstown police officer, Toni McNeice, who had taken a call about drug sales in the building's basement. McNally called her for a briefing.

McNeice said that she'd been working at the front counter of the police station when a caller said that Middle Eastern men were turning up to the car park and buying drugs from an Asian man. They didn't know much more about this dealer except that he lived in the building and owned a Toyota Camry.

McNally got the phone number of the person who'd made the complaint. They were also a resident of the unit block, and he spoke to them at length about the situation. They told him about the building's structure, how it was a confusing series of dual entries, staircases and towers – and how people who didn't live there could find it easy to get disorientated. The dealer himself, the man McNally knew as Miagi, was described as a 'friendly neighbour'.

Meanwhile, Roberts started pulling a team together. The time was approaching 3pm. He liked to use the same entry team for each of his raids; big guys who were trusted and always on game. He soon realised that Nick Glover, one of the regular detectives who was usually the first man through the door each time, had a family commitment – he would have to be replaced.

Roberts looked around the office and spotted the newest recruit, William Crews. He was barely three weeks into the Squad but already he'd fit in fast. Everyone called him 'Crewsy'. He'd just walked in off a nightshift installing a tracking device on a car out in Villawood, a Toyota Camry belonging to Gehad Arja, a target from one of Paul O'Neill's investigations. Roberts asked if he'd be interested in taking Glover's spot on the entry team and, as a sweetener, he offered Crews the position of case officer for the job, meaning he'd be in charge of running the warrant on the ground. Running a case had been something Crews had been trying to do since the first day he'd joined the Squad. In a sense, leading a warrant was a rite of passage, something symbolic. O'Neill had tried to give him the same chance a week earlier when a job to recover some stolen guns had come up, but the informant fell through and the job went with it. The raid at Cairds Avenue, Bankstown, was a chance for Crews to redeem himself and get some runs on the board.

The story of Crews's entry to MEOCS was in some ways an anomaly. Positions in the TAG office were rare and generally they went to officers already working in the Squad's Uniform section. Working in Uniform was like being in a vetting system; it was a feeder group where officers could be tried out and then scouted to progress up the line to the TAG office if they had proven their mettle. Paul O'Neill had joined in this way. So had Ryan Jeffcoat, Vlad Mijok and many others. Beat cops working in police stations who applied for TAG positions were generally ranked as outsiders and told to apply for a Uniform spot first like everybody else. William Crews, one of these outsiders, barely twenty-six years old and not even three years out of the police academy, was an exception to this unofficial rule. He had come to his interview at MEOCS highly recommended – and, in a rare move, he'd been asked to apply.

Mick Ryan had wanted someone sharp and, ideally, experienced with organised crime investigations for the position that had opened up. Applicants were put through a gruelling screening process that began with a longlist of candidates and was whittled down to a shortlist who were brought in for final interviews in Deb Wallace's office, a meet-and-greet to gauge whether their personality was the right fit for the TAG office. Doing the job wasn't enough; TAG was a culture – you had to fit into it.

Crews's career had only just started. When he walked into his interview he had already been awarded two commendations for his work at Campsie with the local Proactive Crime Team. Some cops will spend an entire career chasing down one commendation and still not get it and yet here was Crews with two of them. It's not that his commanders at Campsie wanted to lose him; they put his name forward for the job at MEOCS because even they could tell he was destined for something big.

Ryan was impressed by his CV but told Crews he lacked the experience. He'd done well, but had a way to go. Wallace felt the same; she could see in the way he answered their questions how badly he wanted the position.

Ryan played hardball and asked for specifics: 'How many search warrants have you done? What are your lock-up stats? What's your surveillance experience? How many briefs have you prepared?'

They asked Crews about his upbringing in the country town of Glen Innes – and Ryan, a man of the bush himself, listened closely to his answers. They asked why he had wanted to join the cops and he told them how he'd gone to university in Lismore, moved to Sydney to look for work in IT, and then shocked everyone with his decision. He'd come from a family of cops: his father had served, so had an aunt and two uncles. His brother, Ben, was also in the Force.

On paper he impressed. In person he followed through. When Crews walked out of the room, Ryan turned to Wallace and said, 'I think he's the exception.'

Within a fortnight Crews had been tasked to Paul O'Neill's team in the TAG office and had dived into the work, burning to make an impact. The thought of using tracking devices and listening to telephone intercepts excited him. Every job, every search warrant, every time he snapped on a set of gloves to handle exhibits, he was learning something new.

McNally got off the phone with the Cairds Avenue resident who'd complained to McNeice about drug dealing in the basement car park. Using that conversation and the intelligence from Roberts's source, he began filling out the Operational Orders, the standard set of routine questions and box-ticking exercises required for any raid to go ahead. He cut and paste the surveillance photography of the building, completed the safety checks, and ticked yes as to whether bulletproof vests were available for the mission. Then he flicked a page and started filling out the Risk Assessment matrix, the most important part of the paperwork. A series of questions followed: the likelihood of injury from an assault; the likelihood of injury from animals; the offender's propensity to use violence; and the likelihood of the offender's access to firearms. McNally ticked 'low risk' to each of these questions.

Mick Ryan would have normally joined in for the raid as the overall commander, but by this time he had gone home for the day. In his mind there was no need to turn up to Bankstown – it was a low-risk search of a basement garage. The target was an elderly Asian man who wasn't known to carry a gun. As far as search warrants go, it was as straight as a die.

At 5:05pm, Roberts sent an email to Crews containing a first draft of warrant application 562/10, a document that sought the legal approval of a magistrate to raid garage number 8 of 41–43 Cairds Avenue, Bankstown, and its corresponding apartment in the building upstairs. Crews had never filled out a warrant application form before, so Roberts gave him a head start and completed a few sections, leaving some areas blank. These were questions that went to the need for the raid, its central purpose. Crews took the draft and started typing.

He wrote: 'The Asian male drives a white Toyota Camry ... and on numerous occasions has meetings in his garage with Middle Eastern males. The (Asian) male parks the vehicle at the front of his garage which prevents people walking past from seeing into the rear of the garage.'

Crews added information from Roberts's source, how a recent coke deal with Miagi had included the sale of 125 grams of cocaine to a member of the Kalache family. 'Payment to Miagi was made with three ounces [85 grams] of heroin and cash,' Crews wrote.

At 7:37pm he faxed the warrant application to the after-hours magistrate at Parramatta Local Court and by 8pm the paperwork had come back approved. Roberts called everyone taking part in the raid to join him in the Squad's briefing room.

They were nine men in total, and each man was assigned a role: McNally was on exhibits; Constable Scott Brown and Senior Constable Paul Baglin, partners who worked well together, would search Miagi's apartment. Everyone else was on the basement team: Senior Constable Josh Lavender was on surveillance; the arrest would be done by Senior Constable Tom Howes and Acting Sergeant Fletcher Gentles, a team leader in the Uniform division; Crews was the case officer; and Senior Constable Chris Gerogiannis, another officer in uniform, would do the filming. Having uniform officers involved in the raid was important because most of the entry team were wearing plain clothes and, at first glance, didn't look like cops. Crews was wearing cargo shorts, Roberts a bone-coloured jumper. The idea was to use a mix of cops to keep the element of surprise – send in nine officers in blue shirts and hats and a lookout would see them coming from a mile away. But sending in both allowed for a partial sneak attack.

Before they all headed to their cars, Roberts asked who was 'vesting up'. He always asked that question. Ever since the 2007 incident with Joshua Johns, the Comanchero bikie, Roberts and Howes always wore vests. Low-risk job, high-risk job, it didn't matter; they never left the office without a vest. That night, vests were optional. Most officers taking part in the raid felt they weren't necessary because of the routine, low-risk nature of the warrant. Only a couple of officers reached for them.

Within half an hour, they pulled up in a convoy outside Bankstown Police Station, a seven-minute walk from Cairds Avenue. Roberts stepped through the glass doors and spoke with the shift supervisor working that night. It was a matter of professional courtesy and policy to inform local officers about any raids taking place in their patch. It was also mandatory for an independent officer – someone outside the MEOCS team – to join the raid and make sure everything about it was kosher, an anti-corruption measure. Hussein Mousselamani, an officer working at the station that night, was tasked to the job. He'd worked with Roberts before. Flicking through the paperwork, making sure it had all been legally signed, he turned to Roberts and said, 'Start talking to me, Dave.'

Roberts began reeling off the details, telling Mousselamani that they were looking for drugs and cash in the garage, that Miagi's wife and kids lived in the building upstairs, and that they'd be let into the building by a resident – a 'friendly' – who'd complained about drug activity.

Mousselamani could have rolled his eyes at how routine it all sounded. It was 8:39pm and the warrant was scheduled to kick off in twenty minutes. Roberts picked up the station's phone and called his informant one last time. He wanted to know whether any cash or drugs had arrived. Lavender and Brown were doing surveillance of the apartment, driving past in their unmarked car.

The source told Roberts that Miagi was in the garage with one of his buyers, a man known as 'Hawkie'. None of the cocaine had arrived yet.

What about you? Roberts asked. Where are you?

The source said they were still in the building but had walked away to call in the cocaine for delivery to Hawkie.

How much money is down there? Roberts asked.

'Over fifty thousand,' the informant said.

What about guns? Roberts asked.

No guns.

A few minutes later, the convoy moved out from the police station and drove north along Meredith Street until it reached a roundabout on the corner of Carmen Street. McNally parked his car and started walking, heading down Carmen Street towards the unit block on the corner with Cairds Avenue, about 150 metres away. Everyone else stayed in their cars, including Roberts, who was on a phone call with McNally; he remained on the line with him as he approached the building.

Waiting for McNally at one of the two entrances was the resident who'd made the complaint to Bankstown Police. McNally wedged his foot in the door and took directions to Miagi's garage downstairs.

'The first garage on the left as you're coming from the roller door, the last one on the right if you were to go out through the roller door,' they said.

Roberts was still on the phone. The time was 8.58pm.

'I'm in,' McNally said. 'We're right to go.'

The three unmarked police cars started moving left from Meredith Street into Carmen Street and stopped a few metres short of the unit block on the corner of Cairds Avenue. Roberts stepped out of his car holding a battering ram and walked towards McNally at the entrance. Through the glass door he could see a set of stairs on his right leading down to the basement and another set of stairs above it leading up towards apartments. Roberts called the rest of his team over the radio. 'Form up at the entrance,' he told them.

The plan was to raid the garage, make the arrests and then search Miagi's apartment upstairs where, simultaneously, Baglin and Brown would have already knocked on the door, called out anyone inside and secured the premises. Roberts and Mousselamani had agreed on this plan at Bankstown Police Station – Mousselamani had told Roberts that, as an independent officer, he couldn't be watching two separate raids taking place at the same time.

With Crews and the rest of the team behind them, Roberts and McNally made their way down the cream-tiled stairs and then along a narrow corridor towards a door at its far end. Upstairs, heading in the wrong direction, were the remaining officers assigned to guard Miagi's apartment.

Roberts stepped through the door and into the basement. Facing him was garage number 7, its tilt door covered in wire mesh. To the right were more tilt doors just like it, each one numbered for its corresponding apartment. The car park was shaped like the letter 'T', rotated in an anti-clockwise direction. It was well lit but cavernous, an underground space of concrete walls.

McNally gave directions. He knew the layout and could see a Toyota Camry sedan matching the description of Miagi's car. It was parked perpendicular to three garages, blocking them from opening. Directly opposite the Camry was an open tilt door – garage number

1. A light was switched on inside, the only one with any activity in the basement. It wasn't the same garage described by the 'friendly' in the building – they had indicated Miagi used number 8 – but given that his car was just metres away, and that he was known to use multiple garages for his drug dealing, it seemed an obvious place to go looking for him. Roberts and Crews moved towards it with the entry team behind them. They walked casually, their guns holstered. Roberts held the battering ram in one hand. Crews walked with a notebook under his arm. The time was just after 9:01pm.

As they got closer, Roberts let the balloon up: 'Police! Don't move!'

Crews walked slightly ahead of Roberts and was the first to sight Miagi. He had burst out of the garage in a combat stance, crouched and low. He was screaming in a language no one could understand. Crews saw a pistol in his hands.

'Gun! He has a gun!' Crews called out.

He dropped his notebook, pulled his Glock and rushed ahead to the Camry, closing the distance with the gunman and putting himself in the line of fire, an eight o'clock angle. Barely four metres separated them.

A gunshot rang out. Roberts saw a flash. He rushed to the right towards more garage doors and dropped the battering ram.

Three more shots followed, booming and heavier in sound, a different calibre of bullet. The rest of the team had fallen back for cover. Someone shouted, 'Fucking get back!' The gunman was pointing his weapon quickly, aiming it in in all directions.

Roberts didn't know who was firing anymore. As his battering ram hit the ground he unlatched his Glock, turned to find cover and let off a single shot at the gunman as he raced back to where the rest of his team had taken cover. Heads were spinning. It was still 9:01pm – less than seven seconds had passed since they had walked into the garage. When Roberts looked back, Crews was on the ground.

In another part of Sydney a police radio operator was fielding dozens of calls from squad cars working the southwestern suburbs that night. The calls were typical of the humdrum routine of police work: a caged truck required at Greenacre, officers required for a house that got egged in Punchbowl.

Just before 9:02pm a new voice emerged over the airwaves. It was Mousselamani, the independent officer from Bankstown Police Station, his voice approaching panic: 'Bankstown one three, urgent, urgent, shots fired in Cairds Avenue, Bankstown, shots fired, shots fired.'

The operator was caught off guard. 'Copy 13, situation when you get the chance.' In the background officers were shouting for an ambulance and tactical units.

'We need SPG here ASAP. ASAP. SPG,' he shouted.

Inside the car park, Tom Howes kept his gun trained in the direction of the open garage, ready to shoot if anyone stepped outside of it. Miagi was nowhere to be seen. A no man's land of concrete floor stretched from the covering wall where the officers were standing to the Toyota Camry – where Crews lay on the ground. Untrained in man-down scenarios, anyone who tried to get near him risked getting shot in the process. They were in a siege situation, a stalemate. As they waited for backup to arrive, all they could do was shout across the car park for Miagi to throw out his weapon.

'Put the gun down! We're the police! We just want to help our mate!'

Howes ran upstairs to get ballistic vests. Mousselamani followed, speaking into his radio along the way. The operator wanted more details. Barely two minutes had passed. 'We have an officer down,' he said. 'We have a number of offenders involved in this incident in the garage.' The operator said an ambulance was on its way but a tactical team was forty minutes out. Crews won't make it that long, Mousselamani thought.

Outside, police cars were already converging on the scene. A makeshift command post had been formed on the corner of Meredith and Carmen streets. Mousselamani ran over with tears streaming down his face. Officers were stepping out of arriving cars, unsure where to go and what was happening. He told them William Crews had been shot.

'We have to go and get him, he's by himself,' Mousselamani said.

'What do you mean he's by himself?' an officer asked.

'He's just lying down there, we need to go!'

A short debate ensued. Someone said the tactical teams were en route. Another officer said it was too dangerous to enter. Sergeant Jeff Harkness, an officer from the Bass Hill Region Enforcement Squad, strapped on a vest and said, 'If I was down there, I would want you to come and get me'. He raced towards the entrance with Robert Hogan, a supervisor from Campsie. Hogan had virtually jumped over the counter at Campsie Police Station when he heard Mousselamani's Signal One broadcast.

In the car park, behind the covering wall, the sound of ripping Velcro could be heard as officers strapped vests to their bodies. Shock crept up on everyone; their worst-case scenario was unfolding around them. Some were woefully unprepared. One officer said: 'Man, I don't even have my fucking gun.'

Dave Roberts tried to explain the situation to Mick Ryan in a phone call. He walked away from his team as he spoke. 'Mick, Mick, Mick, he was right next to Crewsy firing shots, mate,' he said, trying to answer Ryan's questions. 'I don't know what happened, mate. We can't get to him. The bloke won't come out and he won't release the firearm.'

By 9:10pm there were almost two dozen officers moving around the covered area of the car park and more were arriving. An ambulance crew was on standby outside waiting for clearance to enter. A Dog Squad officer, David Wynne, arrived with his police dog, Abel, and peered out at the garage down the end of the car park. Everyone was trying to figure out a way to end the siege. Ideas were thrown out. Someone asked Wynne what would happen if the dog was let off his leash. Wynne said there were too many people in the immediate area for the dog to perform its duties. The animal wouldn't be able to tell people apart, including Crews, who might be mistaken for the offender. And there was another problem. The gunman was still at large. 'The dog would get shot,' Wynne said.

Suddenly, a noise came from another section of the basement. Someone saw a firearm.

'There's a gun! Drop the gun and come out!' an officer called.

The weapon belonged to Terence Robinson, a leading senior constable from Campsie Police. He had shown up at the entrance to the Cairds Avenue complex, walked past a set of stairs guarded by officers and taken a second unguarded set to the basement. At the bottom was a doorway into the car park with a clear view of the silver Toyota Camry and Crews's body on the ground. With his gun drawn, Robinson stepped inside and into a blind spot behind the covering wall where the rest of the officers couldn't see him. Within a few steps his gun and body became partly visible.

At the sound of the shouting to put down his weapon, Robinson called out, identifying himself as a police officer. His colleagues asked him to prove it.

'I'm going to put my left arm out,' he said, extending his jacket sleeve until his police patch was visible past his own covering wall to those on the other side of the car park. Two officers rushed over to meet him, discovering the second entrance. They had no idea the doorway existed. Robinson looked ahead to the open garage and, using hand signals, motioned to the officers to cover him as he moved around the side of the Camry. With his gun pointed at the garage, he inched along behind the car and cleared a line of sight. When he was finally looking into the open garage all he could see were boxes and furniture. There was a laundry hanger and a set of drawers. Miagi was nowhere to be seen. At some point, they figured, he must have escaped via the second entrance.

With the basement declared empty, officers rushed towards Crews to check his pulse. Someone shouted for the paramedics. By the time they arrived, it was 9:23pm. Nearly twenty-one minutes had passed since he'd been shot. A paramedic rendering aid said Crews had gone into cardiac arrest and had no pulse or breathing. His injuries were most likely fatal. An officer, overhearing the comment, ordered the ambulance worker to keep going. 'Don't you ever stop,' he said.

Elsewhere in the car park, the MEOCS officers involved in the raid that night paced through the garage, walking in circles and clenching their hair. The reality of the nightmare was settling upon them. Every few minutes an anguished, choking shout would echo through the garage. Some were down on one knee.

As officers moved in and out of the basement, one of the garage doors – number 8 – began to open. Three men were standing inside.

They'd been hiding in there throughout the gunfight. 'We were just playing cards in here and we heard gunshots,' one of the men said as he got on the ground. An officer wrote down their names as they were each searched for weapons – Geehad Ghazi and two friends. A cursory search of the garage revealed no card table or cards, but there was an ice pipe sitting in an ashtray.

Outside, a PolAir helicopter hovered over the unit block and kept a light pointed at one of the apartments on the first floor. Two Asian men had been spotted walking onto the balcony, checking the streets – Miagi and Hawkie. A MEOCS officer who had seen them got onto the police radio. 'The people in that unit are the offenders from this shooting,' the officer said. Angry residents bombarded Triple 0 with phone calls about the chopper, complaining about the noise and unaware of the situation in the garage.

Chris Gerogiannis, the MEOCS uniform officer who was filming the warrant that night, was standing guard next to the apartment block's entrance running a crime scene log when an officer appeared in front of him, a member of the Tactical Operation's Unit Alpha Team. He wore a facemask and had a sub-machine gun across his body.

'I need you to step away from the building,' the officer said. 'This area's being locked down.'

As Gerogiannis left, the tactical team moved inside, taking up positions close to Miagi's apartment with negotiators stationed outside his door.

It was nearly 9:45pm. Crews was en route to Liverpool Hospital in an ambulance being prepped for emergency surgery. It was around this time that Detective Inspector Mick Sheehy received a phone call from his commander at the Homicide Squad, Peter Cotter, briefing him on the events at Bankstown. Sheehy was in another part of Sydney observing a controlled meeting between an undercover operative and target being pursued over a murder, the execution of Michael McGurk, a shadowy businessman and money lender, who was killed outside his home in Cremorne on 3 September 2009. Within minutes, Sheehy had stopped what he was doing, handed over to the person sitting next to him, and was on his way to Bankstown.

After twenty-five years as a police officer, Sheehy had already managed six Critical Incident Investigations and reviewed an untold number of others for his colleagues at Homicide. Few cases can be ranked as more difficult or more exhaustive. For a Critical Incident Investigation to be invoked someone has to be injured or killed at the hands of a police officer. On average, they run for years, taking the most traumatic moments of an officer's career, often their lives, and pressure testing every reflex, every instinctive decision made in a heartbeat against departmental protocols, criminal law and civil liability. In a best-case scenario, the officer is cleared of wrongdoing and walks away spent. At worst, they can end up in prison, or on permanent stress leave, or emotionally shattered with their careers finished.

Sheehy arrived at the command post on Meredith Street and was given a briefing on the current status of the operation. Top brass had gathered as well, senior officers ranking from superintendent right up to deputy commissioner. Sheehy was told that, for the moment, the building remained in lockdown. Negotiators were on standby trying to coax Miagi out of his apartment. He had barricaded himself inside his unit with his ex-wife, two stepchildren, and Hawkie, who, from the little that the negotiators had pieced together, had been with him inside the garage. The negotiators had been using a mobile phone to speak with Miagi, but had started using a loud hailer, urging him to come outside and surrender.

At 11:10pm the door to his apartment finally inched open. A table and couch had been blocking the entry. Miagi emerged from the unit and presented himself to police with his hands up above his head. He walked towards the tactical officers and then dropped to his knees to be searched and cuffed, and then walked outside for a handover to members of Sheehy's team.

By that stage investigators had built a profile of him. He was no longer known by the nickname 'Miagi'. His real name was Philip Nguyen. He was a 55-year-old Vietnamese man who had been married twice, divorced twice, had a drug habit, and had a previous conviction for supply for which he had spent time in prison. Intelligence checks came up clean: nothing for firearms, no history of assaulting police.

He was met on the footpath by a Homicide detective and placed in the back of a police truck to be taken to Bankstown Police Station, where Sheehy's team were settling in for a long night of interviews. Each of the MEOCS officers involved in the raid had already been taken back to the station, along with the three men allegedly playing cards in the garage, and the five people inside Nguyen's apartment – his ex-wife, stepson, stepdaughter, and Tan Hung Chung, the man known as Hawkie. Dave Roberts had been excluded from this interview process for the evening. In the immediate aftermath of the shooting he'd flown into a visceral rage, punching the brick walls of the garage and headbutting a car. He and two others had been taken to hospital and sedated.

Sheehy spoke to Roberts only briefly before he was taken away from the scene. By then the Homicide detective had seen photographs of Crews's injuries, taken by an officer at Liverpool Hospital. While nothing had been confirmed, images of the injury strongly suggested that Crews had been struck by a police-issue bullet. Roberts, while not in a state to do any interviews that night anyway, would from then on need to talk to Sheehy with a lawyer present.

With the building secured, crime scene officers moved into the basement to process the scene. Near the Toyota Camry they collected deformed bullets, copper jacketing and cigarette butts. Swabs of bloodstains were taken. The imprint of a shoe was photographed. Yellow exhibit markers were laid out next to metal fragments, an aqua-coloured t-shirt, and a Glock self-loading pistol belonging to William Crews that appeared to have jammed mid-fire. The layout of the car park was sketched and the erratic trajectory of each bullet was chased down. There were ricochet marks along the walls of Nguyen's garage. One shot had flown through a clothing rack, a rolled-up carpet, an armchair, and then had finally fallen to the floor after losing its speed.

Bankstown Police Station became the epicentre of the trauma, a scene of raw emotion – pale faces and tears. Current and former members of MEOCS walked through the station's doors, having heard the reports on the radio. Their arrival was like a sad reunion, tragedy bringing the old faces together. Guys like Dave Adney, who no longer worked at the Squad, felt compelled to turn up in support. Several dozen others jumped out of bed or stopped what they were doing and hopped in their cars.

For the ten officers involved in the raid, the hours that followed were an isolating experience. Sterile investigative procedures had kicked into gear as each of them was placed in separate rooms. They had colleagues around them for support, but conversations were limited to basic facts, words of comfort. Someone kept tabs on these discussions and steered them back each time they veered anywhere close to the events of the night. It was forbidden to discuss what had happened, but, really, what else was there to talk about; a friend and colleague had just been shot – the nightmare scenario – and no one could breathe a word about it. In the cops this was called 'due process', and it always took priority.

For those further up the MEOCS chain of command the night represented an extraordinary set of pressures. Moving around the station was Mick Ryan, the TAG commander, going room to room, running on adrenaline, and checking on his team who were all in various stages of grief. He was on autopilot, betraying little emotion, but the scenes would stay with him. In one room sat a member of the entry team, an officer who'd gone into the basement car park. When Ryan walked in, the officer looked up and burst into tears. 'I'm so sorry, boss,' he said.

As the overall commander of that night's operation, it was on Ryan to shepherd his team through the crisis. In his own mind he was running over the mechanics of the incident, trying to figure out what processes were followed, what was missed, what – if anything – hadn't been done properly that day. *How had it all gone wrong?* Complicating his position was that he, too, had technically been involved in the raid as the overall commander, even though he wasn't physically present at the scene.

A few minutes after midnight, word filtered through from Liverpool Hospital. Mick Ryan gathered everyone together and delivered the news: Crews had died from his injuries, a gunshot wound to his neck and another to his shoulder. The post-mortem, due to take place in the morning, would determine with more certainty what had happened. Questions about friendly fire were already being asked.

One by one, officers were called out of their rooms to provide urine samples or get breath tested to check for any traces of alcohol; this was standard procedure during a Critical Incident Investigation. Their guns were collected, placed in an evidence bag and locked in a safe at the station. Their hands were swabbed for GSR testing – gunshot residue – to determine with certainty who had fired their weapons. And as the night continued they were each interviewed by members of the Critical Incident Investigation Team for their version of what happened, their stories all pivoting on the same sequence of events: they had walked into the car park and shots were fired a few seconds later. Some saw a muzzle flash. Some heard five shots while others heard a dozen – the cavernous space and concrete walls could make one bullet sound like three. No one knew who had fired first, but many suspected it was Nguyen, the man with the gun. For some officers, these interviews ended as the sun was coming up on a new morning. Standing by as they emerged from the interview room were members of the MEOCS Highway Patrol, volunteering, insisting, that they shuttle each officer home once their statements were complete. It didn't matter if they lived in Coogee or Windsor, they got home in a MEOCS car, stopping for McDonald's along the way.

Nguyen, a harmless-looking figure with a slouch and receding grey hair, seemed to lie repeatedly during his three-hour interview, telling detectives he had been unarmed during the gunfight and hadn't actually fired any shots. He said he was in the car park smoking heroin with a friend, Hawkie, when he heard shouting and saw several men with guns approaching. He thought it was a robbery. He'd been robbed a couple of weeks earlier, but the story of how that happened seemed to change depending on who was hearing it. He told the detectives his earlier assailants had come at him with knives, but to his ex-wife he'd said they had cricket bats.

She and her two children were in separate rooms giving their own statements to police.

A detective asked Nguyen what type of guns he'd seen the police holding and he responded that the two men closest to him – Roberts and Crews – each had a weapon. One of them, he said, was holding a very big gun but had dropped it to the floor, allowing him to pick it up, hoist it to his shoulder and fire it like a bazooka to force their retreat. The gun didn't fire, but the men backed off, he said.

'So you say that you pointed the gun at those people?' the detective asked.

'Yeah, yes,' Nguyen replied. He was talking about Roberts's battering ram.

Another tactic he'd tried was to point his fingers into a gun shape and use that to try to scare off the men, he said. By then Sheehy's team had an overwhelming number of statements indicating Nguyen had genuinely fired at Constable William Crews. Nguyen's stepson had given a statement indicating that once the gunfight was over, Nguyen had raced into the apartment with Hawkie and said, 'I shot someone who was breaking into garage. I think I killed him.' Coupled with the corroborating statements of nearly a dozen police officers, by sunrise Nguyen was charged as the gunman and was told he would face court on a single count of 'shoot with intent to murder'.

In a separate room of the station, Geehad Ghazi was giving a statement explaining his role in the basement car park that night. His account maintained that he had gone to the unit complex with his two friends in order to play cards with Nguyen. Within minutes of their arrival some gunshots had rung out, forcing them to stay quiet in their separate garage where they were waiting for a deck of cards to be brought out. Ghazi's only concession was to reveal that he'd shown up to the card game with a gun, and that he'd hidden the weapon once he heard police arrive at the scene. Tests later revealed that the firearm, recovered from the armrest of a sofa, wasn't used in the shooting, but an admission by Ghazi that he'd tested the weapon at his house in Chester Hill would see him charged with possession. Neither of the two other men found in garage number 8 co-operated with police that night.

Nguyen would later tell police that he and Tan Hung Chung (Hawkie) went to the garage that night to smoke heroin and await a drug deal. Tan Hung Chung was never charged with any offences in relation to that night. He gave evidence at the Coronial enquiry confirming he was in the garage and was a witness to the shooting.

Mick Ryan was one of the last people to leave the station, staying back with Deb Wallace, the Squad's commander, until about 6am. She had watched him closely through the night and could see him bottling up what had happened. Governed by the rules of due process, there was little she could say or do for him except be there if he needed it. She stayed until long after everyone had left and until Ryan finally decided to sign off.

He left Bankstown and drove east, stopping at a swimming pool for a few laps, a 6am ritual he had gotten himself into each morning before work. He figured some exercise would be a release after the events of that night – storm clouds were gathering in his mind and it would be a way to zone out in the focused concentration of each lap. He pushed off the wall, but the relief was only temporary. The race was rigged; no one can outrun a storm. Halfway through a lap he stopped and got out of the water with red eyes, the events of the night catching up with him. As he found out, you can't cry and swim at the same time. He got dressed, walked to his car and drove himself home, defeated.

*

Deb Wallace tried to calm tensions during a debriefing session that morning with staff. They were enraged about the loss of their colleague. Details of the critical incident were scant and most of the officers had been misinformed about the circumstances, unaware of Nguyen's role. They thought that the Middle Eastern men in the garage had somehow instigated the violence, an act of war. The few people aware of the real story, such as Wallace, were not allowed to discuss it.

Riled up, demanding action, some officers suggested turning up at Geehad Ghazi's court appearance on the gun possession charge as a show of force. Wallace was firmly against it. She urged cool heads. 'We don't want to look like vigilantes,' she said. 'We're not going to do this emotional outburst.'

The atmosphere grew tense as the merits of the gesture were argued. Wallace stayed firm. An officer asked if she was making an order. Wallace was shocked that someone would even ask.

'Just think about what you're saying,' she insisted. 'We're in a process of raw emotion.'

Among the officers listening was Detective Sergeant Brad Abdy, the officer who had been investigating the shooting of Fadi Ibrahim. He felt a compulsion to intervene. 'This isn't how we do things. Where you will show respect to Bill is to go out and do what he loved,' Abdy said, referring to proactive, diligent police work. 'Want to show some force? Then double-down on work: jack up some dealers, raid some houses, tip over a few cars, show people what happens when shots are fired at police.' His words silenced the room. That night, he stood watch as three high-risk warrants were executed on an organised crime family at Merrylands, each one planned ahead before the events at Cairds Avenue, but brought forward in response, a small salute for a fallen colleague.

The post-mortem determined the cause of death had been a single gunshot wound to the neck. Nguyen's weapon, which had also jammed, was a .22-calibre handgun found at the bottom of a hot water tank on his balcony, but the bullet and jacketing recovered by forensic pathologist Stephen Wills were consistent with a police-issue Glock .40-calibre round. The finding confirmed that the fatal bullet had not been fired by Nguyen, but by Roberts – the shot squeezed off in the split second as he dropped his battering ram and turned to take cover behind a wall of the car park.

The news, which until then had been all but confirmed, was delivered to Roberts later that afternoon at his home. A car pulled up outside just as Roberts approached his front gate. Deb Wallace stepped out of the car with Peter Cotter, the commander of the Homicide Squad. With them was Pamela Young, a senior investigations co-ordinator at the Homicide Squad.

Roberts had been heading up to his local church to find a quiet space for reflection. He was on about three hours of medically induced sleep and had a bandage around his right hand. His knuckles had split open after he'd punched walls in the car park. Two friends were standing next to him for support.

Visits had been taking place throughout the day and slowly Roberts had learned of a few facts in the case. He knew that Crews had passed away from his injuries. He knew that Nguyen was still alive, untouched by any gunfire, which meant the bullet he'd fired had missed its target. In Roberts's mind, that gave rise to a prospect too painful to say out loud. All he could do was hope, and now pray, that his bullet had hit a wall, a car, or anything else in the garage. Cotter delivered the post-mortem findings in the living room. Wallace had to repeat them for Roberts because they didn't sink in at first. But when they did, the words wandered through him like an illness, causing a harm that can't be done with a physical wound. From that point forward, Roberts – an indestructible figure at MEOCS, a leader of men – was changed forever.

Roberts provided his statement to the Critical Incident Investigative Team the next day, an interview that canvassed everything that had happened leading up to the shooting – from his meeting with the original informant who had led them to the building, to the preparation of the search warrant's paperwork, to the moments following the gunfire. Roberts's memory was hazy. He could remember seeing the open garage door and hearing someone yell out. Nguyen fired first, he said. The sequence of shots wasn't clear, but the gun was going everywhere and it looked like he was squeezing the trigger several times.

'How many shots did you fire?' Detective Joe Doueihi asked.

'I fired one shot,' Roberts said. He tried to answer more of Doueihi's questions but the trauma had erased part of his memory. He still had a walk-through of the crime scene to complete, which would take several more hours. Doueihi suggested they pick up the interview at another time. He asked Roberts if there was anything he wanted to add, and Roberts thought about it for a moment. Then he spoke. There was a reality about the situation that people were only partially acknowledging.

'We were being shot at,' he said.

Police officers and emergency service personnel packed St Andrews Cathedral in Sydney six days later for Crews's state funeral.

Hundreds of ordinary citizens turned out to pay their respects. Some watched from their office towers as the funeral procession made its way down George Street. Inside the church, Police Commissioner Andrew Scipione spoke at length to mourners and described Constable William Arthur George Crews as being on a rapid upward ascent before his life was tragically cut short. His recruitment to the Middle Eastern Organised Crime Squad was testament to this promise.

At the end of his speech, Scipione announced that Crews had been promoted to the rank of Detective, a designation he had been working towards at the time of the incident, and posthumously awarded the prestigious Police Commissioner's Valour Award for 'conspicuous merit and exceptional bravery' in the line of duty. By then it had become clear to investigators that Crews had not only moved towards the line of fire, but that he had also advanced into it as he was being shot.

It took almost four years before the Critical Incident Investigation Team's findings could be delivered to the NSW Coroner in May 2014. Nguyen's criminal proceedings had to play out first before the coroner's inquest could begin. Detective Inspector Mick Sheehy concluded in his 72-page report that both Crews and Roberts had been within their rights to fire back at Nguyen. He ultimately found that Detective Constable Crews's death had been caused as a result of a 'tragically misdirected' bullet.

Sheehy could not say with certainty how this had occurred, but spent a considerable amount of time examining Crews's service weapon and the position of his body on the ground. He found that Crews had fallen away from Nguyen's garage at the time he was shot, which tended to support the hypothesis that he may have turned to take cover as his gun failed and 'in doing so stepped into the line of fire'.

The question of why his gun had jammed at all became a separate line of enquiry to the Critical Incident Investigation, one that saw Sheehy speak with the weapon's manufacturers. Studies of Crews's Glock had shown that its fourth bullet had entered the chamber backwards, making it inoperable. How this happened couldn't be determined with certainty, but Sheehy believed the most likely scenario was that the bullet had been loaded backwards into the magazine.

The weapon's manufacturer said that wasn't possible – the Glock magazine would not allow bullets to be loaded the wrong way around. Several ballistic tests were conducted and, in some cases, it was possible in Glock magazines with significant wear.

Sheehy's investigation conducted acoustic testing of the crime scene and reconstructions of the incident in order to confirm that Nguyen had fired his weapon first. Both the Coroner and the Counsel Assisting the Coroner were also brought to the building and shown its structure. They, too, got disorientated as they tried to navigate its staircases and doorways.

While Sheehy's report exonerated Roberts and his team of any wrongdoing in the preparation of the warrant and the incident itself, the NSW Coroner found there was still cause to suspect the officers should have prepared for a possible gun on the premises. This was based on the notes taken down by Detective McNally in the back of the police car hours earlier when he wrote the word 'gun' and struck a line beneath it. While McNally maintained it was done for no other reason than to remind himself that questions about firearms had been asked, the Coroner instead chose to give more weight to the informant's account of the conversation, a version of which was provided to Sheehy's investigative team. The informant, whose name and gender cannot be identified, told Sheehy's detectives that the word 'ammo' had been mentioned in the car. Asked what that meant, the informant said 'ammo' meant a firearm. This account was flatly denied by Roberts and McNally and discounted by Sheehy in his final report, whose findings were backed by both the NSW Supreme Court in the Crown's case against Nguyen and, later, the NSW Court of Criminal Appeal.

In doubting McNally, a sworn police officer, and accepting the evidence of the informant, a documented liar, the coroner seemed to suggest the TAG officers wanted to hide or ignore the fact that a gun might be on the premises that night in order to get their warrant approved. But this makes no sense. If the goal of both Roberts and McNally had been to raid the unit block as quickly as possible – a fact clearly accepted by the coroner during the inquest – then any hint of a gun would have only ramped up the urgency of their warrant and expedited its execution. In other words, had there been suggestions of a gun the incentive was there to highlight and maximise them. By ignoring or overlooking these suggestions, as the coroner seemed to suggest, the officers would have only been doing themselves a disservice. They also would have been diverging from years of precedent they had helped set. A cursory check of past Operational Orders filled out at MEOCS, particularly those completed by Dave Roberts, would have turned up scores of examples where firearms were clearly flagged in advance.

Included among these examples would be the arrest of Remeh Ghazi, an Auburn crime figure, on 11 November 2009. Remeh's Union Road home was searched on the suspicion he was harbouring a firearm, the risk printed in detail on the opening page of the Operational Orders. The raid ended up yielding the gun plus 156 rounds of ammunition. As it turned out, it was Ghazi's brother, Geehad, who was found hiding in the basement car park during the Cairds Avenue shooting. So why would the risk have been amplified in one case and not the other? Or in the countless other MEOCS raids seeking to recover weapons? Wouldn't the raid on Cairds Avenue, Bankstown, conform to the same standards if the possibility of a gun was present?

To anyone familiar with the nuances of the case, this is not a divisive issue. Despite the coroner's findings, the overwhelming view is that neither Roberts nor McNally were ever told about any gun or 'ammo' on the premises at Bankstown that night.

Sheehy's report made several policy recommendations to the NSW Police Force, among them being that all officers attached to MEOCS and other specialist squads should receive formal tactical training for search warrant entries. It was a finding that seemed to support what many in the Squad had been pushing for since its inception. For years they had been flying blind in some ways, particularly those in the Target Action Group, whose bread-and-butter work was to raid houses.

One of the few aspects of the warrant preparation that Sheehy criticised was the Risk Assessment process, which he found was not completed correctly. This was due in part to a lack of training and a misunderstanding about how to grade the risks themselves. But, even so, his report still concluded this was a technical error only. Had everything been done properly, he found that the warrant would have been graded as a 'moderate risk' rather than 'low risk'. This still, as his report noted, would have ultimately had 'no bearing on the manner of execution' that night.

Nguyen contested his charge of shoot with intent to murder and subsequently pleaded guilty to a charge of manslaughter on 19 July

2012, a plea that saw him admit he'd been armed at the time of the gunfight and had shot at Detective Constable Crews, hitting him with a single bullet to his left arm. He was sentenced to a minimum term of seven years in prison, which was later revised up on appeal to a minimum of thirteen years. In May 2016 he lost a High Court challenge to this sentence. He will become eligible for parole in 2023.

Detective Senior Constable Dave Roberts returned to work within a month of the Cairds Avenue shooting, placing himself on restricted duties. The first thing he noticed when he walked back into the MEOCS office was Crews's desk, which hadn't been touched since the night of the incident. When Roberts loaded up his computer he found emails from Crews that he'd forgotten about, messages exchanged between them in the hours leading up to the search warrant. Staring at the screen, he weighed up whether or not to delete them. They were painful reminders.

It took another four years before he could bring himself to do it.

For a long time, grief was a prism through which he viewed the world. Questions, impossible questions, about that night would trigger mentally exhausting spirals. *What if I'd aimed higher? What if I hadn't fired at all? What if the bullet had been two millimetres to the right? Should I have fired in the first place?*

There were panic attacks, something he had never experienced before. They came on suddenly and with the force of a heart attack. Prescription medication, something he had never needed before, became a crutch to get to sleep at night. Poker machines, something he had never even been tempted to go near, suddenly dominated his days. Weeks were lost pushing fifties into slot machines and he barely cared about the winnings. Thousands of dollars were lost. 'It was an expensive way to numb the mind,' Roberts said later in an interview.

Running parallel to his private grief was the public scrutiny into what had happened. The Cairds Avenue warrant had cast a pall over his career and reputation. Never mind that a year earlier he was Roberts the machine, the decorated police officer, one of the most exceptional cops in the TAG office who had been personally responsible for generating thirty search warrants, 214 arrests and the charging of 119 people. Now, there were clumsy, careless headlines. Journalists incorrectly described the raid as a 'botched' operation, hinting that it was sloppily prepared and suggesting cowboy behaviour.

Sometime during 2011, a few months after the tragedy, Roberts returned to the basement garage with three police colleagues. They were people he trusted to give him a brutally honest assessment of what happened that night. Together, as a group, they recreated the event, step by step, an unofficial account of the lead-up and a breakdown of what had occurred when the shots were fired. At that stage the Critical Incident Investigation was still many months away from handing down its official findings. Roberts needed answers. His colleagues with him in the car park mulled over the complexities, but they all arrived at the same conclusion: it was a freak event, a one in a million, a scenario so improbable that it couldn't be replicated.

That point marked an important step for Roberts to settle the matter in his mind. He tried to put his life back together. He enrolled himself into a treatment program with The Brothers of St John of God, an organisation that assists people suffering from post-traumatic stress disorder. There he saw for the first time other men like him: strong, proud members of the armed forces or law enforcement organisations struggling with their own demons, struggling to admit vulnerability, struggling to ask for help when they had never needed it before.

He weaned himself off the Xanax (though he remains on other medication), gave up gambling cold turkey, and threw himself into fitness – weight lifting, swimming and amateur boxing, putting himself forward as a sparring partner for much more experienced fighters. In a way, the hits were therapeutic, he said. They were a form of catharsis; it can't be explained.

He and other former cops suffering the same post-traumatic stress disorder (PTSD) would get together, pummel each other mercilessly and then hug it out when the fight was over. The hits, in a way, brought Roberts back to life. 'You feel awake,' he said.

Doctors told Roberts that the death of William Crews had been the precipitating factor in his PTSD. For almost a decade, criminals from Arncliffe to Guildford had been talking about him. There were threats so serious that his home had undergone fortification upgrades, giving it the appearance of a fortress – the windows were replaced with bulletproof glass and iron bars, security cameras were installed with a back-to-base alarm system, and a huge wall was erected across the front of the property. He was granted permission to take his gun home too.

There were other factors, the same litany of unacknowledged traumatic events that most police officers encounter daily, sometimes without even realising it. These are the suicides, the child sexual assaults and the near-fatal car accidents where the sight of the injuries lingers in the back of the mind for years afterwards.

In Roberts's case this trail of damage went back to his first year in the job, to the scene of a horrific car crash. It was two in the morning and the driver had wrapped his car around a power pole. Roberts's partner, a former paramedic, had reached into the man's mouth to clear his airway; he was choking on his own teeth. The car's engine had been pushed into the cabin and was crushing the man's legs. He had a sucking chest wound – an open hole in his body. Roberts was told to put his hand on top of it to keep the air out.

Those were the big things, but there were little ones too that crept up slowly: the realisation that the world isn't a safe place, that people can be cruel, and that some are just plain evil. Mick Ryan called this 'the poison'.

Roberts transferred out of MEOCS and moved to a suburban command in a different part of Sydney. Friends, fellow officers and family members told him to consider a retirement package and seek out a peaceful existence elsewhere. He couldn't do it. Sharon Crews, William's mother, had told him before Crews's funeral at Glen Innes that if he, or any of the other officers involved in the raid, left the NSW Police Force then it would only compound her grief.

Roberts is no longer in contact with the Crews family but still thinks about his colleague most days. Each year on 8 September, the anniversary, he visits the police memorial, looks at William Crews's name and quietly, privately, remembers that night.

Today, despite it all, Roberts is still a serving NSW police officer.

For the rest of the Squad, it was a slow return to normalcy. Morale was low. Some officers took time off to deal with their grief. Investigations were put on hold.

To try to help her staff, Deb Wallace reached out to the Special Air Service Regiment to ask how they dealt with death when it occurred in their tightly knit teams. A senior officer told Wallace they had struggled with the same issue. 'We've learned our lessons,' the SAS officer said. 'You have to let people grieve when they're ready. If someone wants to be at work, let them be at work. Don't wrap them in cotton wool; they'll feel like they're victims.'

Wallace kept this in mind as she kept an eye on several officers who'd been involved in the warrant. One of her biggest concerns was for Mick Ryan, who had returned to work immediately after the incident, stoic as ever. His office had been crowded with cards and flowers sent in by colleagues from across the state in condolence.

Most of the detectives tried not to speak about the incident, but the topic was sometimes inescapable. Crews's desk was itself a reminder; it stayed untouched for months, everything left as it was with a jacket slung over the chair and pens still in the drawers. One day, without saying a word, Ryan walked over and began gathering up these personal belongings, packing the items into boxes to send home to Crews's family. He made no announcement of the move and didn't delegate it to anyone else. Those in the room stopped working and watched with respect, a moment of silence in a way. Today, Crews's portrait hangs at the entrance to the MEOCS office, the first thing officers see as they walk through the frosted glass door.

Wallace eventually took Ryan aside and told him he needed to take time off, to disengage. She expected resistance, but by then he too had come to the same conclusion. A long period of stress leave followed and in 2013 he confirmed his retirement.

Now out of the cops, aged fifty-six, his spare time is mostly taken up with working on a 34-foot flybridge cruiser. He says he doesn't miss police work. Thirty years of dealing with criminals and seeing the worst aspects of society has left him with bitter memories. 'It does take a while to get the poison out of your system, to stop seeing the badness in people,' he said during one of several long interviews for this book. 'You become very cynical.'

As a result of the tragedy at Bankstown, search warrant protocols were overhauled and replaced with strict new criteria requiring several additional layers of command approval for raids to be carried out.

This course of action divided police. Some saw it as an overcorrection. They asked why procedures should be rewritten over what was, at its core, a tragic one-off occurrence. Others saw a benefit in the changes, arguing that it was a small price to pay for an added layer of safety in a job that had never been able to guarantee it.

As a result of these changes, most police commands across New South Wales saw a significant drop in the number of raids being carried out. Approval times blew out from hours to days, to sometimes weeks, which impacted severely on some cases. There were instances where detectives would arrive at a house only to find the evidence they had been seeking wasn't there anymore. Too much time had elapsed – the guns or the drugs they'd been told about on Monday had been moved by Friday. At the time of writing, the Force is still adjusting to this overhaul of search warrant procedures.

What was certain was that the raid at Cairds Avenue, Bankstown, had marked a monumental shift, one from which the NSW Police Force would never return. If its lasting legacy is a safer environment for officers, then few can argue with that.

EPILOGUE

The years after the death of Crews saw a rise in gun crime, public place shootings and an even stronger synergy between Middle Eastern criminals and outlaw motorcycle gangs. By 2012 the Squad's work had become enmeshed with that of the Gangs Squad, both sharing crossover targets and strike forces as biker gangs increased their recruitment of MEOC figures.

As a result, gangs went to war, dominating headlines and prompting numerous investigations. Strike Force Felix worked the Hells Angels City Chapter in their war with the Nomads. Then came Strike Force Kinnarra, a Gangs Squad investigation staffed with MEOCS detectives. These cases were both the same old story: two gangs, a turf dispute, a series of shootings too hard to solve, and the perpetrators eventually in prison for drug offences.

Newspaper headlines depicted Sydney as being awash with illegal firearms, either imported from overseas or stolen from legitimate owners. Crackdowns followed, weapons were seized, and the price of guns soared. The economics seemed reasonable enough: it was basic supply and demand.

In response, arms dealers got creative, recruiting backyard machinists to manufacture their own weapons capable of holding extended magazines and shooting on automatic fire. For some this became a big business.

Take, for example, the case of Paul Francis. A 55-year-old fitter and turner, Francis had previously held a firearms licence, had no criminal record and lived in a house at Greystanes with a shed out the back. Inside the shed was an industrial-sized lathe that he used to make handguns and rifles, beautifully crafted weapons fitted with spotting scopes, tactical lights and front grips. It was clear Francis took pride in his work.

'I built this from scratch,' he told two undercover officers from Strike Force Centre who were posing as enthusiasts. They had met him over the internet, contacting him seemingly out of nowhere. Francis later fired one of the guns in front of them to show that it worked. It was a tense moment for everyone involved, including the backup police team listening nearby; had they known shots would be fired they would probably not have sent in undercover officers. Three months later when MEOCS detectives arrived with a search warrant, Francis fainted. He pleaded guilty to his charges and was sentenced to less than four years in prison.

The Squad's ten-year anniversary fell on 1 May 2016, and in the decade since its formation there has been little adjustment to its underlying mission statement. While the problem of Middle Eastern organised crime is no longer treated with the same urgency as it once might have garnered, it continues to be a principal driver of specialist police work. Not much has changed since 2006.

The number of MEOC targets operating in the community hasn't decreased. Some first cropped up on police running sheets during the late 1990s and are still carrying on their criminal tradecraft. Others are new names, second-generation criminals, up-and-comers lured by the wealth promised through the drug game or the sense of identity and belonging provided by gang membership.

In that sense, even less has changed, though more broadly the face of ethnic-based crime, particularly Asian crime, has undergone an evolution.

Asian organised crime once operated under the banner of large gangs. These were groups with names like Big Circle, 14K and Singh Ma. It has since abandoned this structure and corporatised itself into smaller, sleeker groups. Ex-members of these crews still operate in the world of organised crime but are no longer confined by cultural barriers. They work with criminals outside their ethnic circle to achieve their aims. The result has been a far more sophisticated and discreet form of crime, focused less on petty drug runs, turf, distribution and extortion of businesses, and more on large-scale drug importations that, when successful, deliver multi-million-dollar profits. Any violence carried out is also discreet. Houses don't get shot up, and people don't get publicly slain – they simply vanish, their names going into a special file at the Homicide Squad marked 'missing, presumed dead'.

The syndicates involved in these imports, unlike outlaw motorcycle gangs or Middle Eastern street groups, work under no banner. They can be a seemingly random selection of individuals and criminal contacts who come together and then disappear as quickly as they formed once the drugs arrive in the country. 'You might have someone from the Italian mafia, someone from Lone Wolf, someone from Hells Angels, and an Asian triad all working together to get a couple of hundred kilograms of drug into Australia,' Scott Cook, the head of the Organised Crime Targeting Squad, told me during an interview. If there was any proof of the changing nature of organised crime it's the fact that Cook was, until recently, the head of the Asian Crime Squad, which operated alongside the Gangs Squad and MEOCS. Today, it no longer exists.

The decision to disband it was not made lightly, but Cook himself told me that there were certain realities at play. 'There's no more cultural boundaries,' he said. While Middle Eastern organised crime has never been strictly governed by cultural boundaries, the issues of culture, religion and ideology have been earmarked as key for the future.

In a conceptual sense, Middle Eastern organised crime resembles a bratty child: it's loud, kind of stupid, and always seeks attention. The feuds are petty and immature. Its perpetrators revel in notoriety and don't mind being named in the newspapers, seeing this as a channel of building their own status and reputation; it is, in some ways, an honour to be notorious. But beneath this facade are more meaningful traits: a need to belong, a need to be accepted. This, however, is not confined to criminals in the Middle Eastern community. Warren Gray, a state manager with the Australian Crime Commission, told me that most gang members across the spectrum come from torn family backgrounds and carry sad stories of rejection from childhood. Some have tried out for the army or a state police force in order to find a sense of order, structure and belonging. Criminal histories make such career paths near impossible. 'One guy told me that he tried out for the army, then the cops,' Gray explained to me. 'Both rejected him, so he went and joined a bikie gang.'

Today, however, a new challenge presents itself for law enforcement. Socio-economic factors, technology and geopolitical events taking place overseas are resulting in a new breed of criminal who will forgo the membership of an organised crime group for a different kind of social circle. 'What we're seeing now is a whole group not just wanting to join a gang, but wanting to join a radicalised group,' Deb Wallace told me.

The clearest example of this took place in December 2015 when fifteen-year-old school student Farhad Jabar put on flowing black robes and paced up and down outside the NSW Police Headquarters in Parramatta, before aiming a gun at a civilian staff member, Curtis Cheng, and shooting him point blank in the back of the head. Security officers quickly mobilised at the sound of the gunfire and shot Jabar dead on site. At the time of writing, the investigation into the murder and events leading up to it had established that Jabar was recruited by a group of older and similarly radicalised youths, some of whom had already been under investigation by counter terrorism agencies. Police believe members of this group were responsible for sourcing the firearm and giving it to Jabar, having first obtained it from a well-known Middle Eastern organised crime family – the Merrylands-based Alameddine group, several of whose members had been long-standing figures on the MEOCS radar.

For law enforcement officials the case seemed to prove several key points. Firstly, there were links between the worlds of organised crime and terrorism. Secondly, that perpetrators of extremist violence were not necessarily entrenched criminal targets with long criminal histories (Jabar had been unheard of prior to the shooting). And thirdly, the shooting seemed to confirm police suspicions that religious extremism had become its own type of banner and lure into organised crime, one that could give disaffected, vulnerable people a sense of identity, status, structure and belonging – similar to outlaw motorcycle gangs. The ongoing concern for law enforcement is that future recruits to these gangs will continue to be young and impressionable teenagers. And without established criminal records, or a known profile with police, the challenge of interrupting this new breed of target will increase.

It is for this reason, among many others, that Detective Superintendent Peter McErlain, the current boss of MEOCS, says the Squad must continue to exist. It still has important work to do, and the workload is increasing.

McErlain told me that when the Squad first started the vast majority of crime was geographically concentrated in southwestern Sydney, almost as though an invisible border had been created from Burwood to Greystanes down to Green Valley and back to Lakemba, making it easy for officers to find their targets and monitor their movements. But the situation has changed. Investigations are taking officers into regional parts of NSW where drug labs have been set up in difficult-to-reach locations. Cases are multi-jurisdictional, requiring the co-operation of police in Queensland or Western Australia, the Australian Federal Police, the Australian Taxation Office and even partner agencies overseas. The Squad has closer working relations with ASIO and the Counter Terrorism Squad; it's a new and fluid area of complexity, both sides exchanging intelligence on targets.

But if there's one area that constantly being improved and sharpened it's the co-operation and support of the Middle Eastern community. Ever since the Squad started, it has weathered accusations of racial bias and unfair profiling, a charge its officers have worked constantly to annul. At a corporate level this was always rebuffed – the Squad targeted criminals, not ordinary members of the community. But on the streets that didn't wash. Officers had to find their own way of dealing with the race card, or what Ken McKay would term the 'Ace of Race'.

Generally the community supports the work that MEOCS is doing, McErlain told me, who receives feedback through various channels – mainly community leaders and victims of crime. For some, the MEOCS brand has become a source of comfort rather than threat. But this mission remains a work in progress.

In July 2015, mourners gathered at Rookwood Cemetary for the funeral of Hedi Ayoub. Ayoub's coffin was wrapped in black plastic, and it had white bricks placed on each corner. Dozens of men packed together around the open gravesite, standing, crouching, jostling each other for space, some holding telephones and filming. Mohammad Hoblos, a religious leader of the Muslim community spoke to the mourners, his speaking style a mix of Koranic philosophy and street slang. Using words like 'mad' and 'hectic', it was a fresh take on the speeches of traditional religious preachers. Hoblos told them he was frustrated that funeral attendance had become trendy, a place to be seen.

'I'm starting to see a lot of regular faces at this place,' he told the gathering. He asked them what they had learned since their last visit, and why they bothered to even show up.

Ayoub, twenty-two, a body builder, had been shot dead in a children's playground at Punchbowl during daylight hours. His body was found bullet-ridden and slumped against a tree, another victim of apparent gang activity in southwestern Sydney's Middle Eastern community.

There had been several other funerals just like this one, Hoblos told the crowd, each one attracting large numbers of young men, many of whom show up for the voyeurism, to film the grave and post it online later in a kind of perfunctory attempt to appear virtuous. Few people, he said, were actually heeding the messages from the funerals they had come to witness: that life is precious; that material wealth, and their aspirations for it – a thin reference to the promises of gang life – were meaningless.

'What good is a house to this brother?' Hoblos said, pointing to Ayoub's casket. He was exasperated and nearly shouting. 'What good is all the money in the world to this brother? What good is an AMG or a Lambo? What use is that to him? What good is a six-foot-two blonde?

'It's of no benefit now – granite bench tops, timber bench tops, ensuite, not ensuite, is it a double-storey, is it a split level … this is of no benefit.' He clapped his hands together as if cleaning dust from them.

The crowd was silent, most of the men looked down sullenly, as if in shame.

'It's all a dream,' Hoblos said. 'And to believe in the dream you have to be asleep.

'My brothers, life is not a joke. You could be living in a mansion, [but] this is where you're coming. This is the real home,' he said, pointing back at the grave. 'No ensuites here. No granite benchtops here. No women in there, brother. You're alone. That's the reality of life, here in this hole. When are we going to change our life? Do you not see what's happening in the community?'

But even as he spoke, Hoblos noticed some in the crowd were growing weary, already bored and checking their phones.

For them, this was all routine. People in the game get killed – it's a fact. You show up at the funeral, pay your respects, grab some lunch with the boys and then it's back to the dream, or the chase for it anyway. It takes a jolt to the system to interrupt this cycle, to wake up. Hoblos said death is one way, but there are others.

A strong hand at home is one. A brush with the law is another.

ACKNOWLEDGEMENTS AND A NOTE ON SOURCES

In the autumn of 2015, while writing a series of newspaper articles about the Brothers 4 Life street gang – the crew first conceived by Bassam Hamzy in Lithgow Correctional Centre back in 2008 – I was approached by a small group of detectives who suggested I write a book chronicling the gang's downfall.

They thought it would make a great story and, of course, I agreed. Over the following weeks I mulled over the logistics and legal limitations, including the threat of limbo-like court delays and lengthy appeals. The timing seemed off.

On hearing this, one detective offered an alternative suggestion: 'Why don't you write a book about us?' he said. 'There are so many untold stories.'

So began my journey into the world of the Middle Eastern Organised Crime Squad (MEOCS). Reporting for a newspaper had made me familiar with MEOCS, but I had little actual knowledge of its inner workings. There had always been an air of mystique about the Squad and its people – a black-ops feel, something akin to a clandestine service. This might have just been my imagination, but, looking back, this doesn't feel so far off.

On Tuesday, 14 July 2015, I drove out to a southern suburb of Sydney to meet the Squad's former commander, Ken McKay, who had retired from the NSW Police Force at the rank of Assistant Commissioner of Police. McKay had agreed to be interviewed on the record, and garnering his cooperation was something of a coup for me. As a young reporter I'd written some fairly bold articles about him that led to a lawsuit and some bad blood between us. We hadn't spoken in years. But a book about MEOCS without McKay's input would be a failure, almost illegitimate. In my mind, McKay was the core of MEOCS. He was the frontman, the rockstar – Page and Plant, Mick and Keith, all rolled into one. I'd already signed the contract to start writing and, frankly, without him I'd have been screwed.

Daniela Ongaro, a mutual friend and colleague, kindly lay the groundwork for me by calling McKay on my behalf, putting in a good word, and paving the way for our first meeting at a boathouse café. It turned out to be one of many long interviews. Retired and no longer duty-bound by the NSW Police Force's corporate policy restraints – the kind that limit frank, open and honest opinion due to the crime of releasing insider information – McKay could say whatever he liked during our subsequent meetings; no subject was off limits and nothing was off the record. He was as sharp as ever, full of scintillating stories. He was also a doorway of sorts, an all-access pass to many other officers. Once they heard McKay was onboard, people I barely knew, or had never spoken to at all, felt much better about talking to me.

The following weeks and months became a fact-finding mission. I wanted more people, more stories, more anecdotes, any insight into life at MEOCS and the mechanics of its investigations. Each new person I interviewed steered me towards more vitally important people: friends of friends, old police colleagues, living legends who had seen things and were forced out by retirement or PTSD – it wouldn't be a book without them, I was told. Time out from the job had given each one of these people a chance to reflect deeply on their policing careers and when they spoke it was with superb recall and clarity about daily life 'in the job', as they called it. There are too many to name here, but I am especially grateful for their time, advice and patience with my questions.

I approached the NSW Police Force at the start of this project in the hope they would work collaboratively with me. They declined the offer but instead permitted interviews with serving officers upon request, and on a case-by-case basis. Some of these interviews were conducted in the offices of MEOCS, where on one occasion I was given a lengthy tour by Detective Superintendent Peter McErlain and afforded enough time to take notes and familiarise myself with each space – the intelligence division, the commander's office, the gun room, the briefing rooms, and even the kitchenette where you can buy a can of soft drink for $1. All of the interviews were chaperoned by a media liaison officer (MLO), and were still overwhelmingly candid and invaluable. The MLOs – Georgie, Ainslie and Michelle – also responded to countless emails and requests, rarely saying no to anything. To them, and to the police hierarchy authorising these requests, I say thank you.

In addition to these on-record interviews were more than 100 off-record conversations and interviews with various people: serving members of MEOCS and the wider NSW Police Force who were not given formal approval to speak with me; former members of MEOCS who had moved elsewhere within the organisation; serving law enforcement officials with knowledge of operations and staff (who asked that their names be withheld); and retired police officers who preferred not to be quoted or named in any capacity. I found myself calling these people repeatedly (often at antisocial hours) to clarify details and fact-check information. In some instances the conversations ran for several hours and my hand muscles cramped up in protest as I furiously scribbled notes. Pens were chewed to oblivion.

All of the insight provided in this book comes from both primary witnesses and hundreds of paper records and documents. Second-hand information was only used after extensive corroboration and any quotes featured in a scene are verbatim, or provided to the best recollection of either the people saying them or those privy to the conversation. The manuscript was not provided in full to anyone, but certain sections were shown in advance to some individuals upon request. These readings resulted in some factual clarifications and, in some cases, more insight through elaboration. No information was removed.

Court files were immensely helpful in piecing together the undisputed facts of each investigation and I'm indebted to the staff of the NSW Attorney-General's Department for making this material available. On several occasions I found myself locked in a room with nothing but my notepad, a table, and some boxes pulled from the state's archives. These files held a trove of invaluable documentation: autopsy reports, police logbook entries, crime scene photographs, witness statements, investigative timelines, records of interviews, statements of fact, ballistic reports, forensic testing results, hand-written letters to judges begging for leniency, drawings of suspected killers, telephone intercept and listening device transcripts, custody records, pre-sentence reports, and psychiatric assessments of criminals.

I also spent many hours closely examining the coronial brief of evidence tendered during the inquest of the death of Detective

Constable William Crews, which comprised a ten-folder compendium of police radio logs, policy documents, walk-through interviews, confidential briefing notes, statistics and organisational documents specific to MEOCS, investigative plans, operational orders, diary entries and, of course, dozens upon dozens of witness statements. This material was not only forensic in its account of the events of that night, but also of the processes and culture in place at MEOCS, including how they handled informants, selected their teams and assessed operations leading up to each arrest. Coupled with documents provided to me by some sources – without which this book would not have been possible and who, really, made it all possible – this information was illuminating about the Squad's operations.

As with any true crime book, a handful of names have been changed or omitted for legal reasons; this is specified in the body of the text. All other names, facts and stories mentioned over the course of the book are real and unchanged.